Michael + Liz
Thanks for your
witness! Shalom
Justin
Barringer

# A FAITH NOT WORTH FIGHTING FOR

# The Peaceable Kingdom Series

The Peaceable Kingdom Series is a multivolume series that seeks to challenge the pervasive violence assumed necessary in relation to humans, nonhumans, and the larger environment. By calling on the work of ministers, activists, and scholars, we hope to provide an accessible resource that will help Christians reflect on becoming a more faithful and peaceable people. The series editors are Andy Alexis-Baker and Tripp York.

**Volumes include:**

VOLUME I: *A Faith Not Worth Fighting For:*
*Addressing Commonly Asked Questions about Christian Nonviolence*
Edited by Tripp York and Justin Bronson Barringer

VOLUME II: *A Faith Worth Embracing All Creatures:*
*Addressing Commonly Asked Questions about Christian Care for Animals*
Edited by Andy Alexis-Baker and Tripp York (Forthcoming, 2012)

VOLUME III: *A Faith Encompassing All of Creation: Addressing*
*Commonly Asked Questions about Christian Care for the Environment*
Edited by Andy Alexis-Baker and Tripp York (Forthcoming, 2013)

Visit us at www.peaceablekingdomseries.com.

# A FAITH NOT WORTH
# FIGHTING FOR

Addressing Commonly Asked Questions
about Christian Nonviolence

EDITED BY
*Tripp York and*
Justin Bronson Barringer

FOREWORD BY
Stanley Hauerwas

AFTERWORD BY
Shane Claiborne

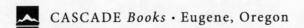 CASCADE *Books* · Eugene, Oregon

A FAITH NOT WORTH FIGHTING FOR
Addressing Commonly Asked Questions about Christian Nonviolence

The Peaceable Kingdom Series 1

Cascade Books
An Imprint of Wipf and Stock Publishers
199 W. 8th Ave., Suite 3
Eugene, OR 97401

www.wipfandstock.com

ISBN 13: 978-1-61097-499-8

*Cataloging-in-Publication data:*

    A faith not worth fighting for : addressing commonly asked questions about Christian nonviolence / edited by Tripp York and Justin Bronson Barringer ; foreword by Stanley Hauerwas ; afterword by Shane Claiborne.

    xii + 244 p. ; 23 cm. —Includes bibliographical references.

    The Peaceable Kingdom Series 1

    ISBN 13: 978-1-61097-499-8

    1. Nonviolence—Religious aspects—Christianity. 2. Pacifism—Religious aspects—Christianity. I. York, Tripp. II. Barringer, Justin Bronson. III. Hauerwas, Stanley, 1940–. IV. Claiborne, Shane, 1975–.

BT736.6 .F25 2012

*In memory of Philip Berrigan (1923–2002) and Art Gish (1939–2010),*
*who lived the kind of peace we can only hope to describe.*

# Contents

Foreword  ix
*Stanley Hauerwas*

Introduction:
Why Refusing to Kill Matters for Christian Discipleship  1
*Justin Bronson Barringer and Tripp York*

1   Isn't Pacifism Passive?  11
    *C. Rosalee Velloso Ewell*

2   What about the Protection of Third-Party Innocents?  18
    On Letting Your Neighbors Die
    *D. Stephen Long*

3   What Would You Do if Someone Were Attacking a Loved One?  31
    *Amy Laura Hall and Kara Slade*

4   What about Hitler?  44
    *Robert Brimlow*

5   Must Christian Pacifists Reject Police Force?  60
    *Gerald W. Schlabach*

6   What about Those Men and Women Who Gave Up Their Lives
    so that You and I Could Be Free? On Killing for Freedom  85
    *Justin Bronson Barringer*

Contents

7    Does God Expect Nations to Turn the Other Cheek?  107
     *Gregory A. Boyd*

8    What about War and Violence in the Old Testament?  125
     *Ingrid E. Lilly*

9    What about Romans 13: "Let Every Soul Be Subject"?  140
     *Lee C. Camp*

10   Didn't Jesus Say He Came Not to Bring Peace, but a Sword?  154
     *Samuel Wells*

11   What about the Centurion?
     A Roman Soldier's Faith and Christian Pacifism  170
     *Andy Alexis-Baker*

12   Didn't Jesus Overturn Tables and Chase People
     Out of the Temple with a Whip?  184
     *John Dear*

13   What about the Warrior Jesus in Revelation 19:
     "He Has Trampled Out the Vintage"?  192
     *J. Nelson Kraybill*

     Conclusion:
     A Faith Worth Dying For: A Tradition of Martyrs Not Heroes  207
     *Tripp York*

     Afterword  227
     *Shane Claiborne*

     Contributors  232

     Bibliography  235

# Foreword

I SHOULD LIKE TO think that this book represents a new stage in the conversation between Christians about the viability of nonviolence as a stance necessary if we are to be adequate witnesses to Jesus Christ. Too often, past discussions of Christian alternatives for justifying Christian participation or nonparticipation in war or other forms of violence address their interlocutor as if he or she is tone deaf. By contrast, the authors of the essays in this book take seriously objections to their commitment to nonviolence. As a result, these essays help pacifist and non-pacifist alike better understand that a commitment to Christian nonviolence is not so much a position but rather a declaration that requires ongoing reflection.

In their introduction to *A Faith Not Worth Fighting For*, Barringer and York observe that it is hard to imagine what nonviolence might entail—an astute remark that can too easily be overlooked for its significance. Yet I think they rightly call our attention to the necessity of continuing reflection by those committed to nonviolence. For example, the very description, "nonviolence," can be quite misleading, suggesting as it does that we know what violence looks like in a more definitive way than we know the alternative to violence. But that surely cannot be right if peace is a more determinative reality than violence.

I feel confident that John Howard Yoder would have read this book appreciatively. That is a high compliment. Yoder was a demanding critic, particularly of pacifists who claimed to represent Yoder's position as if Yoder had said all that needed to be said. *The Politics of Jesus: Vicit Agnus Noster* was first published in 1972. Yoder did not think the book was the last word about Christian nonviolence, but rather he thought the book represented a report of New Testament scholarship that was best understood as a "first word." The authors of these essays have clearly absorbed what Yoder began in *The Politics of Jesus*, but they have done so in a manner that extends Yoder's willingness to entertain challenges to his account of nonviolence.

Accordingly, the essayists in this book exemplify the nonviolence they advocate—that is, they refuse to ignore or dismiss those who would raise objections to their position. Nonviolence is not a stance that is to be limited to being against war, but rather nonviolence requires that every aspect of our lives be open to listening to those who differ from us. That means that those who are not committed to nonviolence should find their objections to nonviolence fairly represented by the authors. I hope, therefore, that those who justify violence in service to the neighbor will find this an important book to read just to the extent that these essays have avoided caricatures of their position.

It must be said, however, that these essays represent the christological pacifism that was at the heart of Yoder's work. That is the uncompromising heart of this book. The responses to the challenges to nonviolence presented in the various essays turn on this determinative conviction, that is, that any adequate understanding or defense of nonviolence will entail christological considerations. That does not mean that the readership of this book is restricted to Christians, but it does mean that the challenges, as well as the response to those challenges, are shaped by christological considerations. That, moreover, is the way it should be.

The editors of *A Faith Not Worth Fighting For* defend the title as an appropriate description of their understanding of Christian nonviolence. I confess that I do not like the title, because I think that there is a way to fight nonviolently—as do, I am sure, the editors of this book. But that is a small matter. Another title did occur to me that I think nicely characterizes these essays; my title is, *But What About . . . ?* What about the need to defend the innocent? What about the pacifist dependence on the police? What about the good people in the military? What about the role of government? What about the violence of the Old Testament? What about Romans 13? What about Jesus' appeal to the sword? What about the moneychangers? What about apocalyptic imagery? All good questions that most people would ask and desire to have addressed in a way that is not evasive. I think these essays provide just that.

This is a book, therefore, that is written for anyone. Of course no one is "anyone," but the appeal to that mythical person indicates the attempt to write essays that are accessible to those who have not followed the scholarly debates about Christian nonviolence. I think these essays have admirably fulfilled that ambition, but I hope those who have been engaged in past debates about nonviolence will find this book extremely important for their ongoing reflection. For as I suggested above, this book represents a stage of development that was made possible by the work of John Howard Yoder. We can, therefore, see by the substantive character of these essays what a fruitful beginning Yoder represents.

Stanley Hauerwas
Gilbert T. Rowe Professor of Theological Ethics
Duke Divinity School

# INTRODUCTION

## Why Refusing to Kill Matters
## for Christian Discipleship[1]

Justin Bronson Barringer *and* Tripp York

Behold, your king comes to you . . . humble and riding on a donkey. He will cut off the chariot from Ephraim and the war horse from Jerusalem; and the battle bow shall be cut off, and he shall command peace to the nations.

—ZECHARIAH 9:9–10

IN 1569, A CHRISTIAN by the name of Dirk Willems was burned at the stake for committing a capital crime: being an Anabaptist. It has been jokingly said that the only thing Catholics and Protestants could agree on in the sixteenth century was that it was a good thing to kill

---

1. The very title of this introduction sparked an interesting debate between the editors. One of us wanted to replace the word "kill" with "do harm," the argument being that the practice of nonviolence extends far beyond the reach of killing. This is absolutely correct. Our relationships with one another, with animals, and with the earth—are all tainted by various forms of systemic violence. For the purposes of this book, however, we agreed that it may be something of an achievement to be able to first problematize killing prior to moving on to other forms of violence. Volumes II and III of this series will deal with some of these other modes of violence.

1

the Anabaptists.[2] While that may or may not be true, it is certainly the case that neither Catholicism nor Protestantism tolerated the dissenting "heterodoxy" of the Anabaptist movement. The Anabaptists were a body of Christians who, among other things, would not swear oaths, argued for a believer's baptism, resisted clerical hierarchy, and refused to wield the sword. Though they claimed such practices were scripturally accurate, the powers that be (the Catholic and Protestant state churches) concluded otherwise. The Anabaptists were a threat to the social order. They had to be put to death. On the dual charges of sedition and heresy, many Anabaptists underwent public executions (oftentimes after enduring excruciating bouts of torture). This was a case of Christians killing other Christians over issues regarding both orthodoxy and political allegiance. As you can well imagine, it was not the most grace-filled period in the history of Christianity.

Amidst the chaos and violence of sixteenth-century Christianity, there were, on all sides, moments of authentic Christian witness, as the case above illustrates. Dirk Willems offered what we imagine to be an incredibly difficult, odd, subversive, yet faithful response to his killers. As he was fleeing from a hired "thief-catcher," he crossed a frozen river in an attempt to escape his pursuer. As he cleared the ice, he heard a crack and a splash. He looked back to find the pursuer drowning in the icy water. Some would view that moment as providential. God was providing Willems an easy escape. Others may view it as just desserts or karma for the thief-catcher—that's what he deserves for attempting to be complicit in the death of an innocent human being. Others still may see it as nothing more than a natural consequence: ice cracks under a certain amount of weight, nothing more need be said.

Willems saw it differently. He viewed it as an opportunity to help a suffering neighbor—one who also happened to be his enemy. Willems turned around and helped the man out of the icy river, saving his life. Overwhelmed by the mercy shown him, the thief-catcher wanted to release Willems. Regrettably he was unable to, as the thief catcher was instructed to remember his oath and detain him. Willems was appre-

---

2. We are not sure who originated this comment, but it may not be too big of a leap to imagine it was Stanley Hauerwas.

hended, tortured, and burned at the stake. He was killed by those who claimed to know the peace that is Christ.[3]

Gandhi, it is said, once famously quipped, "The only people on earth who do not see Christ and his teachings as nonviolent are Christians." This is, of course, not entirely true. The Christians of the first three centuries are known for their refusal to participate in violence, and the history of the church is replete with numerous examples of theologians, bishops, saints, mystics, monastic groups, historic peace churches, and all sorts of Christians committed to the practice of nonviolence. In the past century alone, witnesses have revealed a Christian commitment to peacemaking, including the Catholic Worker Movement, the Anglican Pacifist Fellowship, the descendants of Anabaptism (Mennonites, Brethren, Hutterites, Amish, etc.), as well as leaders of the Restoration Movement, to name just a few.

Unfortunately, it can certainly be argued that, generally speaking, Gandhi may have been right. For as adamant as many Christians are about practicing their biblically based faith, the majority of us struggle to understand why the practice of violence may be at odds with the life and teachings of Jesus. Granted, in the case of Dirk Willems, it may be easy to spot the error of his Christian executors from our contemporary perspective. But it wasn't easy then, and we don't imagine it is easy always to spot how we are disobedient to Jesus now. Part of the project of this book, therefore, is to complicate things a bit. For too long, the lure of violence has gripped and owned much of Christian thought and practice. We have assumed its necessity for so long that it remains easy to justify any present situations in which we imagine that the potential ends of violence outweigh the potential problems it causes for those serious about following Jesus. To be sure, we rarely engage in violence unless we think it is for a good reason. Much of why we resort to it is rooted not in what we hate, but in what we love. It is out of our many loves that violence so often becomes a great temptation. We wish to protect our loved ones, our families, our friends, and ourselves. Of course, these very reasons have led to many wars, pogroms, inquisitions, and public executions. Dirk Willems was executed because he was thought to be a threat to the common good. Better to kill him than allow him to

3. Braght, *Bloody Theater, or, Martyrs Mirror of the Defenseless Christians*, 742.

live and potentially infect a larger section of society with his heresy. It was specifically out of obedience to the command to love one's neighbor that Willems, theologically, had to be executed.

We do believe that this was the conviction that led many Catholics and Protestants to kill one another (along with the Anabaptists) in the sixteenth century. It was due to their concern for the preservation of civil society that they thought it necessary to wage violence against their enemies. The Anabaptists, however, were peculiar because they were the only ones, as a group, who refused to retaliate.[4] Though they gladly died for their faith, they refused to kill for it. They could not reconcile resorting to violence, even in terms of protecting themselves or their children, with the path of Jesus. We imagine that for many people, even Christians, this seems counterintuitive.

Part of what we want do in this book is discuss why refusing to employ violence is so important to Christian discipleship. We do not think nonviolence is a tangential matter. It is crucial for us to understand how, for example, Willems' extension of a helping hand to his enemy is irreconcilably at odds with those who would rather put their enemies in a grave. In the case of Willems, he was taking up his cross and denying himself as he obeyed Jesus' command to love his enemies. This cannot be said of those who decide to resist evil by treating their enemies in a way contrary to what Jesus demands. We believe that how we respond to our enemies reveals the reality of our ultimate commitments. If Jesus really is Lord, then to respond to our enemies with anything less than what he demands makes us liars (1 John 2:4). If this sounds a bit combative (ironically), it's because it probably is a bit combative. Such concern was even expressed, rightly we think, by one of our contributors about the book's title. It was suggested that *A Faith Not Worth Fighting For* conjures negative and polemical images that may be antithetical to our project. This is certainly a valid concern. Such a title can be off-putting and runs the risk of alienating a potentially

4. Notice, we said the Anabaptists, *as a group*, were the only ones to resist using the sword against their enemies. We do not want to dismiss the peacemakers in each tradition nor to gloss over an early Anabaptist group, the Münsterites (quickly decried by all other Anabaptists), who did resort to violence. Anabaptism did, however, evolve out of this century as a body of people principally defined by their pacifism. This is a form of life not widely shared by these other two Christian traditions.

larger audience. At the same time, we think the title is worth the risk. First of all, it *is* a negative title. It is negative in the sense that we wish to avoid doing something in particular: violence (though we also have no desire to be defined by what we are against). Second, it is polemical inasmuch as it purposely strives to attract critical readers with the hope that we can offer an explanation as to what we mean when we claim that Christianity is not a faith worth fighting for. We do not think it is worth fighting for if fighting suggests that we can maintain the radical path of Jesus while simultaneously employing violence as a means of dealing with our enemies. This refers to forcefully protecting our lives, the lives of our friends, our faith, or, as in the case of sixteenth-century Christianity, our doctrines and convictions.

On this latter point, we should be reminded that Christian faith is precarious. Its many fine theological points, historically shaped, are never a given. Our best theologians are capable of making tremendous theological errors. We cannot statically secure all the grammatical specifics of the Christian faith. The faith cannot be "fixed."[5] When it is settled or becomes a given, it becomes an ideological construct that tempts us toward idolatry and, often, toward utilizing various modes of violence against the other. We end up having faith in our carefully constructed system rather than in the one who bids us come and die; and we are tempted to protect that system against those with whom we disagree. For this reason, we invite others into this discussion and ask that readers remain open to the arguments that lie within—just as we will do our best to remain open to correction. We hope this book produces healthy dialogue, the kind of conversation in which we do not commit violence toward one another by refusing to hear one another. Violence is certainly not limited to the realm of the physical, and we understand that there can be violence in the militancy by which some people defend the practice of nonviolence (as if nonviolence were an end in itself). All we hope for within this book is to be faithful to the vision of God's peaceable kingdom as lived by Jesus. This is certainly no easy task, so we ask that you struggle along with us as we attempt to understand what it means to be called by God to be a people who are not of this world.

5. See Chris K. Huebner's *A Precarious Peace*, 134–44.

## A NOT SO MODEST PROPOSAL

*Those who say they live in God should live their lives as Jesus did.* (1 John 2:6)

We begin this book with the audacious hope that you will accept our proposal to concede that following Jesus *could* demand a lifelong commitment to nonviolence. Granted, we agree with Stanley Hauerwas that it may not be clear to us what such a life should look like, nor is it even safe to assume that we understand the meaning of words such as *nonviolence* or *pacifism.* Inasmuch as we say something like "Christian nonviolence," it tempts us to imagine that whatever peace is, it is "not violence."[6] This surely limits the conversation and sells it short in terms of the reality that is the peace we find in Christ. Those of us who utilize the language of nonviolence must also guard against the tendency to be defined by what we are against. This makes the mistake of allowing that which is the object of protest to define what one is for. To be clear, we stress nonviolence not because we are *against* something called "violence," rather, we emphasize nonviolence because we believe Jesus is resurrected from the dead. For in light of his resurrection, what else can we do but follow him?

We do not, therefore, begin this book with a chapter arguing for something called Christian nonviolence. Instead, we assume that if Jesus is who he says he is, and if the Gospels are to be taken seriously, then what must be addressed are the important questions that often tempt us to ignore, neglect, explain away, or flat-out reject the difficult teachings of Jesus that could potentially require us to give up our lives, and those of the ones we love, at the hands of our enemies. We view this as a matter of both faithfulness and obedience to Christ.

For this reason, we have attempted to bring together the knowledge, experience, and wisdom of numerous pastors, professors, and

---

6. Hauerwas, "Explaining Christian Nonviolence," in Chase and Jacobs, eds., *Must Christianity Be Violent?*, 173. We admit to such a shortcoming implicit within this terminology. We will, however, use such language if for no other reason than to signify a certain way of life that, at minimum, problematizes Christian complicity and participation in violence. Yet, as Hauerwas rightly points out, it is by no means clear that we can always know what constitutes violence. He suggests that only against a backdrop of peaceableness can we come to name violence well.

practitioners of Christian nonviolence in order to address why it is the case that the idea of Christian pacifism is so difficult for many of us to imagine. As the subtitle suggests, the goal of this book is to address questions that are routinely posed by Christians who have concerns about the morality, practicality, and theology of Christian nonviolence. Many of us do wish to live peaceable lives, but we fear that in doing so we will somehow neglect our responsibilities to those we care for, to our nation, or to any temporal good that demands our attention. Our chief task, therefore, is to provide serious yet accessible responses to the kinds of questions that render difficult a commitment to the nonviolent path of Jesus. Such questions are quite prominent: What do I do if someone is harming a loved one? What about violence in the Old Testament? What about the warrior Jesus in Revelation 19? These are all very serious and important questions. We aim to answer them as faithfully as possible, for what we feel matters most are the practical implications of our arguments. The various contributors to this volume deal accordingly with issues of biblical interpretation, theological analysis, historical problems, hypothetical situations, and matters of daily living in hopes of, at least, complicating the manner by which many of us avoid the subversive nature of Jesus' message. We hope such a format takes seriously the concerns of the reader as we respond to a number of very important objections to Christian nonviolence.

We end with an essay chronicling the tradition of martyrs who declared in their lives and deaths that, while we may not have a faith worth killing for, we do have one worth dying for. It attempts to show how important it is to embody the claim, "Jesus is Lord." This chapter endeavors to negotiate how it is that two different Christians can make this same confession, yet one could be true and the other false. Jesus makes it clear that we cannot claim to be his follower if we do not do what he commands. It is not enough to claim that Jesus is Lord; we have to embody this claim if we are to be truthful. We have, therefore, called upon what the Christian tradition has deemed the ultimate imitators of Jesus, the martyrs, to illustrate how at odds the path of Jesus is with retaliation, revenge, and current popular conceptions of what passes for justice. By making connections between the early church's commitment to nonviolence and martyrdom, the last chapter hopes to establish an argument as to why Christian participation in warfare and/or self-defense is antithetical to the path of Jesus. At the very least, this chapter, along with the others, demands that those who do resort to violence justify such violence in light of what Jesus said and taught. That is, we begin with the assumption that the Christian's refusal to participate in violence is something that does not require justification (though we obviously do provide an account as to why violence is adverse to Christian practice). We believe, along with the just war tradition, that Christianity favors the practice of peace and that, if violence is to be practiced, it requires an account as to how it is possible to disobey the clear instructions to love our enemies, to turn the other cheek, to not resist evil and to put away the sword. Of course, as a matter of full disclosure, we do *not* think there is a faithful justification for the overriding of these commands—hence, we address the variety of what-ifs that many assume legitimate the use of violence.

While many of these difficult questions have been answered in volumes of academic and popular works alike, there has yet to be a book that seeks to directly answer the most prominent questions about Christian nonviolence in an easy-to-read (yet academically thorough) edition. This book seeks to answer the questions that many of us are often asked in a way that is accessible to anyone curious as to why this form of Christian discipleship may be at the heart of following Jesus. To be sure, this is not a comprehensive articulation for a theology of nonviolence. For that we strongly suggest that you begin with the writings of John Howard Yoder and Walter Wink. Of course, we hope that we make a strong case for the practice of nonviolence; we will do so simply by engaging those questions that seem to suggest the impossibility of such a way of life rather than constructing a systematic theology of nonviolence.

It was important for us to include a variety of voices representing a number of ecclesial traditions. We are quite proud of the diversity of theological traditions represented herein. We believe such diversity strengthens our arguments, as we emphasize the strong commonalities across denominational lines. The contributors to this book come from a number of backgrounds: Wesleyan, Church of Christ, Catholic, Mennonite, nondenominational, Episcopalian, and Methodist. Though different ecclesial traditions are represented, and people in different lines of work have contributed, what is central is the conviction that through the life and teachings of Jesus, God has called us to live a life that offers an alternative to that of a violent, vengeful, and hate-filled world. We are called to embody a different kind of ethic, one predicated on the life, death, and resurrection of the Jewish Messiah who demanded of us the unusual and difficult way of dealing with our enemies by loving them. Contributors to this volume share not only a commitment to such a claim but also a commitment to, with the help of others, embodying it. It is certainly not always easy. Honesty requires us to admit that we do not know for certain what we would "really do" in any given situation; but we hope that we have at least achieved some clarity about what we should do—that is, if we wish to follow Jesus precisely when it may matter the most.

Finally, a word of gratitude is in order. As always there are way too many people to thank in a book of this nature. Clearly, such a book would not be possible if not for the wonderful contributions of our authors. We are grateful for both their witness and their friendship. We are also indebted to Cascade Books for adopting not only this particular volume, but the series as a whole. (We hope it will not bankrupt your fine press.) Many thanks to Jonathan Melton for nurturing and shaping this idea from its beginning. We are especially grateful to Cori Cypret for her diligent efforts formatting the essays and her keen editorial eye, and to Andy Alexis-Baker, general coeditor of The Peaceable Kingdom Series. Without the meticulous help of either of you, this book could not be what it is.

We extend thanks, of course, to our friends and families for their support, criticism, and care. We are who we are only because of you. Most importantly, thanks to the readers for taking a chance on these reflections. For those of you seeking to take Jesus at his word and to pick up a cross instead of a sword, we offer you what we hope are straightforward responses to some very difficult questions. If nothing else, we trust this book will function as an invitation to better understand the radical nature of God's love for all human beings—even those who wish to do us and other's harm.

# 1

## Isn't Pacifism Passive?

C. Rosalee Velloso Ewell

### An Introduction by Way of Assumptions

Isn't pacifism passive? Perhaps. But that depends on your definition of passive. If by passive you mean one who sits back and does nothing, then yes, pacifism can be passive, but that is not what this book is about. In fact, if you see such pacifism, it is not the type of pacifism to which Christians are called, nor is it in following with the life, teachings, death, and resurrection of Jesus of Nazareth.

In this chapter, I will look at some of the ways this question can be addressed, but first, a few assumptions must be made plain.

First, I assume that the one we call Lord lived as a first-century Jew in Palestine about two thousand years ago, was tortured, tried, and convicted of treason, and was hung to die on a cross. Three days later God raised him from the dead. This God-man, Jesus, is also the one through whom all things were created. After Jesus returned to the Father, he sent the Holy Spirit to guide, comfort, and inspire God's people and to enable them to live genuinely as a holy nation.

Second, Christians are called to witness to the story of Jesus through their lives, in word and deed. Such witnessing is essential to the life of the church and is inherent to God's saving plan for the world.

Third, all our thoughts, our languages, our theology and ideas are part of creation. Therefore, they are never perfect and never complete this side of the new heaven and the new earth. Ours is always a theology in progress and must always have Christ at its center. We "see through a glass dimly . . . but we do see Jesus" (1 Cor 13:12; Heb 2:9). Such a realization should call us to humility and thankfulness towards God.

Fourth, Christian discipleship is a journey. Questions, difficulties, and celebrations come up along the way; people join us on this road, and we join others. We must always ask ourselves who are our friends on this way and whether we're making the trip visible so that others may want to take a look and, hopefully, come along.

Fifth, our understanding of what it means to be human depends on how we see Jesus. He is the standard and the model for what faithful obedience to God looks like. Any form of living that is not in line with the life, teachings, and death of Jesus falls short of the life for which God created us.

## What Does It Mean to Be Passive?

Generally speaking, the word *passive* is used today to describe doing nothing. In most contexts of violence, it is understood as sitting on one's bum, watching the world go by, observing one's life and the lives of others without taking any action either to stop or to promote the violence. In cases of war or a criminal act by an individual, passivity is often a charge made against someone who does not use violence to stop the crime. It is presumed that to stop the criminal—either to defend oneself, one's loved one, or an innocent victim—one must make use of violent means. Might there be other alternatives?

Such an understanding of the term *passive* is a fairly recent development and owes much of its meaning to the ways in which the term is employed in psychological idioms (e.g., passive-aggressive behavior). Earlier uses of the term carried the connotation of nonviolence, especially in contexts of public protests or resistance to wars and other types of violence. Passive did not mean doing nothing, rather, it meant doing something specific (e.g., protesting the apartheid regime) without resorting to violence. Thus, in the early years of the twentieth century, the term "passive resistance" was supposedly coined by Gandhi while he spoke during a public protest in Durban, South Africa.

The root of the word *passive*, from the Greek *pascho* or the Latin *passio*, should recall to Christians a particular story—the passion of our Lord. One who is passive in this older sense is one who suffers. In Christian history, it is one who suffers on behalf of others or in place of others. It is anything but sitting back and doing nothing—quite the contrary, it refers to taking on suffering in a very active way, subjecting oneself to torture or potential death as a way to affirm and stand according to one's convictions. It can also be understood as an active form of obedience: "obedience to the point of death—even death on a cross," as Paul states in Philippians 2:8. There is nothing passive (i.e., nonactive) about Jesus' passion.

Keeping with the word study a bit longer, it is indeed strange that pacifists should often be accused of passivity, in the negative sense of the word, as those who do nothing. Another term, also from the same Greek root, would more adequately describe the pacifism to which we are called: *passionate*. In today's usage, to be passionate about something or someone is actively to pursue, to seek out, to understand, to express one's longings for an object or person of desire. Lovers seek to understand and learn about each other's preferences in music, food, books, and other interests. Such passionate affections serve as a drive and motivating factor toward certain types of behavior and action. Being passionate is not being inactive.

Christian discipleship, understood as the radical call to follow Jesus, is a passionate affair. It is a journey and a lesson in obedience, in which Christians actively engage in the work and mission of God. There is no such thing as an inactive disciple. Pacifism, understood as a particular way of being in the world that is consistent with the life of the one we call Lord, is anything but passive. It is the way to obey the commands of Jesus and to live in the reign of God—a way of living that challenges the powers of this world, for which violence is god.

Passivity, Neutrality, and the Fight for Justice

Let us assume that Christian pacifism is not an individualistic under-taking, but rather reflects part of what it means for Christians to live as the people of God. This is an important assumption because most un-derstandings of pacifism presume an individualism that is completely foreign to the biblical texts. The logic and reasons for such presupposi-tions are discussed elsewhere in this book, but it is necessary to mention them here again. This is because the accusation that pacifists are passive also presumes an individualism, plus the autonomy and power of the individual to make certain decisions in contexts of great trauma and danger.

The struggle for justice and human rights is one such context in which this accusation of passivity is made. For example, how can a Christian claim to be a pacifist and do nothing to stop the systematic rape and genocide of Muslim women and girls in the former Yugoslavia in the early 1990s, or in present-day Sudan? Not to take (violent) ac-tion against the soldiers carrying out these horrific acts is tantamount to being unchristian—so goes the argument against pacifism, and thus explains the accusation of passivity.

In *What Would You Do?*, John Howard Yoder and others have raised questions about the assumptions and the logic of these argu-ments against pacifism. Arguments between Yoder and people like John Milbank (who accuses pacifists of being passive) have filled too many pages of academic books and journals, and in the meantime, pastors and church folk who find themselves in places of violent conflict struggle to learn and live what it means to be a faithful follower of Christ in such contexts. So we must ask, what actually is the shape of Christian witness in the fight for justice?

Christian faith and practice are never neutral. If we say our Lord is both the Prince of Peace and the bearer of justice, how can both peace and justice be embodied in the context of war and violence? I would agree with those who say that it is wrong for Christians to stand by and do nothing to save or protect the innocent. But agreeing that it is wrong to do nothing goes beyond my mere personal opinion—it is a matter of Christian conviction. There are ways for Christians to seek justice and to protect the innocent that are not simply the annihilation of the perpetrator of the violence. Furthermore, seeking justice should not be something optional for Christians in the first place—it is a calling for all Christians—and demands of us that we stand with those who are oppressed, recognizing that we do not stand alone.

The character of Christian witness is one shaped by the biblical narratives—by the stories, the lives, the commands that form a people into a community that loves mercy and seeks justice. Neutrality is not an option for such a people. Therefore, the ways in which justice and mercy play out will be as varied as the people themselves, scattered over all parts of this globe. Furthermore, such character requires trust and creativity. Christian pacifism is not passive because it creatively seeks alternatives to the violence of this world. Christian pacifism is not passive because it actively engages the powers of violence, even to the point of death. Christian pacifism is not passive because it is courageous enough to act like Esther and to face the earthly powers—to the point of putting one's own life on the line. Christian pacifism is not passive because it takes responsibility for not killing the oppressor and for finding another way forward. Christian pacifism is not passive because it presumes that prayer is an essential aspect of the Christian life, and prayer is actively participating in the life of God. To pray for, to bless, to love an enemy and to find creative ways of doing so is anything but being passive.

## Pacifism and Evangelism

Genuine Christian pacifism requires boldness and courage because it is very likely to be scorned both by the world and by other Christians. This is so because such pacifism witnesses to the lordship of Christ in such a way that it challenges the power structures of our churches, our communities, and even world governments. It is evangelistic in its very nature. That is, it tells the good news of Jesus' death and resurrection and announces the reign of God and the transformation of the world. Thus powers and authorities ought to be threatened by it, for it reveals their ambitions and makes relative their claims to glory.

Pacifism is not passive because it is evangelistic. If it is not evangelistic, it ceases to be authentically Christian. In word and deed,

Christians testify to a vision of God's care and providence that offers the world an alternative to violence. But more than this, pacifism witnesses to our trust that God will act—and in fact does act—in all situations. The ways in which God will act cannot be controlled or manipulated, but we can trust that they will be consistent with the way in which God has acted already in Jesus of Nazareth. Therefore, to argue that the only solution to a violent threat is to react in violence (and anything else is simply being passive) points to the pride of self-determination and a lack of trust in divine providence. It presupposes that there are only two alternatives: to watch violence happen or to fight violence with violence. But the evangelistic nature of our calling reminds us that God's way of acting in the face of violence was revealed in the death and resurrection of Jesus. Such an act was not simply God's way of surprising us then, but sets the framework for how we should expect God to surprise us in present and future circumstances.

Mere passivity (i.e., not doing anything) is also a mistake and indicates a failure to trust God. It points to a determinism that is fatalistic at its core, and therefore allows no room for Christian hope, let alone the practice of prayer.

Christian pacifism is not passive because it is an embodiment of the life of discipleship. It is standing where Jesus stood, finding ways to disarm the powers and seek justice for the oppressed. As Dale Aukerman points out in his reading of the story of the woman about to be stoned in John 8:2–11, Jesus did not stand by passively. Rather, he stood between the woman and her attackers, taking upon himself their attack on her.[1] Jesus' mode of defense was not to attack the mob, but rather creatively to disarm them, and in doing so, to offer a glimpse of the grace and forgiveness of God. Whether or not the attackers then become followers is not the point, though it is a desirable outcome. The point is that God acts in ways of justice and mercy that do not impose or force violence even upon those who threaten the weak. Therefore, as Aukerman rightly asks, "Would God ever expect from us a mode of defense which we do not see in Jesus?"[2]

1. Yoder, *What Would You Do?*, 75.
2. Ibid., 76.

As witnesses to the power of the resurrection, passivity as inaction is not an option. Evangelistic pacifism is rightly understood in terms of the passionate nature of our discipleship. It refers to the creative ways of God that we are called to embody as we show others that another world is not only possible, but that it has already been made available to all who join on the journey of following Jesus.

# 2

## What about the Protection of Third-Party Innocents? On Letting Your Neighbors Die

D. Stephen Long

### A Reluctant Pacifist

I AM A RELUCTANT pacifist. In one sense I am uninterested in being a pacifist at all because I find so many kinds of pacifism unconvincing, if not silly. I once worked and lived in a seminary community where nearly everyone was a pacifist of some sort. Yet people would drive luxury vehicles and SUVs with bumper stickers that read "no war for oil," and no one laughed. No one asked, what are the social conditions that necessitated war and how might we be responsible for them? It was blithely assumed that war was perpetrated by vicious men who took delight in violence and destruction, and who had no ability to imagine any alternatives. I found this to be an inadequate analysis then as I do now. It is based on a far too easy distinction between oppressors and oppressed, where both groups are readily identifiable based on the rigid application of a code drawn from a metric of race and gender. I have no interest in being a "pacifist" as one plank in a progressive platform perpetuated by a putative political "left." For me the question of pacifism only makes sense in terms of Christian discipleship. It is the question, how do we follow Jesus?

It is true that Stanley Hauerwas's work deeply influenced my pacifism, but oddly enough, it was not his defense of pacifism that first moved me in this direction but his defense of war as a serious moral activity. I don't think I could be a pacifist if it were not for his essay, "Should War Be Eliminated?"[1] It was the first defense of pacifism that did not characterize war and soldiers as so blatantly immoral that pacifism won by default. Hauerwas conceded that war could be a serious, moral act that required self-sacrifice, disciplined community, and moral attentiveness. His pacifism was not a reaction against a caricatured version of warcraft, but it raised this question: Even if war has this moral seriousness, is it possible for a people who confess the Nicene Creed? In other words, given that God definitively speaks to us in Jesus and nothing more needs to be said, how are we to witness to this Word? This spoke to the reality I knew as a boy growing up in Indiana, where the soldiers in my family were not vicious or immoral, but people who sought to be good and decent human beings. Had Hauerwas simply rejected war out of a liberal opposition to war's moral seriousness, I would not have found him convincing. In other words, it was not what Hauerwas opposed that attracted me to his position (war) but what he affirmed (Jesus).

Hauerwas's work was by no means the first time I was confronted with the question of Christian participation in violence. I had been baptized by the Anabaptists in Goshen, Indiana, at the age of twelve, and I remember my parents discussing the church's commitment to nonviolence. We went to the church because it was within walking distance of our home. We only went for two years. Before and after that brief sojourn among the Anabaptists we were Methodists. Despite being baptized by the Anabaptists, I didn't give much consideration to the question of war until I had an evangelical experience in my late teens and then began considering where I would go to college. My father wanted me to attend the Air Force Academy. He had served in the military and knew of its moral and intellectual seriousness. He had grown up in White County, Indiana, which was notorious for its racism. When Joe Louis

---

1. In Hauerwas, *Against the Nations*, 169–208.

held an exhibition fight there, he was not allowed to spend the night. My father left a job as a factory worker, and left White County, to enter the military, much to the chagrin of his family. The military provided him with an education and a commitment to social justice; it was through his friendship with black soldiers that he most fully recognized the deep evil of racism, something he made sure his children recognized as well. He was never a violent man, and one of the few times I saw him visibly angered was when I repeated a racial slur I had learned at school.

He had admired his uncles for their bravery in battle, as I had. My great Uncle Skeeter was in the "Sawdust Commandos" who built bridges for tanks in World War II. He fought in the Battle of the Bulge, and was once admonished by General Patton. My great uncle Cleon spent two years in a Nazi prisoner of war camp. He was a tail gunner on a bomber that was shot down over German territory. He parachuted to safety but was quickly identified by civilians. He said he could have fought his way out, but knew it was futile. He threw his handgun into a lake and surrendered. Surviving artifacts of his time in that concentration camp can be found in the Air Force museum in Dayton, Ohio. I observed these men while I was growing up. These Indiana farmers wanted nothing more than to work the fields and tend to their families, but they found themselves catapulted into events halfway around the world.

## Haunted by Pacifism

When I was a boy, my father and I visited the Air Force Academy, where we purchased an Air Force Academy pennant that hung in my room until I left for college. Then I read the Bible and became haunted by pacifism. I wondered how Christian participation in war, for all its moral and intellectual seriousness, fit with Jesus' Sermon on the Mount. That question still troubles me, and despite all the attempts, ancient and modern, to make it fit, Jesus' words will always haunt the Christian Church with the specter of pacifism. It is the uncomfortable guest who will not leave. I was confronted with it when I attended the evangelical Taylor University, where, for my senior capstone in Physical Chemistry, I read Mark Hatfield's *Between a Rock and a Hard Place*, which explained his opposition to the Vietnam War based on his Christian faith.

We discussed Christian participation in violence and war during that capstone, but I came to no conclusions. When I went to seminary I was quite taken by Reinhold Niebuhr because, unlike much of the liberal Protestantism I received in my first semester, he seemed to take sin seriously. One of the first works I read was his famous *Moral Man and Immoral Society*, which argues that while an individual may in himself or herself be moral and live out the Gospel, this was not possible for societies that had to be politically responsible. In other words, pacifism was fine for individuals or a witnessing minority who didn't seek to be political, but it was wrong, and even immoral, for a political society responsible for the lives of others not to use violence in order to protect the innocent. This is the central question posed to pacifists. It is not the question, Are we willing to die?, but rather, Are we willing to let others die for our convictions? I will address this most important question at the end of my essay.

Niebuhr's position has a kind of plausibility. It acknowledges what Jesus taught with all seriousness: "You have heard it was said, 'An eye for an eye and a tooth for a tooth.' But I say to you, do not resist an evildoer. But if anyone strikes you on the right cheek, turn the other also; and if anyone wants to sue you and take your coat, give your cloak as well; and if anyone forces you to go one mile, go also the second mile" (Matt 5:38–41). It does not simply dismiss this teaching, but it privatizes and depoliticizes it. Those who are called to be saints, or to be holy, can live this out as individuals, but those who are responsible for political orders *must* not.

Yet at least two problems exist with this argument. First, it is a poor reading of Scripture. Nowhere does Jesus' Sermon on the Mount suggest that it is only for individuals. There is no footnote or proviso where Jesus says, "You are to live this way except when it comes to the defense of your neighbors, then you must use the violence at your disposal to protect them." In fact, the Sermon on the Mount is not private instruction for individual consciences; it is the political platform for the new kingdom or city that Jesus proclaims, the city that is to be "set on a hill" and illumine the world (Matt 5:14–16). He gives this platform to the twelve disciples, who represent the restoration of Israel and the return of God to the temple, a return found in Jesus' own body, in Jesus who is fully divine and fully human. The Sermon on the Mount is also, as John Wesley noted, Jesus' autobiography.[2] He is the one who embodies it and demonstrates what a blessed life and city look like. The Sermon is not some moral teaching separate from his life, death, resurrection, and ascension. It shows us God's purposes for God's creation. This leads us to the second problem with the Niebuhrian interpretation of the Sermon on the Mount: all Christians, like Jews (and ultimately all creatures), are called to embody God's holiness, to be a dwelling place for God. This too is found in the Sermon when Jesus commands us, "Be perfect therefore as your heavenly Father is perfect" (Matt 5:47). This is why he also taught us to pray, "Our Father in heaven, may your name be holy on earth as it is in heaven." These are a Christian's political marching orders. We are to make God's name holy by the way we live. Can we do so at the same time that we take up arms?

That Christians should not defend themselves through the use of violence is a long and venerable teaching in the Christian tradition. St. Augustine, who in part also gave us the just war teaching, taught this in the fifth century. We still see vestiges of it in the teaching of Thomas Aquinas in the thirteenth century. He too recognizes that on the whole a Christian should not protect himself. However, if he has responsibility for others, then he can protect himself only as a means to protect those others. (He never tells us what that means for those who are not responsible for others. Does this mean they die?) Because their use of violence is solely for the sake of the protection of the innocent, Aquinas and the just war teaching offered strict guidelines on when and how violence could be employed. Whether or not these strict guidelines have ever been adhered to is beside the question; they are a rigorous ethic that requires incredible self-restraint in the employment of violence. Only enough violence should be employed to protect the innocent neighbor, and because the purpose is to protect the innocent neighbor, violence cannot directly target those who are noncombatants, that is to say, those who are not directly prosecuting the unjust aggression.

2. See Long, *John Wesley's Moral Theology*, 125–70.

## Haunted by Just War[3]

So as much as I'm haunted by Jesus' hard teachings on forgiveness of enemies and the demands of the "new city" formed through his bodily death, resurrection, and ascension, I confess I'm also haunted by the challenge the just war tradition puts to pacifism. It is this: "Okay, we have Jesus' teaching in the Sermon on the Mount; his refusal to use the sword on the night of his arrest, his command that takes the sword away from the disciples (Matt 26:52; Luke 22:50; John 18:11); and the example of his own crucifixion and resurrection. Nonetheless, we also have his command to love our neighbor as ourselves. Although we may not employ violence for self-defense, we must do so for the sake of the neighbor." This is the strongest possible defense of Christian participation in war and violence. It is both what authorizes and limits it. It says that I cannot simply intend to defend my own life against unjust aggression. However, if a neighbor—near or far—is unjustly aggrieved, then I am called to love both neighbors, the oppressor and the oppressed. Circumstances demand that I must make a choice, and I must choose to defend the innocent by doing all that I can to resist the aggressor. This also limits what can be done. If my intention is to defend the innocent, I cannot do so through indiscriminate uses of violence, which kill both aggressor and innocent. The violence must be both proportionate to the end it serves and executed in such a way that it never directly intends to kill the innocent. This would not be an act of war, but murder, which is clearly prohibited in the sixth commandment: "Thou shalt not kill."

## Pacifist and Just War Presumptions

This strenuous interpretation of the just war tradition would seem to have a great deal in its favor. Some have argued that it and pacifism share a common presumption against the use of violence, and that may be, but if it is, it is not very illuminating. The heart of these two traditions is not that they share in common a presumption against violence—after all, who wouldn't share such a presumption? Who is actually in favor of

3. For the best contemporary account of the just war, see Bell, *Just War as Christian Discipline*.

violence? Who would say, given the opportunity to resolve differences through peace or violence, "I prefer violence"? Of course there are such people in the world, and sometimes they do find themselves in political office. But on the whole I think no one directly wills the suffering and death of others without some justification. Only a sociopath or a particularly immoral person would affirm that. This is, of course, the nature of sin. It always seems justified, as good for our sustenance, a delight to behold and desirous for the sake of wisdom (Gen 3:6). The assumption that war occurs because oppressor males seek violence seems to me to give pacifists a Pyrrhic victory; it smacks of that silly pacifism I mentioned in the first paragraph where oppressors and oppressed are too easily characterized based on an empirical code.

That pacifism and just war share a putative common presumption against violence says next to nothing. What differentiates pacifism from just war is that the former, at its best, only makes sense because of the christological convictions we hold about what God has done in Christ. If Jesus is not the unique and definitive expression of God's economy, of how God redeems the world and engages it politically through the cross, resurrection, and ascension—if he were not bodily raised from the dead—then pacifism makes no sense. For pacifism asks you to take a serious risk—not only that of your own life, but also of those you love. Life is good and not to be squandered. If there is no resurrection of bodily life, if all we have is this life, then such a risk would not be worth taking. The presumption of Christian pacifism is not a presumption against something, but for something, for the holiness God calls us to embody as a faithful people redeemed by Christ's blood.

Likewise just war, at its best, is not a presumption against something, but for something. It is a presumption for a well-ordered justice, or as well ordered a justice as can be had this side of Christ's return, which allows us to fulfill our vocation to neighbor love. Just war only makes sense if it is an alien work of love to protect the neighbor from an unjust aggression. It is "alien" because one does not usually think of "love" as killing other human beings. Just war may have a presumption against something, but it is not against violence; it is against the disorder that threatens our everyday lives. Just war tradition says the use of violence is sometimes necessary and we should be prepared—ethically, politically, practically—to use it when necessary.

Pacifism has more than a presumption against violence. It opposes it. Now, different kinds of pacifism oppose violence for different and incommensurable reasons. Pacifism is not a monolithic stance or approach to war, violence, or politics. There are varieties of it, some as alien to the Gospel as are certain affirmations of war. Some argue that violence is always unnecessary in order to accomplish good political ends, and if we were only more imaginative we could always achieve those same good ends through nonviolent means. This is often referred to as "liberal pacifism" or "pacifism as a political strategy." I don't find it very compelling. While it is true that every use of violence brings with it blowback—that is, unforeseen consequences that will create further problems—I think it is impossible to deny that, at least in the short run, violence and war do sometimes work. The allied forces that liberated the prisoner of war camp where my great Uncle Cleon was imprisoned for two years brought him and others liberation from political oppression, which in all likelihood they would not otherwise have had. It allowed him to return to Buffalo, Indiana, and take up his occupation as a farmer and father once again. So I am not taken by pacifist claims that argue with dogmatic certainty that we can always achieve through nonviolent means the same goals that violent means achieve.

## Christological Pacifism

The pacifism that has haunted and always will haunt the Christian Church is something other than this. It assumes that we have seen and heard God's purposes for creation in Jesus. The pacifism I cannot discredit, and have not yet been able to deny, is the pacifism that claims that we are called through our baptisms to participate in the life of Christ and bear witness to the world as God has borne witness to us. It asks us, what happened to us at our baptisms into the life and death of Christ? This position is sometimes called "christological pacifism," and it only works when we take seriously dogmatic Christian convictions.

It only works when we assume what the fifth-century ecumenical council at Chalcedon affirmed about Jesus. He is fully God and fully

human, yet a single acting subject. As such a subject, his perfect obedience is what repairs the wound of creation and sets us right with God
and our neighbors. This perfect obedience required the cross, not of
course because God will only be appeased by blood. This is not something that one can find in the Christian tradition prior to the modern
era—not even in Anselm. As John Wesley taught, Jesus' active obedience—the fact that he embodied God's righteousness through his actions—led to his passive obedience. He gave himself over to human sin
and violence in order to suffer it and thereby confront and heal it.[4] Yet
we were commanded not to defend him. If ever there were an innocent,
it was Jesus. If ever there were a reason to use the sword, it would have
been when he was arrested. Yet in all four Gospels, his words to us are:
"Put away the sword." Is this just a limited, contextual claim, or is it not
better interpreted, as many Church fathers did, as a universal command
transcending all places and times, a call for all baptized Christians, for
this is how God intends God's creatures to live together? It is because
we confess Jesus as "truly divine" and "truly human" that his way of life
must also be *the way* that leads to truth and life (John 14:6).

Christ's incarnation and crucifixion cannot be well understood
apart from his teaching, particularly his pronouncement of "beatitude"
in the Sermon on the Mount. These beatitudes are the forms of life that
are necessary for us to live as citizens of God's coming Kingdom, the
one we pray for everyday in the Lord's Prayer. God does not simply seek
to save individuals from hell if they recite some prayer. The purpose
of creation and redemption is for God to dwell with God's creatures
and vice versa. This cannot, however, be accomplished in any haphazard
way. It is not simply a function of will; it requires that we participate in
the holiness that characterizes God's own perfections. This can only be a
shared participation, but in Christ, God shares it with us. God makes us
into his city, the "new Jerusalem" of which Christ is the temple (Revelation 21). Our task in these times between the times is to prepare ourselves for that citizenship. Of course, that will only be fulfilled when our
bodies are resurrected and creation is restored, but we have no excuse
for failing to participate in Christ's blessedness.

4. See Long, *John Wesley's Moral Theology*, 139.

Along with the incarnation and Christ's teachings, christological pacifism only makes sense if we affirm, as the creed professes, bodily resurrection. Pacifism is not a celebration of death and suffering. God does not affirm death, nor does it somehow get the better of God. Although we worship Jesus as God, and this necessitates a cross, we do not worship death. We can only take the risk of faith that pacifism requires because resurrection is certain. We learn this from the book of Hebrews where we are told that Abraham could gesture toward the sacrifice of Isaac only because he knew God would raise Isaac from the dead. The most difficult aspect of pacifism is not that we might lose our own lives, but that we might lose those we would want to defend. Only the hope of resurrection makes that possible. But that hope is certain because Christ is already enthroned as our "priest-king." This leads to another essential christological dogma: the ascension.

Christ is already enthroned as our "priest-king," even if not all things are yet subject to him. He will not require subjection by force, for this would speak a word contrary to the definitive Word God speaks in Jesus' life, death, and resurrection. We expect him to complete his rule when he returns, and to do so in a way that will be consistent with how he came the first time. It is not as if the second time he comes he does so as a commando ready to conquer through force![5] He has already triumphed through the cross. We await the perfection of the rule he has already established. This is why we announce, hopefully every Sunday, "Christ has died, Christ is risen, Christ will come again."

So the question is, how are we to participate in his rule? We are, I would suggest, called to repeat his life—nonidentically of course—by cultivating his righteousness as our own, seeking to be nothing less than perfect.

## On Letting One's Neighbors Die

Christological pacifism does not begin by reacting against something. It does not need a caricatured version of war or soldiers to win by default, but it must then take seriously the question posed by the just war tradition: Are you willing to let the innocent die at the hand of aggressors? If

5. See J. Nelson Kraybill's essay in this volume.

we don't caricature warcraft as simply irrational blood sport, then christological pacifism must not shy away from the just war claims to moral seriousness. This does not mean we capitulate to every claim made by politicians and soldiers about the moral justness of any particular cause. They could be wrong about such claims. Perhaps this war or military action is simply out of self-interest, but that would not mean that every use of military action is. It was not for my great uncles. So the question put to pacifists at its boldest is, Are you willing to let your neighbors or other innocents die for the sake of your dogmatic theological convictions? And the first answer that must be given, before it then gets qualified, is yes. We look at this tragic reality caused by human sinfulness and confess that not everything we do to protect the innocent prevents the violent, who refuse God's vocation, from wreaking havoc upon God's creation. Is this immoral? Is it disobedient to God's call to love one's neighbor? This question must haunt the Christian pacifist if he or she is not to gain a Pyrrhic victory.

Having confessed that this "yes" is something christological pacifism entails, the next question is, Does this render that position immoral? The first thing that must be acknowledged here is that just war and pacifism *both* say yes to this question. If it makes pacifism immoral, the same must apply to the just war. For just war also recognizes that in any military action, "collateral damage" occurs. The innocent will be killed along with the aggressor. There is no way to wage war without this taking place. The drones that target terrorists also target incidentally their families and neighbors. Any military action will take out the innocent men, women, and children who are not directly prosecuting the war but simply happen to be in close proximity to those who are. In just war teaching innocent civilians cannot be directly targeted, but they can be legitimately killed insofar as their deaths are the "indirect effect" of directly targeting the aggressor and for that reason do not fall under the prohibition of the sixth commandment. If pacifism is to be condemned because it says "yes" to allowing innocents to die, then so too must just war be condemned.

Could the just war advocate say rightly that it at least *intends* to defend the innocent with proportional reason? That is to say, a just war does not seek to kill the innocent, but pacifism gives them up *intentionally* as a sacrifice to its dogmatic theological convictions? This would be to attribute an intention to an action because of others' abuses of such convictions. Such an argument has a recursive structure that finally leads to horrible consequences. If the pacifist is accused of *intending* the death of the innocent because she or he refuses to use violence, then couldn't the same be said of the person who, when confronted with a violent action, wasn't prepared? Perhaps he left his gun at home, was out of bullets, or had not been to the firing range for practice and simply missed? In truth, we live in a sinful, fallen world where we cannot secure our existence, or that of our friends and families, against all potential aggressors. To live as if we can is simply to deny the reality of sin. To live as if we must is simply to deny the reality of resurrection. What disarms the aggressor is not our better ability to use and implement violence, but to be freed from the grip of fear it has over us. Life belongs to God. Its unjust ending cries out for justification, and we cannot but believe that God will somehow justify those who suffer such a fate. "We believe in the resurrection of the body."

Of course this will raise another question, one where the political right and left quickly join forces, for they both immediately raise the same question almost every time this argument is made: How is this not quietism? How is it not an invitation to allow abuse against the oppressed by the oppressors? Despite the predictability of the question, it gets raised because it is an important and just question. Christological pacifism, grounded in the hope of the resurrection, could lead to such quietism. It could lead to the kind of "liberal pacifism" I already mentioned where those who are already secure by their position, wealth, or access to power allow those who are not so secure to die for their convictions. (Is not the same the case with a volunteer military?) This is immoral. However, "the abuse of a thing does not take away its usefulness." For this reason christological pacifism can only be taken seriously where it calls those who affirm it to take the risk, at some point in their lives, to be insecure and vulnerable through their service to those who are likewise vulnerable. I don't intend to be romantic here. No one should *will* such vulnerability throughout his or her life unless he or she has a special vocation, just as no one should will a permanent state of war. God is a God of life, not death. Poverty, vulnerability, and insecurity are not states anyone should will if he or she has seen Jesus raised from the dead. But they are states that accompany a fallen world, and we all must share the burden. For this reason I would advocate for a national policy of universal conscription that would also allow for alternative service to the common good through works that provide ways for securing the life of our neighbors by means other than violence.

Christological pacifism, grounded in the hope of the resurrection, could lead to quietism, but it could also lead to a profound risk for faithfulness and hope on behalf of those whom Jesus says will inherit the Kingdom (Matthew 25). It can lead to a profound commitment to do all we can—without employing violence—to make the world habitable for those who find it uninhabitable. Does it ask us to let our neighbors die? No. It finds life good and affirms it, acknowledging that in a sinful world this affirmation will sometimes be thwarted. It also acknowledges that God has done the one thing necessary to repair the wound: God has definitively spoken in the cross and resurrection of Jesus. All Christian thinking about war and violence must begin there.

# 3

## What Would You Do if Someone Were Attacking a Loved One?

Amy Laura Hall *and* Kara Slade

SOME OF THE QUESTIONS in this volume clearly resound in the registers of scriptural interpretation or of the intersection of faith and public policy. At least initially, we may be able to consider our reading of Romans 13 or the case of Nazi Germany from a safely analytical remove. This question, on the other hand, is troubling precisely because of its personal specificity and because of the visceral reaction it evokes. *You* are present as one of your own *loved ones* is being *attacked*. And *you* are being asked to respond as you would, or as you hope that you would, in that moment of crisis. It carries within it so much particularity, so many implicit assumptions, that we believe the best response is to trouble this troubling question itself.

Who is the *you* in the question, who is the *loved one*, and who is the attacker, the *someone* whose violence may in turn require a violent reaction? What sort of *attack* is implied or brought to mind in the scenario? By drawing out these initially peripheral issues, we hope to show that even in the face of the most personal violence, a nonviolent response becomes more than a theoretical possibility once we recognize and name the particularity that underlies the generally assumed *other* possibility, that of violently protecting one's beloved. Of course, we also bring our particularity to bear as we question the question: as women, as feminists, as pastors and scholars of an evangelical bent in mainline Protestantism (where pacifism is, admittedly, usually treated as a minority position, an optional add-on to personal holiness rather than a confessional commitment). But as a dead Danish philosopher—to whom we are both indebted—wrote as he began his series of deliberations on Christian love, "Every discourse, particularly a section of a discourse, presupposes something that is the starting point. Someone who wishes to deliberate on the discourse or statement therefore does well to find this presupposition first in order to begin with it."[1] Our task, then, is to find the presuppositions in this question, to uncover the starting points, and so hopefully to make it possible for our readers, in their own particularity, to discern an answer to the question along the way.

## What Would *You* Do if Someone Were Attacking a *Loved One*?

In the prepublication format, this question appeared with my name under it. What would *you* do, Amy Laura, were someone attacking your loved one? This reads as humor. I weigh "about 100 pounds soaking wet" (as we would say in Texas) and I am about 5'2". The *you* of this sentence is presumably someone who could, should the need arise, be a *you* of the assumed query. The *you* is someone who could take out someone else should the need arise. I could only be such a *you* were I to purchase a weapon, or to employ another *you* or a set of other *you*'s who could do my bidding. On my own, I am no such *you*. The question appears to me as a joke, or, perhaps, as a reminder that I am a little woman in need of protection. Which, of course, I feel sometimes in a salient way—that is, I feel like a little woman in need of protection.

But to this point, even with nonlethal force, say, a baseball bat or pepper spray, I could only be such a *you* if I were facing a *someone* who is considerably smaller than I am. And that *someone* would need to be as ambivalent about power and force as I am, truth be told. I would need some equalizing factor in order even to get the chance to spray or to batter up. In order for me to be the *you* at the heart of the question, I would

1. Kierkegaard, *Works of Love*, 17.

need to face a small someone who would, not incidentally, have to be divided in his or her soul about the faithfulness of violence. I would need an opponent who also flinches. Otherwise, this presumed scenario of *me* taking on a *someone* evokes laughter—like a short wherein Nancy Drew faces Godzilla.

And that laughter comes out of an irony that is at the heart of the question. A little lady is not the *you* of the question. She is the *loved one*. And, as the presumed beloved, my challenge—the "feminine" challenge, so to speak—may be to relinquish my carefully taught desire to be protected. Sadly, I have heard from some pacifist men over the years that they have lost courtship efforts when their hoped-for beloved asks them *what they would do if* . . . Basically, these men have failed a cultural test of their fitness for holy husbandry. In a dog-eat-dog, post-9/11, China-owns-us-economically sort of world, some young men who unequivocally reject the terms of this question will, apparently, appear less worth an investment of affection. How may heterosexual women in the church resist this pull toward a security that has more to do with cultural tropes than with christological truth?

Even if the irony of the question here has some root in what we sometimes call "nature"—in the apparent "fact" that women are generally less capable of upper-body strength and that during certain times of our "natural" cycle we prefer certain set-male jawlines to other male profiles—that says little for Christians, I think, about who we are called by God to be.[2] Just because scientific research, gleefully reported in the popular press, tells me that I might "naturally" prefer a muscular Jesus during ovulation does not mean that I can know fiddle about which Jesus I am to follow to the cross.[3] Neurobiologists may attempt to tell us these days just who we "are" and who we are "naturally" summoned to be, but Christians know better than to accept this new version of determinism.[4,5]

2. Penton-Voak and Perrett, "Female Preference for Male Faces Changes Cyclically," 39–48.

3. "What an Ovulating Girl Wants."

4. DeYoung et al., "Testing Predictions from Personality Neuroscience," 820–28.

5. Gray and Thompson, "Neurobiology of Intelligence," 157–62.

At the risk of being overly autobiographical, I will note here that our conference "Toward a Moral Consensus Against Torture" fell a few weeks after my separation from my husband. I was reading paper after paper on torture while living for the first time as a single mother of two daughters. We also had the complicated blessing of being covered in an online article that provoked dozens of unhinged comments by (mostly, it seemed) lonely, scared men accusing me, personally, of being soft on terrorism. I had the urge, on more than one occasion, to call the fire department and ask them to send a firefighter to sleep on my couch. Frankly, I am not sure if I wanted just a housemate. There is something fairly visceral about a desire to be protected during a time of physical and emotional vulnerability. But, somehow, the Holy Spirit granted me the courage not to call a firefighter or police officer to come live with me for a week. I will admit, here in print, that having two rude and excitable rescue dogs helped. If I am honest with myself, I have to admit that Bertha and Mabel function as alarms and implicit threats to anyone who might think about breaking in. Of course, that history in the South is fraught: dogs were used as weapons and implied threat all throughout the fight for Civil Rights.

Inasmuch as Christian women engage in resistance to these patterns of fear, perhaps even women in our current neoconservative corseted/sexy/"protect me" culture may seize back and reclaim the *you* of the sentence. What would *you* do if the wider world told *you* to want a man who can take on an attacker? I suggest we teach the wider world a little song: "I have decided to follow Jesus; / No turning back, no turning back." I sang this to my daughters when they were little, as a lullaby. Their lives as girls are not going to be easy, but they need to live into courage, not fear and a longing for false shelter.

## What Would You *Do* if Someone Were Attacking a Loved One?

The question hinges on a decision to act: in the heat of the moment, in the split second of crisis, *you* are called upon to *do something*. I am reminded of the dialogue between Keanu Reeves and Dennis Hopper in the otherwise forgettable (but entertaining) thriller *Speed*: "Pop quiz, hotshot: there's a bomb on a bus . . . what do you do? *What do you do?*"

Of course, Reeves, playing the heroic and handsome off-duty police-man, saves the passengers and wins the heart of Sandra Bullock in the process. But while situations requiring instantaneous acts of daring may make for exciting cinema, they make bad cases for moral-theological reasoning—especially when the question is posed to test the consis-tency of opposition to war, which is anything but an instantaneous act. "Surely," the argument goes, "in that case you would *do something*, and if you would *do something* then, your squeamishness about violence conducted by the state would be revealed for what it is: trendy political posturing of the worst sort. Or, if indeed you would *do nothing*, you are revealed as less than responsible, less than a man." The question, with its implicit presupposition in favor of protective violence, is bound up intimately with particular assumptions about masculinity and the role of violence in the performance of masculinity, whether in a Christian context or outside of it.

One must look no further than a relatively recent presidential campaign to see those assumptions worked out on the national stage. In 1988, Massachusetts Governor Michael Dukakis, a noted opponent of the death penalty, was asked a variant of this question in a televised debate with then-Vice President George H. W. Bush. The debate mod-erator, CNN's Bernard Shaw, asked him if he would support the death penalty if his wife, Kitty, were raped and murdered. His response struck a fatal blow to his presidential aspirations: "No, I don't, Bernard, and I think you know that I've opposed the death penalty during all of my life. I don't see any evidence that it's a deterrent and I think there are better and more effective ways to deal with violent crime."[6] Dukakis' answer played directly into the media narrative of the governor as an effete technocrat, as *less than a man,* incapable of filling the role of national father/protector included in the office of President of the United States. Two other aspects of the Dukakis story should be named explicitly here. First, according to *Time* magazine's coverage of the event, viewers saw the answer as "dispassionate," when clearly *passion* was expected. But is passion only acceptable in men when it appears as anger or violence? Is there room in this discussion for returning evil with good, for pa-tient suffering, for *passion* of an explicitly christological sort? Second,

6. Stephey, "Top 10 Memorable Debate Moments."

although it was completely unnecessary for the purposes of the debate because the hypothetical murder in itself would have constituted a capital crime, the issue of rape made its way into the discussion. And, as we will examine in more detail in a later section, rape makes its way into the discussion more often than not.

In his short book, *What Would You Do?*, John Howard Yoder addresses this question in detail, and in the course of his argument he identifies a number of possible actions and their outcomes: tragedy, martyrdom, another way out (either "natural" or "providential"), or attempted killing (either "successful" or "unsuccessful").[7] As it is usually posed, the question assumes that either tragedy or successful attempted killing—that is, violence that stops the attacker, regardless of whether or not anyone is actually killed—are the only possibilities. But as Yoder makes clear, this is a false dichotomy, and its applicability to institutional violence is negligible at best. And as part of a peculiar people who reject the notion that moral agency occurs in a hermetically (and hermeneutically) sealed system of human deeds and consequences, we as Christians must take God and God's actions—past, present, and future—into account: "There are more options than the evident ones; miracle and martyrdom are possibilities not to be excluded. [. . .] I do not claim to know ahead of time that either miracle or martyrdom is promised or commanded. I know I can never justify killing, or adultery, or blasphemy. I know I can never approve institutionally and in principle of preparations before the fact to be in a position to do those things, as war does."[8] Yoder's position, here and elsewhere in his work, is relentlessly christological and eschatological. Any desire, any perception of a need to individually save the day *à la* Keanu Reeves, must be tempered by the knowledge in faith that this day—and indeed all days—has already been saved by the one Individual who is both our eternal Savior and our pattern for earthly life.

7. Yoder, *What Would You Do?*.
8. Yoder, "'Patience' as Method in Moral Reasoning."

## What Would You Do if *Someone* Were Attacking a Loved One?

Jennifer Mackenzie found for me, years ago, the Disney short from 1952 called *Uncle Donald's Ants*. Jenn pointed out at the time that the ants are a perfect combination of Asian and African, marching in time to invade Donald's home, and take his sugar. Kara suggests in the next section that a very particular kind of sugar is implied in this question, that is, the sugar that is a female beloved's sexuality. I think she is quite right, and I believe that, for some people, the *someone* implied in the question is tacitly brown. For others, that *someone* may be poor or homeless or struggling with a severe mental illness, but I believe that a common factor in our visualization of the *someone* is that "their" bodies are marked as different from "our" bodies such that the perceived threat to the body of the hypothetical beloved in the question is multiplied exponentially.

This type of comment landed me in hot water last year, when I suggested in a *Sojourners* interview that torture is a racial issue. My comment offended an older generation of scholars in theology, who want to keep torture a purely principled issue, apart from postcolonial and racial modes of self-interrogation, confession, and repentance. I would humbly submit that this offense is a crucial point of discussion for pacifists.[9] How does pacifism, as a mode of Christian consideration, prevent us from digging into the racial and colonial aspects of warfare? How might it encourage willed blindness to the isolation of "people like us" in the academy and in most churches from "other people" of a different socioeconomic class, or those with disabilities that cause them to be feared rather than cared for? When kept as a principle, or even as a Christian virtue, apart from truly probing questions about the *who* implied in the *someone*, we are left with something only partly radical, and mostly useless in the real world of resisting domination. To resist a culture of domination and violence, Christians have to dig into questions about who "we" deem to be, implicitly, after "our" stuff, "our" children, and "our" women. The supposedly raw, masculine impulse to fight off

---

9. Roberts, "Torture and the Biopolitics of Race," 229.

an attacker is itself culturally taught, carefully, in terms of the contours of the potential attacker(s).[10,11]

The youngsters living into their early adulthood right now watched as their parents watched an unparalleled display of emasculation. White Protestant young people watched as their parents watched the future shift from cultural confidence to a sense of impending cultural impotence. I recall, myself, praying under my breath, "Please dear Lord, do not let the attackers be Muslim," over, and over, and over again. I prayed hard that the attackers would be white, as in the case of the Oklahoma City bombing of 1995. This sounds ludicrous to some. Why would I pray that the attackers be white? Because, and this is controversial, I believe that always simmering under the surface of American mainstream culture is a fear of variously brown people, and especially the physical power of brown men. My prayer came out of a knowledge that American history is replete with images like those on the Donald Duck short, whether subtle or overt. The sense that nonwhite male creatures are going to come in, and take our sugar, is an American trope that is always ready for deployment. In the case of 9/11, it united African-American and Anglo-American men against Muslim men. Today, in some regions, it unites African-American men and Anglo-American men against Latino immigrant men—who are presumably taking the few remaining jobs that have not been sent over to the other region of anxiety, that is, China. A Disney short today would need to combine the menace of inchoately Asian men (yesterday, Japanese/Chinese, today mostly Chinese) and the foreboding of what Samuel Huntington called the "Clash of Civilizations" with Islam. The vaguely brown ants would need turbans, perhaps.

I would submit that the sentence implies not only a male *someone*, but a male *someone* whose body marks them as somehow *other*, somehow not part of "us." *Someone* who "we" have been "carefully taught" (to quote from *South Pacific*) to see as wanting what we have, and being willing to take it (or them/her) with a force that *someone else* must counter. I cannot, because I am the presumed endangered/beloved/damsel in distress and not the agent of moral action in the sentence. And so the

10. Gunning, *Race, Rape, and Lynching,* 5–6.

11. McMaster, "Torture from Algiers to Abu Ghraib," 1–21.

task is left to *you*, the *you* whose protection I have been taught to desire, which, if I can trust in my own baptism and face an uncertain future with graced courage rather than fear, I do not truly need.

## What Would You Do if Someone Were *Attacking* a Loved One?

> Me: (in the midst of a conversation) "... actually I'm a pacifist."
>
> Person X: "Really?"
>
> Me: "Yeah."
>
> (After a brief pause.)
>
> Person X: "What if someone was raping your wife?"
>
> First off, what makes people jump from pacifism to rape? Why does every person on the planet do this? It's never: "Pacifist, eh? Like Dr. Martin Luther King, Jr.?" or "Pacifism? Isn't that the opposition to war or violence of any kind, culminating in a refusal to engage in any military activity?" Nope, no Merriam-Webster here; just the same fictitious rape of my invented wife.
>
> —*English teacher and amateur blogger Nathan Rex Smith*[12]

As it poses a hypothetical situation that is intended to provoke a visceral response, this question presupposes a certain kind of attack. It may be possible to reason through a response to a robber on the street, it may even be possible to think through possible courses of nonviolent action in the hypothetical case of a home-invasion burglary, but sooner or later the question will be reduced to its bare, emotive essence: what would you do if someone attempted to rape your own beloved? We saw, for example, the addition of rape to the debate question posed to Michael Dukakis, and we have both seen this rhetorical move being made time after time, in both online and in-person discussions among young Christian men, when the question is raised. Sooner or later, the prospect of rape enters this discussion, and it should be addressed directly—not as the spectral superlative example of the larger category of

---

12. Smith, "First Question about Pacifism Which I Will Never Answer Again."

violent crimes, but as rape in itself, as a particular intimate violation of the body of a particular other.

The notion of rape as a particularly egregious offense is intertwined with its early history as not only a crime against the person but as a crime against property, specifically against the property rights of the husband or father of the victim. And it is intertwined with ideas (still very much alive in evangelical culture) of the substantive value and irreparability of female virginity outside of marriage—or marital chastity within it. It is enmeshed with the idealization of female sexuality and with the location of its control under the authority of particular men. This is an old story, as old as the Pentateuch. We read in Deuteronomy 22 that "if a man meets a virgin who is not engaged, and seizes her and lies with her, and they are caught in the act, the man who lay with her shall give fifty shekels of silver to the young woman's father, and she shall become his wife. Because he violated her he shall not be permitted to divorce her as long as he lives."[13]

Within this worldview, once it is transferred to the husband, the control (and use) of a woman's sexuality becomes exclusively and ultimately his. But this is also a story that we carry with us into the present. Our own home state of North Carolina, for example, was the last in the United States to eliminate the spousal exemption to its statutes defining rape, only removing that clause in 1993. It remains a matter of prayer as to whether women in our state have internalized this removal, or whether instead most of us, when faced with the requirement to do what must be done to salvage a struggling marriage, are willing to undergo whatever might be necessary to *keep the peace*. Of course, I do not mean to suggest that the control or commodification of female sexuality is the only factor in play in this discussion. Husbands, fathers, and lovers have—both historically and today—earnestly felt the desire to protect their beloved ones from the physical and emotional trauma of rape, and have responded to those traumatic events in women's lives out of a place of genuine love and concern. However, the history of the way that rape has been thought of and talked about, especially by men, remains a considerably complicated and contextually laden topic.

13. Deut 22:28–29, NRSV.

By way of conclusion, I also would like to trouble the idea of considering the rape of one's beloved *as an idea*—that is, considering it in theory as part of a theological object lesson or subject of debate. As a woman, my thoughts immediately jump from the rape of another to my own hypothetical rape. The potential situation shifts from "someone is attempting to rape a loved one" to "someone is attempting to rape *you*."[14] It is a question that every woman, pacifist or not, has probably thought about (or worried about), and it is also a question that for far too many women brings to mind the intrusive memories of assaults that they have survived. It is tied tightly to cultural expectations that say, on the one hand, a virtuous woman should resist an assailant as vigorously and loudly as possible, but on the other hand, "nice girls" don't question expressions of male power in impolite ways. And tragically, it is also linked to the lingering and destructive distinction between forcible rape by a violent stranger and rape by someone known to the victim, especially when the victim is under the influence of alcohol or drugs. For me, and for many other women who have written to me about this question, its most off-putting feature may, in the end, not be the *pacifism* or the *protectiveness* at all, but rather the *pontificating* about what my coauthor has previously described as "a horrible rupture of God's intent for gracious human intimacy."[15]

## What *Would* You Do if Someone Were Attacking a Loved One?

The format of our response in this chapter, as a reprisal of the approach in chapters IIA, IIB, and IIC of *Works of Love*, was chosen not only out of a desire to make use of Kierkegaard's method, but also to point to the content of the original work. As he digs through the assumptions lurking within the commandment, "You shall love the neighbor as yourself," Kierkegaard pulls each reader—each "single individual"—up short and

14. I would especially recommend Angie O'Gorman's treatment of the possibility of nonviolence in the context of attempted rape, "Defense through Disarmament," which appears in Yoder's *What Would You Do?* as well as in O'Gorman's *The Universe Bends towards Justice*. It is an important piece that raises a number of unsettling and unsettled questions, and may be used fruitfully if this topic is discussed in the parish.

15. Hall, "Unwanted Interruptions."

shows him (or her) the false starts, misapprehensions, and entirely human failures that inevitably accompany our attempts to love anyone as God would have us love them.[16,17] We would suggest that recognizing the fallenness revealed in each of us as we try (and fail) to love faithfully is an essential part of the struggle with this question.

Any consideration of what *you*, the "single individual" reading this essay, *would* do or *should* do if *someone* attacked your own beloved is first complicated by the presence of the beloved *as the beloved*. If you find yourself constructing a series of hypothetical situations and hypothetical responses involving her—testing them for plausibility or consistency, analyzing what you would or would not do for her, pulling away from the immediacy of your love—do you then truly love her? Or do you instead love the reflection of your *other self* in her, as you are unable to see her without the objectifying lens of objectivity?

The question is further confounded by the fact that within the category of *neighbor* stands both the *loved one* and the attacking *someone*. And the commandment to love the neighbor requires the unequivocal rejection of preferential love (*Forkjerlighed*) and its replacement by Christian love (*Kjerlighed*), which "means not to exclude a single one."[18] The duty to love all people based on our kinship before God asks us to transcend our cultural and personal fears of *someone* else. If I err by reserving my love for only the friends I deem to be safe, and withhold it from those I name as my enemy, then maybe I should "shut [my] eyes . . . become all ears to the commandment," and find that "the enemy looks just like the neighbor."[19]

It may be helpful here to suggest a series of other questions that may point the reader in far more fruitful directions than the original one. How has my love gone astray if I conclude that violence is the only possible response to the threat of violence between neighbors? If I as-

16. Kierkegaard, *Works of Love*, 47.

17. The pronouns in this section assume a male reader and a female beloved, as we have focused primarily on culturally constituted gender norms within heterosexual relationships. The presumed male *you* in the chapter's question is here imputed to *you*, the reader.

18. Kierkegaard, *Works of Love*, 52.

19. Ibid., 68.

sume that the attacking *someone* is uniquely undeserving of love and I cannot see him as a neighbor, will I then be blind to Yoder's nonviolent "another way out" if it appears? Is it possible that Christian discipleship may indeed call me to witness in a cruciform way to my love of both the *someone* and the *loved one*?

We end this essay with a note of caution, an emphatic "yes, but . . ." attached to the last question in particular. As Thomas Becket faces temptation and despair in T. S. Eliot's *Murder in the Cathedral*, he says of his longing for sainthood, "the last temptation is the greatest treason: to do the right deed for the wrong reason."[20] In our efforts to push this question out of the range of facile and orderly analysis, we do not wish to drive the reader into the opposite philosophical end zone in search of a poetic answer either. Both miracle and martyrdom are indeed possible, but miracle is beyond our capacity for faithful expectation and martyrdom is beyond our capacity for faithful desire. For some Christian men and women, the thought of martyrdom (especially in the presence of one's beloved) may be strangely compelling. However, the casual allure of this most radical and rigorous act of faith is more closely aligned with baptized aesthetics than with faithfulness. Thus trapped between the "either" of ethical abstraction and the "or" of the desire for a poetically satisfying witness to love, the reader looking for answers in terms of a path to faithful action may have found far more frustration than moral clarity in these pages. In the end, to encourage persistence in that frustration is the clearest guidance we can give.

20. Eliot, *Murder in the Cathedral*, 44.

# 4

## What about Hitler?

Robert Brimlow

"Sleeper, awake!
Rise from the dead,
and Christ will shine on you."

Be careful then how you live, not as unwise people but as wise, making the most of the time, because the days are evil.

—EPHESIANS 5:14–16

It is a curious sensation to write for, or speak to, an audience that agrees with you. I am assuming that if you have read this far in this fine book willingly—that is, you are neither a student slogging through an assignment nor my wife being her dutiful self—you are most likely in accord with the views that have been presented thus far. And that is not at all surprising. Even if you were not initially inclined to understand the meaning of Jesus' call, my colleagues have presented persuasive, scholarly, and perhaps even holy reflections and arguments about what discipleship and the faithful following of the Lord demands for our interactions with others.[1] Being called to follow Jesus and responding to that call means that we lead lives of nonviolence. Yet, I am still confronted with the prospect of that curious sensation.

On those rare occasions when I have been asked to speak about faith, nonviolence, and peacemaking, they have usually been to audiences who already agreed with the views. Invariably the curious sensation felt as though I were talking in an echo chamber, or, perhaps more accurately, resembled those times in the car when I speak to myself. At times like those—and this might well be a time like those—I recall the old adage that if two people are in complete agreement, then at least one of them is not thinking. I hope you will not be disappointed if I do not offer a scholarly or theological chapter to you at this juncture. Prayerful and, therefore, honest reflection is what I wish to engage in.

The questions we all eventually have to confront once we put this book down is how far this peace thing extends, how seriously we want to treat Jesus' commands, and what's the cost in real (that is, material) terms. Let's be honest—and we can start obliquely: Jesus was quite explicit in Matt 5:28 and 5:32, and how many of us believe and (let's not forget) conform our actions to his proscriptions against lustful looks and divorce? We are awfully willing to go through all sorts of spiritual and interpretive gymnastics to get Jesus not to mean what he clearly says, and for what purpose? We want to preserve the purveyance and consumption of sex and soft-core pornography, at least for advertising campaigns, movies, the Net, and the swimsuit edition of *Sports Illustrated*, as well as the freedom to marry and remarry and remarry. Jesus clearly wasn't factoring in how modern marketing techniques need to function in a free market economy, nor could he have known how contemporary cultural values have evolved. No, no. His message must have a deeper, spiritual meaning that doesn't address our behavior or material attitudes. He couldn't have meant what he said.

---

1. Not having read the manuscript as yet, I assume my friends have laid much of the scriptural and theological groundwork for this essay. Needless to say, I also assume that I am not in significant disagreement with large parts of whatever they have said; their views should not be tarred with the brush meant for mine.

If we are so willing to sacrifice the gospel for what some may regard as a "recreational" attitude towards sex, what are we willing to do with his other commands regarding turning cheeks, walking extra miles, giving our shirts as well as our cloaks, forgoing the law courts . . .? All well and good for first-century Jerusalem, but what happens to me in Rochester and you in Cincinnati, Detroit, Tuscaloosa when we're confronted by the jonesing junkie with a knife? We are sensitive in many of the areas the gospel touches, and that means we should poke those areas and try to draw out some pus. Before we can speak truth to power, we have to learn to speak it to ourselves.

So, yes, we read that Jesus calls us to nonviolence and peacemaking, but also to care for the poor, the hungry, prisoners, the enslaved, the suffering, and the oppressed. Jesus came to declare the coming of the Kingdom, what John Howard Yoder explains as the Time of Jubilee.[2] This is the time when all debts are forgiven; and, what's more, it's a gospel declaration I can get behind because I have lots of debts of lots of kinds. This is quite a beautiful thing for us debtors, but I don't think it is so great for our debt holders.

I do not want to suggest that I have any sympathy at all for whatever financial losses accrue to Goldman Sachs or Bank of America if the debts they hold are canceled, especially if one of those canceled debts is my Bank of America Visa account. But "debt" means more than just cash that is owed. Those who are oppressed and who suffer are also debt holders: they have been abused and deprived, imprisoned and killed by evildoers, and we are called to help them and alleviate their suffering. Alleviating suffering must mean more than wiping their brows and uttering sympathetic sounds, or tossing ten extra bucks in the collection plate. When someone is hungry, we feed her; when someone is naked, we clothe him; when someone is suffering, we try to stop the pain. It does not seem right to look at those who are suffering and think, "Well, since the debt that is owed to them by the sin of the evil-doers is continually being canceled with the arrival of Jubilee, all is right with the world," and we can go on and wipe their brows, placidly humming "Amazing Grace." We are not called only to aid, abet, or ignore injustice;

2. Yoder, *Politics of Jesus*.

we are also called to redress the balance as well as we are able—to restore to victims what is theirs.

And this is where our dear brothers and sisters, the just warriors,[3] come in to ask us to be honest and thereby poke a sore spot. To put this in a slightly different context, we who oppose violence are apparently engaged in a debate, a war dialogue—political, academic, and ecclesial—with just warriors. And the interesting thing about this dispute or dialogue is that we are tending to talk past one another. Focusing on our side of the discussion, we zero in on and analyze the *war* aspect of their justification; whereas I think the just warriors zero in on and elaborate upon the *just* aspect of that same justification: they are speaking in reality of justified violence in support of a just cause.

This is something that we need always not simply to bear in mind but also to keep in the forefront of our hearts, and it has two parts. First of all, we must avoid the temptation to demonize the just warriors; I believe that in most cases they are indeed guided by a motivation that is rooted firmly in the aspiration to follow the gospel. When we engage in hyperbolic, rhetorical characterizations, we may derive some satisfaction but ultimately we are engaging in a verbal violence and are not telling the truth. Second, what motivates the just warriors in the specific situations we examine together—those reflections on concrete examples that guide us—what concerns the just warrior needs to concern us explicitly as well. Those concerns are important, they are significant, and it is incumbent upon us to address them directly rather than to let them dwell in the background.

In this regard, I am concerned that, when we talk about Christian nonviolence and characterize or think about ourselves as proponents of a nonviolent gospel message, we unconsciously focus on the negativity of our position. If we focus excessively on what we are against, it becomes quite unclear (and perhaps even elusive) to others and even to ourselves just what we are for.

---

3. A just warrior is one who believes that under certain circumstances, and only as a last resort, violence may be employed—for example, to protect innocents from death at the hands of an evildoer. For one analysis of the just war theory, see my *What about Hitler?*, 37ff.

So what is it that we are for? Perhaps we want to say that we are called to help bring the Kingdom of God to the world nonviolently, a Kingdom where the slaves are freed, the mournful are soothed, and the suffering victims are healed.

To find out how good that answer is, let's return to the just warriors, mainly because I think we can learn important truths even from those who oppose us—maybe especially so since they are eager to point out our faults, which may, at the end of the day, really be our faults.

Again, let us grant the just warrior goodness of will—after all, what kind of warrior without a good, moral will worries about and takes seriously the question of the justice of war in the first place? I think we will find that she is concerned and confronted with a serious moral issue or serious moral problem involving the suffering of innocents.[4] Considering the specifics of the situation, she has arrived at the conclusion that violence—usually, though not necessarily exclusively, exercised by nation-states—is the *only* way to reestablish justice and end the suffering of the innocent. What is our position here as proponents of Christian nonviolence—that is, accepting that there is a serious moral issue we are called to settle or a moral problem we are called to solve, any specific situation which involves the suffering and death of innocents we are called to end, but which cannot be ended except through violent means? It is all well and good to proclaim as some dogma that our call to nonviolence is always compatible with our call to alleviate the suffering of innocent victims, but the just warrior is telling us that is false. The just warrior accuses us of choosing to maintain our mistaken notion of spiritually pure nonviolence at the expense of the lives of the innocent when confronted with the inescapable alternatives. We are like Pilate, keeping our hands clean while the victim goes to her death.

So we need to examine this compatibility thesis (by which I mean the notion that nonviolence is compatible with justice and the alleviation of the suffering of innocents) if we are to assess the charge of the

---

4. I am introducing a vague notion of morals here, primarily because I am convinced that the just warriors' argument is fundamentally based on a secular rather than a Christian ethics. If that's true, all sorts of underlying assumptions about describing situations and solving them get introduced into our dialogue that we should be cautious about accepting.

just warriors against us, as well as our charge against them—namely that violence is forbidden by the gospel. For it must be clear that our claim that discipleship means nonviolence entails that our warrior brothers and sisters are terribly wrong.

I believe that the compatibility thesis amounts to two claims:

1. No war has ever been justified because the nonviolent alternatives have never been exhausted.

2. All disputes can be settled through nonviolent means, for example, by truthful, rational discourse and compromise. And there is a corollary to (2):

2c. Violent action does not yield solutions; it only exacerbates injustice and suffering.[5]

Before proceeding, I want to point out an interesting grammatical technicality.[6] It is common for us to say that we are called to be nonviolent. In that sentence, "nonviolent" is a noun and has a certain status in the proposition. In the compatibility thesis, "nonviolent" becomes adjectival, that is, it is something that modifies and is therefore dependent upon some noun—behaviors or actions. Leaving aside the wealth of other grammatical implications, we have very subtly been led to assert that we are called not to be nonviolent but rather to engage in nonviolent methodologies to achieve certain other ends. In other words, we are implicitly led to grant priority to what is precisely in dispute.

That first claim of the compatibility thesis—that no war has ever been justified because the nonviolent alternatives have never been exhausted—well, that's an empirical claim and I don't know that it is, in fact, true. I'm not an historian; heck, I'm just barely a philosopher what with my concerns with adjectival function. But even if it is true, it implicitly grants the possibility that nonviolent alternatives might be

---

5. Proponents of 2c seem to argue two things in support of it: i) No matter how careful the just warrior is, there will always be innocent victims of violence—so-called collateral damage. ii) Responding to violence with violence initiates a never-ending cycle of violence.

6. I am a philosopher, after all, not a theologian; thus grammatical technicalities of this sort have great appeal to my analytic sensibilities.

exhaustible, in which case violence would be justifiable. So that claim doesn't work for our purposes.

That leaves the second claim, which appears to be the more interesting one. My problem is that I don't think the proposition that all disputes can be settled through nonviolent means is true. In addition, many of us seem to treat the corollary—that violent action does not yield solutions—as though it were *a priori*, that is, self-evidently true. Yet that proposition also strikes me as palpably false: my killing the evildoer most definitely does solve the problem of how I can end the suffering of the innocent victim, and does so efficiently. If someone has to die in this situation, it is better that the guilty evildoer be the one and the victim be saved rather than the other way around; there is no third alternative. Secondly, while it may be true that in some situations some other innocents will die as collateral damage through the actions of the just warrior, it is not clear that this must always be the case, nor that this result is completely unacceptable[7] should it occur.

I think it's important to discuss in a little bit more detail why I think the second claim and its corollary are false, especially as that conclusion seems to put me outside the nonviolence camp and might well embarrass the editors of this volume. To say that all disputes can be settled by nonviolent means, such as through truthful, rational discourse and compromise, assumes that the disputants are both rational and willing to compromise their goals. Even if this is accurate for the vast majority of cases, it is not warranted for all cases, and this is a point that deserves more elaboration.

What I have spent some effort in examining in my work over a few years is Adolph Hitler. He is the paradigmatic example of a target for justifiable and justified violence—violence when there is absolutely no acceptable alternative. I don't think it's necessary to go into any great detail regarding Hitler's and Germany's actions during the 1930s and 40s except to specify their aggressive invasion and control of numerous European countries and, of course, the Holocaust. I think that any

---

7. For example, President Truman reasoned that the thousands of deaths of (presumably innocent) Japanese civilians and noncombatants—a result of the atomic bombing of Hiroshima and Nagasaki—were preferable to the estimated death of a million innocent Allied soldiers if an invasion of Japan were required.

assessment of the Holocaust alone is enough to show that even if we could possibly characterize that slaughter as "rational" in some abstract, theoretical way, it displayed a rationality that is impossible to comprehend. The Holocaust is impossible as a subject of rational discourse; the Holocaust is impossible to compromise upon. It is the programmatic, industrialized slaughter of innocents—what's to talk about? What's to compromise? The Nazis' single-minded devotion to the extermination of Jews strikes us as so psychotic because they even devoted scarce resources to the Final Solution when those resources could have been used against the increasingly victorious and threatening Soviet Army in the last years of the war: rail cars and rolling stock that could have brought needed supplies to German troops in the east were used to ferry Jews to the camps.

Now as to the corollary of the second claim—that violent action does not yield solutions—again, in this case it is clearly false. Waging war against Hitler and the Nazis, using violence as a methodology, clearly achieved the end: it stopped the horror without initiating a never-ending cycle of violence. Further, the war against Hitler, Nazism, and the atrocities they perpetuated certainly satisfies all the requirements for a just war: even if no other war was justifiable, even if every other dispute could have been settled by nonviolent means, that dispute could only have been solved through violence. Again, an empirical claim, but one that is most likely true.

Let me offer two cautionary examples that show the weakness of nonviolence as a methodology in the confrontation with Hitler. Two men who have exalted places in my personal pantheon of intellectual giants: Bertrand Russell, the philosopher who espoused nonviolence throughout his long life and argued against the First World War to such an extent that he was jailed for his activities, came to support the war against Hitler as the lesser of two evils.[8] And then there is Dietrich Bonhoeffer, the theologian whose work *Discipleship* in the 1930s still guides Christian nonviolence. Ironically, Bonhoeffer ends up conspiring to kill Hitler with a suitcase bomb in 1944, even offering to be the courier. In the face of Hitler, nonviolent methodologies melted away for both Russell—a leading secular pacifist—as well as Bonhoeffer, a

8. Russell, "Future of Pacifism," 7–13.

leading Christian pacifist. In Bonhoeffer's case, he came to reject the compatibility thesis, at least for the specific situation Hitler presented, and opted to help innocent victims.[9]

Now I mentioned earlier that Hitler is paradigmatic. His name has entered our lexicon in a way that other tyrants' names have not. The word *Hitler* has come to signify the epitome of evil and evil actors in the world. The term *Hitler* in our discourse functions as a way of labeling all sorts of evildoers—it characterizes them as existential threats to other nations, as existential threats to minorities within their own nations, and even, by extension of the predicate "evil," to denominate some domestic criminals within our own nation as existential threats to individual citizens.

The introduction of this term and the concept it represents into our language has an effect on the dialogue of war's justification—the verbal expression, surely, but also more. The term not only delineates that a particular person or phenomenon is a member of a category but it also implies an argument that is supposed to be decisive about what we are to do:

1. There is evil in the world, or so-and-so is an evildoer whose evil actions harm or kill innocents.

2. The evil actions must be stopped: it is our moral/religious obligation to try to stop the evil from spreading further and harming or killing more innocents.

3. There are no nonviolent means or methodologies that will be effective in stopping the evil since it is relentless and ruthless.

4. Therefore, an effective violent methodology is our only available alternative to satisfy our obligation.

5. Therefore, we ought to engage in violent actions to stop the evil from spreading further and harming or killing more innocents.

The availability and simplicity of encoding this argument in a single word leads to what I have called "the Hitlerization of politics." Our political discourse comes increasingly to use this formulation to mount

9. See, for example, the section "The Structure of Responsible Life," in Bonhoeffer's *Ethics*, 257ff.

a justification for violent responses to rampant evildoers: the Ayatollah Khomeini, Idi Amin, Pol Pot, Fidel Castro . . . and so on. All of them have been labeled as "Hitler" because if that label is appropriately applied, then violence against them—violence of one form or another—is justifiable. More recently, Saddam Hussein, Osama Bin Laden, and Kim Jong Il have been Hitlerized. Insofar as those characterizations are justifiable, violence against them, their regimes, and/or their minions is also justifiable. Certainly it is clear that many if not most of these characterizations are hyperbolic—rhetorical devices used in place of clear demonstration. But I think it is also true that we only recognize the erroneous Hitlerization in retrospect, after time has cooled tempers or history has revealed hidden evidence. Yet still, some of these characterizations may well be correct.

Much the same phenomenon applies domestically: think of Jeffrey Dahmer and Timothy McVeigh. They also were spoken of as epitomes of evil who needed to be stopped or eliminated as threats through the mechanism of state violence.

I think it is important for us to bear in mind that when we think of just war and the just war tradition that we are also referring—at least implicitly—to the state's police power as well to the war-making power of the state in international affairs. The justifications for each is the same, so much so that I have referred to police powers and war powers as flip sides of the same coin. And the ultimate source of those justifications is the same. It lies in the fundamental function of nation-states.

So now let's proceed to this fundamental function of nation-states. What is it that states must do necessarily? Why do they exist in the first place, and how does the activity of state violence fit into that picture?

We understand the nation-state to be the locus for the justified use of force; the employment of violence is reserved to the state alone. This provides a way to understand some events in Iraq that occurred in 2006. Shiite President Maliki sent his army against Muqtada al Sadr, who is also Shiite, who was a political ally of Maliki's, and whose support was indispensable for Maliki's election as president. A significant reason why Maliki initiated military operations in Basra and Sadr City is the existence of Muqtada al Sadr's Mahdi Army—his militia. Just having an armed force independent of the central authority of the government is a direct challenge to the state that the state must eliminate. The existence of this independent force proclaims the transformation of an ethnic group, a sectarian group, and so forth into a quasi-state within a state, and usurps the function of the state, rendering it meaningless.

The justified employment of violence is reserved to the nation-state rather than to individuals or groups of individuals—with one significant exception: an individual may justifiably employ violence in those situations in which his life is endangered, that is, in self-defense. At least within social-contract theory, self-defense or self-preservation is proffered as the most basic and fundamental human right, and the individual has moral standing to take whatever means are necessary to preserve his own life, or, by extension, the lives of other innocents. In the mythic formation of states, the power to exercise that right is transferred to the governmental authority. The state is thereby empowered by this transfer of fundamental individual power, rooted in the individual's right to self-preservation, to ensure the defense of the lives of its citizens. This is the primary function of states—their *raison d'etre*—no matter what other responsibilities they take on. States must defend their citizens, provide them with security, and maintain a stable social order to promote that security;[10] should states not perform this necessary function, the power would then revert to individuals to exercise on their own or others' behalf.

I want to emphasize the centrality of the right of self-defense in our most basic intuitions. If you think back a few minutes, I challenged the notion that Hitler was rational in any way we recognize because he was willing to sacrifice his and his nation's self-preservation by devoting scarce resources near the end of the war to the Final Solution. It would seem, then, that even a basic notion of what it means to be rational rests upon an assumption that one will act, using any means, to preserve her life.[11]

10. I've just explained the genesis of the function of states employing social-contract theory, from Plato to Hobbes to Rawls, and its concept of individuals. I think the function of states as the guarantor of security and social order is also assumed by other social/political theories such as MacIntyre's and communitarianism, though the account of the derivation of this power is significantly different.

11. See Boyd's discussion on the foolishness of the Cross.

This basic function of the state is the reason I argue that we ought not to separate police power from military power. The only difference is the arena in which state violence is employed—either against domestic threats and malefactors or against international threats and malefactors. The argument for just war is identical in form, structure, and substance with an argument for just policing, and both are rooted in the right to self-defense.

If this analysis is accurate, then several interesting things follow. Just war theory is not simply a set of prescriptions for the initiation and prosecution of armed conflict but also part and parcel of a politics—political structures and their aims. Their ends are directly linked and apparently inseparable from the justified employment of violence to preserve the life of innocents.

The second interesting thing that follows needs a little bit of a buildup. In *Leviathan*, Thomas Hobbes makes a point that I think is right on the mark when he says that a state of war is not restricted to the actual use of violence in battle but must also include the *willingness* to engage in violence even when one is not actively fighting.[12] If that is accurate—and as I said, I believe it is—then we are in a continual condition of violence simply by virtue of the fact of the fundamental function of nation-states as well as the fundamental role of the right and obligation of self-defense. There is no time during which nation-states are not willing to engage in violence to promote their legitimized ends, and no time when we are not willing to use violence to protect ourselves.[13] To paraphrase Hobbes again,[14] the threat of the sword underlies every statute, every treaty, as well as every interpersonal relationship.

Given all of this, the compatibility thesis is doomed. The moral foundation of the politics of nation-states demands it to be invalid; the preciousness of self-preservation renders nonviolence not only irrational and unnatural but also absurd; and extending those same rights to innocent victims requires that we kill the evildoers whenever that is the only alternative that will end their suffering. Some reasoning like this must have moved Bonhoeffer to his conclusion that the compatibility

---

12. *Leviathan*, I, 13.

13. See Amy Laura Hall and Kara Slade's essay in this volume.

14. Hobbes, *Leviathan*, II, 17.

thesis had to be rejected in favor of violence against Hitler; if he did not become a just warrior, he became the closest thing to it. Given the two alternatives of assassination or allowing the war to continue, killing the evildoer was the less sinful option.

Bonhoeffer was correct, in part. The compatibility thesis is wrong and should be rejected. But Bonhoeffer was mistaken if he believed that killing was in any way required by the faith or consistent with the gospel.[15] His root error is the same one we all have a tendency to make, and it is one that has certainly occurred in this essay. The problem centers on how we understand Jesus' call, and to see it, we have to start again.

We are not called to be nonviolent, nor to be nonviolent actors—Gandhi was many wonderful things, but he was not a Christian. Neither are we called to alleviate the suffering of innocent victims—the church is not a social service agency with pews. We are called to follow Christ, to be faithful disciples. Certainly that involves nonviolence and the alleviation of suffering, but when only *some* of the requirements of discipleship fill our focus, we treat them as though they are isolated principles, and we can lose the context of the entirety of the call that must impact how we are to be disciples and understand Jesus' commands.

We are the people of God, members of the Kingdom, the Body of Christ; and being who we are means that we belong to only One. The call is not one that only affects our souls and dispositions or aspects of our spirituality, leaving our bodies and our actions to the authorities of the world. We are heirs to a new politics of faith and love that overturns the politics of the nations and rejects the violence of states. This new politics makes love of God and love of neighbor our sole virtues from which everything else flows, and thus replaces the primacy of the right of self-preservation.

So what should we disciples do when we are faced with a ruthless evil such as Hitler who engenders such horrific suffering? We confront the powerful evildoer with love and truth; we resist the temptation of power and demand that the evil end; we try to alleviate the suffering of

---

15. This does not reflect Bonhoeffer's thoughts. He believed that his alternatives, killing Hitler and not killing Hitler, were *both* sinful. I argue that this is incoherent. See my *What about Hitler?*, 122–24.

all. Simple. And given that we are dealing with a powerful evildoer, the result is that we will fail.

And yes, we will also die.

The problem with the compatibility thesis is that it is so starry-eyed optimistic. Jesus does not promise us that we will be successful; quite the contrary, he argues against our expectations of success throughout the gospel, most clearly in Luke 6:32–35:

> If you love those who love you, what credit is that to you? Even sinners love those who love them. And if you do good to those who are good to you, what credit is that to you? Even sinners do that. And if you lend to those from whom you expect repayment, what credit is that to you? Even sinners lend to sinners expecting to be repaid in full. But love your enemies, do good to them without expecting to get anything back. (NIV)

What we can expect, in truth, is that we shall undergo a good deal of suffering. If we offer our other cheek to the fellow who has just struck us, we shouldn't be surprised if we are belted again. What we can expect from being faithful disciples is death. We can expect these things because they are part of the call in the first place.

I am a Roman Catholic layman, so one shouldn't expect that I know Scripture all that well, but even I know that Jesus says, often and quite clearly, especially in Matt 10:38 and 16:24, Luke 9:23 and 14:27, and Mark 8:34: "Whoever does not carry the cross and follow me cannot be my disciple," or, more positively, "If anyone wishes to come after me, he must deny himself, take up his cross and follow me." Paul echoes the same sentiment throughout the Epistles, especially Romans 12 and Colossians 1.

I think it's clear that any phrase or idea that is repeated often in Scripture is something that is being particularly emphasized and deserves special attention because of that emphasis. Many of the sermons and homilies I've heard on these passages have tended to focus on the first part of the positive statement—the denial of self—and have interpreted cross-carrying in a figurative rather than a literal way, linking it closely to self-denial. Sometimes this lends itself to rather trivial analysis, such that carrying one's cross is likened to the suffering of giving up indulgent bad habits, like cigarettes or swearing. More often, though, what is referenced is the pain involved in conforming our interior life to the spiritual demands of discipleship. I certainly have no wish to deny that those texts bear that meaning. However, I want to insist, especially in light of what we have examined thus far, that the texts about cross-carrying should also be considered more literally—that the cross really refers to crucifixion, execution. Before he says, "follow me," Jesus says, "take up and carry"—the call is conditioned by our prior acceptance that we bring the instrument of our own execution with us as we live the life of discipleship; the cross becomes the instrument of our execution *because* we live the life of discipleship. It entails a probably gruesome death at the hands of the powers.

Now honestly consider how this answer to the questions posed in the third paragraph of this essay sits with you. If I were to admit to being a betting man, I'd wager the vast majority of you, my blessed readers, would try very hard not to accept this conclusion.

Well, I don't like this conclusion any more than you do, and I like it a lot less than the proscription against lustful looks. And I am sure that God does not care whether we like it or not. The gospel ought not to be treated as we would a new brand of toothpaste that must conform to our tastes before we accept it. We are called, rather, to conform our lives to the gospel. That we are reluctant to do so—reluctant, hell, that we doubt that we are even able to consider it a possibility to do so—indicates that there is something wrong. When we reject the thought of loving Adolph Hitler, Osama bin Laden, pedophile priests and the mendacious, corrupt episcopate that protects them, and further reject the actions that must follow from that love, something is wrong. When Jesus warns us that we will be hated, scorned, and persecuted for following him, and it turns out that we are not, somebody has gotten something wrong, and it ain't the Lord.

The most important reflections I can share with you follow from this, and I am already over my allotted page allowance. We do not accept what the gospel commands because we have not been schooled or trained to live discipleship well, nor have we been taught how to die. We must pray more and hold each other to account with love and truth. We must engage in those constant, daily practices that embody God's love and forgiveness to those who suffer as well as those who cause suffering.

Primo Levi, a survivor of the Holocaust, reminisced in 1971 about his captors in Auschwitz:

> They were not monsters. I didn't see a single monster in my time in the camp. Instead I saw people like you and I who were acting in that way because there was Fascism, Nazism in Germany. Were some form of Fascism or Nazism to return, there would be people, like us, who would act in the same way, everywhere. And the same goes for the victims . . .[16]

Levi's reflection has a double significance for us in the church. In the first place he reminds us that we ought not to regard the evildoers as monsters or demons but rather much as we are ourselves; in Christian terms, they are our neighbors as much as the victims are and bearers of the image of God. "Whatever you did for one of the least of these brothers and sisters of mine, you did for me" (Matt 25:40).

In the second place, Levi warns us that we too will succumb given the right circumstances, and those circumstances include the sin and violence we engage in daily: in the ways we interact with each other, in the politics we practice. They are the foundations for the violence of the Holocaust and the violence of war, and they are the foundations of our unwillingness to believe that Jesus meant what he said. We must obey the call and pick up the cross.

16. Quoted in Griswold, "Forgiveness and Apology."

# 5

## Must Christian Pacifists Reject Police Force?

Gerald W. Schlabach

IT IS ONE OF the most subtle but significant and moving scenes in the 1985 movie *Witness*. As they come over the crest of a hill in response to a shoot-out in one of their barns, a half dozen or so Amish farmers in Lancaster County, Pennsylvania, cast aside their pitchforks or stick them into the ground. It is *their* community that is protecting the Philadelphia detective in hiding among them, *not* the other way around. Now his corrupt police superior has hunted him down. An altercation has ensued. The swelling group of peaceable Amish farmers responds with what is about to become a spontaneous action of nonviolent accompaniment or shielding. But first they block any last-minute, last-resort temptation to turn their farm implements into weapons. The scene is fiction, of course. Nonetheless it offers a vision of the possibility that making a prior commitment to thoroughgoing nonviolence might unleash the creativity needed to find nonlethal responses to violence—perhaps even to do nonviolent policing.

In October 2006, just a few miles away from where *Witness* was filmed, the rolling hills of Amish country presented the world with real-life scenes that were often just as moving, but inevitably more complex. In a way virtually unknown in American society, the Amish community immediately offered forgiveness to the family of a troubled man who had shot ten girls in a one-room schoolhouse near the village of Nickel Mines, killed five, then committed suicide. As media descended on the community not only to cover the gruesome killings but also to try to understand such forgiveness, non-Amish neighbors were protective of "our Amish," while Amish leaders expressed gratitude for the way that the state police helped shield them from relentless scrutiny.[1] Even this most "separatist" of Christian pacifist churches, after all, was in fact intermixed and interdependent with a larger society that does not share all of its ethical commitments and practices. At the crucial moment of the shootings, in fact, the Amish woman who managed to escape the schoolhouse in order to seek help had called 911.[2]

As we turn to ask whether Christian pacifism entails a rejection of police force, readers may quickly realize that this is where those practitioners of nonviolence are often ambivalent. Frankly, Christian pacifists have not had a consistent answer to this question. Historically, the historic peace churches have differed among themselves in their assessment of whether to depend upon or participate in police forces. Ethically, they have not always been sure how to square actual practices with their peace theology. Regretfully, puzzlement seems to have left even leading Christian pacifists as surprisingly mute on matters of policing as they have become increasingly vocal on matters of war.

The challenge is not simply the usual difficulty that all human beings have in living up to their highest ideals. The challenge is that so many other questions converge around the question of policing—about how the community of Christian disciples ought to situate itself in society, and about how it ought to live in time. For if our eyes must be fixed for guidance on the Lord Jesus Christ who has already inaugurated God's Reign, our hands must be sensitive to both the pain and the aid of neighbors right around us. For we can finally only practice hospitality and love of neighbor nowhere except in our present time and place, the present in which God's Reign is breaking in but has not yet fully come.

Policing, then, is unfinished agenda for Christian pacifists. But actually, that makes it particularly instructive. For to examine the chal-

1. Kraybill, Nolt, and Weaver-Zercher, *Amish Grace*, 31–32, 41.

2. Ibid., 23–24.

61

lenge that policing presents to Christian pacifists is to explore nothing less than their continuing vocation.

## Difficulties

The teaching of Jesus about love of enemies that is so foundational for Christian pacifism is not the only teaching in Matthew 5, the first chapter of the Sermon on the Mount. Jesus also taught his followers there to live lives of such integrity that they would not need to swear oaths in order to seal their claims to veracity, but instead could let a simple yes communicate a trustworthy yes, and a simple no, a reliable no. Those in the historic peace churches who would claim to follow Christ as disciples, therefore, must honestly admit:

Some pacifists, in some circumstances, do call the police. A few of their number, in fact, serve as police officers. To be sure, we should not confuse the descriptive with the normative. In other words, what *is* is not necessarily what *should* be. So among Christians who call themselves pacifists, some will admonish others that to call the police is problematic at best, and that to work as a police officer must surely be unfaithful. Still, we must be transparent about the fact that even if Christian pacifists *should* have a stronger consensus around policing, they do not. And we must see what we can learn by asking why not. After all, simply in taking up this question we face at least four difficulties:

*No one pacifist consensus exists.* Diversity of practice among Christian pacifists is nothing new. Those Amish of Lancaster County, Pennsylvania, and many of their Mennonite cousins, have traditionally held to a "two-kingdom theology" that their early Anabaptist forebears had articulated in 1527 in what is known as the Schleitheim Confession. Schleitheim and its adherents have quite consistently concluded that they could no more be police officers than soldiers. Christ's own rejection of the sword led to the conviction that all true Christians must follow him through defenseless suffering. If Romans 13 said that God has nonetheless ordained "worldly magistrates" to wield the sword in order to punish the wicked and protect the good, this was—according to Schleitheim—how God rules "outside the perfection of Christ," not how

God would have believers rule either themselves or others.[3] But should believers never avail themselves of police protection? Schleitheim and Romans 13 do not really address *that* question, and so would give little direct guidance to the Amish woman from Nickel Mines about whether to call 911 at least in such an extreme situation.

In fact, the very location of substantial Amish and Mennonite communities in eastern Pennsylvania is a direct result of divergence concerning policing among Christian pacifists. Mennonites first began to settle in the region precisely because they knew that they would enjoy religious toleration and protection from the Quakers—Christians from another historic peace church!—who then governed colonial Pennsylvania. To be sure, any constables of the period would at most have been lightly armed in comparison even to small-town police of our own day, to say nothing of militarized police forces in large cities. Or they might often have been unarmed, serving more as neighborhood conflict mediators than modern cops. Furthermore, the Quakers could govern Pennsylvania in relatively peaceable ways because they had settled the colony in more peaceable ways than others, through treaties of friendship with Native Americans. Still, govern they did, and this has contributed to a different attitude among the Quakers toward policing, even in international affairs. In the twentieth century, some Quakers suggested that while they must continue to be conscientious objectors against participation in the military of any nation-state, they might be able to participate conscientiously in United Nations peacekeeping operations that model themselves more along the lines of police forces than aggressive military operations.[4]

---

3. Yoder, *Schleitheim Confession*, article VI.

4. For further background on the diversity of Christian pacifist stances toward policing, see the surveys that Tobias Winright has provided in "From Police Officers to Peace Officers," in *Wisdom of the Cross*, 96–108, and "Challenge of Policing," 163–94. Winright finds four or five basic stances: 1. Rejection of all forms of violence, including that of policing. 2. Rejection of policing for Christians, while recognizing its legitimacy for society at large. 3. Rejection of war but endorsement of international policing, and by implication domestic policing. 4. Explicit endorsement of the legitimacy of policing in society at large, and in some cases, of Christian participation as police officers. 5. Acceptance of policing but only if it could be nonlethal.

*Precedents are hard to trace.* A further source of difficulty begins to emerge even in this brief sample of divergent positions on policing among pacifists: Only since the nineteenth century has the role of policing come to be conceptually distinct from that of soldiering. When we look to the Christian tradition for examples that might cast light upon our question, therefore, it is not entirely clear what constitutes a historical precedent. In medieval and early modern periods, princes and "magistrates" had responsibility for regional military self-defense, but also domestic rule and policing. Anabaptists who said faithful Christians could not serve as magistrates, therefore, were not objecting to exactly the same thing as modern cops who walk the beat or try to pull over drunk drivers before they kill someone or intervene to stop domestic abuse.

This is not to say that the modern distinction between soldiering and policing renders police forces benign. The modern era can put quite lethal military technology into the hands of domestic police. And then it often charges them with maintaining order in societies that are quite stratified, economically and racially. The result is that to maintain "order" often means to cement in place a quite unjust *disorder*. Still, a modern distinction between roles has the potential to subject police officers to the rule of law in ways that more easily break down among soldiers amid far-flung warfare.

*Surprisingly little theological attention.* One might think that historical diversity and conceptual fuzziness would invite contemporary Christian pacifist thinkers to take up the challenge of policing. But surprisingly, they have not really given systematic attention to the ethics of policing. Even the work of leading peace church theologian John Howard Yoder, for example, is suggestive but contestable. As part of his argument against Christian participation in war and militarism, Yoder sometimes distinguished warfare from policing. Warfare was far too indiscriminate to qualify as the sort of legitimate practice of the state that Romans 13 authorizes, amid its realism about how God maintains order in a fallen world. To make that point Yoder noted that by contrast, localized police action can be accountable to legislative regulation and

judicial review in ways that mean it at least stands some chance of punishing only the guilty while protecting the innocent.[5]

Did this mean that a faithful Christian could serve as a police officer? Only very gingerly and skeptically was Yoder willing to entertain
the possibility that "the Christian can by any stretch of the imagination
find his calling in the exercise of state-commanded violence." Those
who claim a calling must subject themselves to the most strenuous of
scrutiny in a Christian community schooled in practices of moral discernment and mutual admonition:

> Long enough we have been told that the position of the
> conscientious objector is a prophetic one, legitimate but
> only for the specially called few; in truth we must hold that
> the nonresistant position is the normal and normative po-
> sition for every Christian, and it is the use of violence, even
> at that point where the state may with some legitimacy be
> violent, that requires an exceptional justification.[6]

If Yoder was contemplating the possibility of Christian participation in
policing here, he was being extremely guarded. Furthermore, his discussion of policing is short and he made it in passing, amid a larger
argument. That argument was not really about what the Christian ethic
ought to be, but rather about how pacifist Christians can call people
working within *other* moral frameworks to at least live up to their highest ideals. The take-home lesson of the passage is therefore contestable.
The one thing that should be clear about it is that it does not add up to
a systematic pacifist ethic of policing.[7]

5. Yoder, *Christian Witness to the State*, 36. Yoder continued: "The use of force
must be limited to the police function, i.e. guided by fair judicial processes, subject
to recognized legislative regulation, and safeguarded in practice against its running
away with the situation. Only the absolute minimum of violence is therefore in any
way excusable. The state has no general authorization to use the sword indepen-
dently of its commission to hold violence to a minimum." See also 5 and 46–47 of
*Christian Witness to the State*; Yoder, *Original Revolution*, 74f.; Yoder, "Peace Without
Eschatology?," in *Royal Priesthood*, 159–60.

6. Yoder, *Christian Witness to the State*, 57.

7. For contrasting readings of Yoder on policing, see Schlabach (with Drew
Christiansen, SJ, et al.), *Just Policing, Not War*, 82–84; and Alexis-Baker, "Unbinding
Yoder from Just Policing," in *Power and Practices*, 147–66.

*Call the police for what?—and other reality checks.* The reason to name all these complexities surrounding the question that policing poses for pacifists is to be honest, not to evade the question. In fact, for the attentive reader, one lesson may already be emerging: Policing is not just one single thing. Police officers play multiple roles and Christians relate to their neighbors in multiple ways. We have already had reason to mention a continuum of reasons that police might intervene—to stop a mass murderer, to stop domestic abuse, to prevent drunk drivers from killing anyone, including themselves, or to mediate village or neighborhood conflicts.[8] Yet, lest we portray police institutions too benignly, we also have had reason to hint at more complicated realities: Simple highway patrols to promote safe driving practices can become the occasion for racial profiling. The more an urban neighborhood might benefit from ordinary cops on the beat, the tenser it is likely to be and the more its dangers may tempt police officers to develop an adversarial, us-versus-them relationship with the local population. Police may then take their operational models from warfare after all. And if that local population is largely a minority population, some may then feel targeted for what amounts to repression. But on the other hand, if police reduce their presence, still others within those very communities may feel that municipalities are neglecting them.

In the face of these complex realities, some radical Christians argue that to look to the police to secure order and justice in the first place is a mistake. They argue that justice-minded Christians and other social activists should put their trust and energy into organizing local communities capable of dealing with conflicts through grassroots processes that rely less and less on the state and its top-down intervention, or not at all. This, at its best, is the goal of Christian anarchism—where *anarchy* does not mean "chaos" at all but doing without what the Greeks called "arky" or overarching rule. Here's another reality check, though, and it does not even involve the dismissive worry of critics that such

8. Dave Jackson has noted further distinctions that can be relevant to Christian pacifist discernment concerning when to call the police: "1. Juvenile versus adult crime . . . 2. Crimes against persons versus crimes against property . . . 3. The rational criminal versus the insane person . . . 4. Crimes against others versus crimes against ourselves . . . 5. Deadly or offensive force versus restraining or diverting force . . ." See Jackson, *Dial 911*, 46–52.

a vision is simply unrealistic. No, the reality check is this: The success of any radical Christian or anarchist vision for community would not mean dispensing with the police function at all, but would rather mean perfecting it through humane, communal, nonviolent means.

No community can do without some kind of police function. No Christian community. No human community. The Amish men in the movie *Witness* who stick their pitchforks in the ground so that they can nonviolently protect their guest are not simply fiction. Whether or not such a dramatic instance of nonviolent accompaniment has ever actually happened among the Amish themselves, I do not know. But Amish practices for maintaining communal cohesion and standards are well known. Instead of going by the name of "nonviolent policing," however, they go by the name of excommunication or "shunning." Even though this has its basis in Matt 18:15–20, modern Christians (including many in peace church traditions) are often shocked or embarrassed at the way that the Amish and some conservative Mennonites deliberately ostracize those they believe to be sinning. Yet once we recognize shunning as one nonviolent alternative to potentially violent forms of policing, two striking conclusions begin to dawn. First, the less a community or social movement seeks to depend on state-run apparatuses to exercise the police function, the more it will actually need to develop its own.[9]

Second, once Christian pacifists lose their reluctance to use the words "policing" and "the police function" for naming these models, they will not be without resources. It will obviously take much work to translate older models of communal governance into wider advocacy for social justice, police reform, and alternatives to the criminal justice system, but they do have precedents from within their own traditions. Even while arguing vehemently that faithful Christians should have as little as possible to do with the police, for example, Christian anarchist Andy Alexis-Baker has cited alternative models from premodern Europe in which villages organized themselves to raise a "hue and cry" to gather in order to defuse conflicts and prevent altercations.[10] Though not well

9. Another example: Social movements organizing nonviolent protests have generally needed to train their own marshals in order to maintain nonviolent discipline and isolate provocateurs.

10. Alexis-Baker, "Gospel or a Glock?," 28–29. In a workshop titled "Wrestling

documented, early-twentieth-century Mennonites settling in colonies in the Paraguayan Chaco reportedly appointed members known to have good conflict-resolution skills to intervene in local disputes; these church-led colonies did not have weapons, and the central government of Paraguay was far too distant to provide police, so Mennonite communities exercised the police function themselves, unarmed.[11]

One cannot expect to transfer premodern or isolated examples like this directly into complex contemporary societies, of course, but contemporary peace churches also have fresher raw material for offering and witnessing to the possibility of nonviolent policing. Christian Peacemaker Teams now has decades of experience developing strategies of nonviolent accompaniment and shielding in conflict zones around the world. Peace church practitioners have played leading roles in the restorative justice movement that offers alternatives to dominant approaches to criminal justice.

So does Christian pacifism entail rejection of police force? To answer that question, it seems, we must ask a more precise one: What *kind* of policing must pacifists reject, and when and where?

## Analysis

To ask about the what, when, and where of policing for Christian pacifists is not to fall back upon a relativistic "situation ethics," but to place our discernment within the overarching narrative of God at work in history, patiently calling out a people of witness. Theologians call this narrative "salvation history." The plot of any narrative, as well as the complex unfolding of events in any history, always requires the author, teller, reader, or listener to keep their bearings in both time and space. So just as authors occasionally speak of "the time/space continuum," Christian theologians and social ethicists do well to locate the *what* of

---

with Faithfulness in Peacemaking: Just Policing," at the Peace Among the Peoples conference at Associated Mennonite Biblical Seminary, Elkhart, Indiana, in July 2010, Alexis-Baker read from an unpublished paper that includes a further elaboration of "hue and cry" practices as a positive alternative to modern policing.

11. This pattern had roots in the experience of Mennonite colonies in Russia in the eighteenth and nineteenth centuries. Some evidence is thus available in Krahn, "Government of Mennonites in Russia," 556–57.

any moral discernment about "what to do" within the *when* of God's unfolding action in history, and the *where* that maps the place or social location of the church in the world.

In other words, there are two key variables for understanding how Christian pacifists *have* dealt with the question of policing, as well as for discerning how they *should* deal with the question of policing.

> Variable 1: Where are we in time? In other words, how hopeful are Christians that they can "already" live according to the promise of God's inbreaking Kingdom? Do they see themselves forced to adjust to the reality that God's Kingdom has "not yet" fully arrived? Or do they see themselves living "between the times" where "already" and "not yet" overlap?

The Gospels present Jesus as inaugurating God's Kingdom or Reign. It is, as he proclaimed, "at hand!"—palpable, touchable, breaking into our lives even as we speak! The hopes of Israel and the promise that God's Spirit would anoint God's servant to bring good news to the poor, release the captives, heal the blind, set free the oppressed, and proclaim a new year of Jubilee were being fulfilled right now, in the very presence of Jesus' listeners (Luke 4:16–21). If even John the Baptist could harbor doubts, well, *look around*, said Jesus, at all the tangible signs of healing and resurrection that are confirming good news to the poor (Matt 11:2–6). To be a Christian is to trust that in the very person of Jesus the Christ or messiah, God's Reign has *already* come!

And yet, in a world of exploitation, poverty, violence, and genocide, we would be utterly foolish to claim that God's Reign has come in its fullness. From where we stand, God's Kingdom often appears as a distant horizon, to which we have *not yet* arrived, and which seems to recede whenever we approach it. Like a distant horizon, it may still define our journeys and shape our present by beckoning and pulling us forward to itself. But we will only arrive at the fullness of God's Reign when it arrives as God's gift, at the end or "eschaton" by which God brings history to its purposeful completion.

Thus we live "*between the times*," in a tense and overlapping zone in which the Kingdom of God is both "already" and "not yet." Our moral challenge is to discern our specific callings or vocations amidst this in-between time, leaning into God's "already" even while recognizing the world's "not yet." The "already" by which Jesus has inaugurated God's Reign must guide us. And the "not yet" realities of suffering, injustice, and violence—to say nothing of simple mortality—provide the messy and complex occasions in which we meet our needy neighbors even when we offer the most Christ-like of solidarity and service, or find ourselves needy and indebted too. Theologians use a technical-sounding term, "eschatological tension," to describe this in-between existence. But for any Christian who both lives in trusting hope that God is working to bring history to its fulfillment, *and* lives in loving solidarity with the pain of the world, the concept is altogether and profoundly familiar, with or without the name.[12]

> Variable 2: What is our social location and how do we recognize it? In other words, do Christians map their lives and identity within one universal social geography that expects everyone to live according to a single standard? Do they mark out a separate territory for the life of the church while harboring little expectation that unbelieving society can even approximate the ethic of Jesus? Or here too do they find some way of saying "both/and"?

In this meantime in which we live as Christians—this overlap "between the times"—it sometimes seems necessary to pause the story, pull off to the side of the road, and check our maps to see where we are. Stories always unfold in space as well as time, after all. So *where* exactly is God at work? Where are the pitfalls or temptations we ought to avoid? Indeed, where might we in fact have already strayed from our path?

Pausing the story in time in order to examine spatial locations is both dangerous and necessary. The danger is that we will forget that God's work is dynamic and continuing to unfold, so that we prematurely lose hope that God's Spirit can yet transform some *place*—some community or institution or culture or society—and judgmentally write it

---

12. For a further exploration of how Christian positions on war and the possibly exceptional use of violence track with their respective emphases on the "already" and "not yet" of God's Reign, see Friesen, "Peacemaking as an Ethical Category."

off as irredeemably lost or evil. The story may then move on without us, leaving us the ones who are disoriented and lost in self-righteous pride. Still, to keep our bearings, we do need to make some moral judgments about *where* to invest our time and vocational energy. A Christian with financial skills, for example, might serve an inner-city neighborhood by working at a locally owned bank or credit union committed to socially responsible urban development favoring the poor—but not if it turns out to be a mafia front operation set up to launder drug money. Distinctions matter! Not every moral locale is equal!

The language of "kingdoms" that we have already encountered has been one traditional way of mapping our moral and social geography. "Two-kingdom theology," in particular, marks out life according to God's Kingdom as though it were a clearly distinguishable moral territory, in contrast to the kingdom or kingdoms of this world. Lutheran and Anabaptist versions of two-kingdom theology differ in significant ways, to be sure. The Lutheran version authorizes Christians to act according to quite different ethics as their roles in life take them back and forth between the two kingdoms by which God rules the realm of faith and the realm of the sinful world. The Anabaptist version expects Christians to live always according to the rule or Lordship of Jesus Christ, thus marking the border between kingdoms pretty much on a line between the church and the world. Either way, the territorial metaphors that come with the language of Kingdom, kingdoms, Reign, and realms tend to result in some kind of dualism. Whatever the problems of dualism, it does provide a device for realistically recognizing that vast realms of human life do resist God's Reign and refuse to recognize the paradoxical Lordship of Jesus Christ, who rules not by domineering over others but by bearing the cross of suffering love even on behalf of his enemies.

Still, there is much about the Christian faith that must chafe against any rigid or ultimate dualism. For if the one God created all things with purpose and pronounced them good, evil cannot claim any existence or occupy any territory independent of God's rule or care. Christian hope in turn must trust that God never gives up on any corner of creation, however rebellious. To do so, in fact, risks the ancient heresy of Manichaeism, which saw good and evil as two independent realities locked in eternal combat. Any two-kingdom theology that starkly cements in place the distinctions between those parts of life in which Jesus' teachings do and do not apply will risk sliding into that heresy.

The philosophical opposite of dualism is "monism," the insistence that all reality is one. The truth of monism that is relevant to issues of war, violence, and policing is this: If God has purposefully created one good creation (however richly variegated it may be, both ecologically and culturally), and if God has revealed its ultimate pattern and purpose in Jesus Christ the Logos (John 1:1–4), then Jesus' ethic of non-violent, self-giving love must ultimately apply always and everywhere. Yet monism does not quite seem right either, at least when it fails to acknowledge the gap between those places where we *currently* know how to apply Jesus' ethic and the places where we *ultimately* hope to do so. Arguably, monism too risks heresy insofar as it may tend to under-estimate the grip that sin continues to have on us.[13]

If there is something right about both dualism and monism, yet both are inadequate, is there any way to resolve or split the difference? Starting instead with the temporal dimension of the Christian narra-tive by situating God's people "between the times"—within a dynamic, unfinished story rather than on a static map of our moral and social ge-ography—already gives us our most important tool.[14] For if maps have obvious value they will nonetheless mislead us if we fail to recognize how the realities they point to change through time. We might then speak not so much of two kingdoms versus one (monistic) kingdom, or two ethics versus one ethic, but one missional ethic. For if God's work is to transform the kingdom of this world into the Kingdom of the Lord and Messiah (Rev 11:15), then the overriding moral obligation and pri-mary vocation of the Christian is to participate in God's own dynamic and transformational mission. As soon as we begin claiming to partici-pate in God's transformation of the world we will have crucial questions of power, means, and ends to discern; Christian pacifists will insist that we can only get these right if we follow God's lead by trusting in the

13. This, in effect, was Reinhold Niebuhr's argument for why the optimistic liberal pacifism of the early twentieth century was heretical, even if not all forms of Christian pacifism are heretical. See Niebuhr, "Why the Christian Church Is Not Pacifist," in *Christianity and Power Politics*, 1–32.

14. Schlabach, "Beyond Two- Versus One-Kingdom Theology."

preeminent yet nonviolent power of the cross. But it is this dynamic combination of the temporal and spatial elements to God's saving work in history that John Howard Yoder once encoded in his own alternative to both dualism and monism: "duality without dualism."[15] What that phrase captures is this: We must recognize that believing trust in Jesus Christ and his way makes a decisive difference in the "logic" of how communities order their lives, but do so without speaking of that difference as though it were a static metaphysical difference. Frank and realistic recognition of diverging ethics thus names a "duality" but not a Manichaean dualism.

Already—between the times—not yet. Monism—duality without dualism—dualism. Combining these two key variables, we can chart why Christian pacifists have moved back and forth among a variety of approaches to the question of policing (see page 74). We may also note how Christian pacifism sometimes becomes problematic, when it stresses one ethical impulse or biblical truth in isolation from the full drama of God's saving history (1A and 1C). Finally, we can identify the border zones where Christian pacifists may rightly and charitably engage with non-pacifist Christians about the challenges they share, but should recognize that pacifists verge on adopting some form of just war thought if they actually reside in those zones (3A and 3C). We can thus find guidance not only around the issue of policing, but for discerning the ongoing vocation of Christian pacifist communities.

## Guidance

To recognize ourselves as living "between the times," in a social geography that cannot be static precisely because God is at work to redeem human history and transform our lives, is to locate questions such as policing within a theological framework that has a center (2B on chart). Christian pacifists may and should find ourselves pivoting from that center into various modes of pacifism as we debate how hopeful to be about the transformational possibilities opening up before us in the world, and discern how God is calling us to respond. It is from this

15. Yoder, *Christian Witness to the State*, 31.

← *continuum of social geographies (spatial)* →

| | A. Monism | B. Duality w/o Dualism | C. Dualism |
|---|---|---|---|
| **1. Live the promise of the "Already"** | **1A:** "All we are saying is give peace a chance." Mind and heart reject war and police violence for all people everywhere always. Often serves as starting point for commitment to nonviolence. But without "saying" more about how, it seems to ignore the realities of sin. **(idealistic pacifism)** | **1B:** Draw on older examples of nonlethal policing in churches and local communities to offer society less-violent alternatives, while recognizing that social change will be limited without recognition of Christ's Lordship **(the messianic pacifism of a community of witness)** | **1C:** War and potentially lethal policing seen as God's will for the state, but forbidden for Christians **(stark version of Anabaptist-Mennonite Two-Kingdom Theology)** |
| **2. Discern Vocation "between the times"** | **2A:** Enlightened social reform and Gandhian nonviolence are expected to progressively eliminate the causes of violence, both international and domestic, thus abolishing war and institutionalizing less-violent or even non-violent forms of policing **(progressive pacifism, often Quaker)** | **2B:** Following Jeremiah's injunction to "seek the *shalom* of the city" pacifist Christians cooperate with police and state structures on a case-by-case basis, as required by dynamics of community engagement and congregational responsibility, but guided by a call to mission and their primary loyalty to Christ **(the pacifism of Diaspora Christianity)** | **2C:** Though they could never bear weapons themselves, pacifist Christian lawyers, government workers, lobbyists, office holders, etc. work for somewhat greater justice and less violent policies within the structures of the state **(modified version of Anabaptist-Mennonite Two-Kingdom Theology)** |
| **3. Accept the reality of the "Not Yet"** | **3A:** Christians who refuse military service for any nation-state might nonetheless serve in a United Nations peacekeeping force as a form of international policing (even if they are members of pacifist churches, their ethic = a variant of the **just war tradition**) | **3B:** Christian pacifists call the police in emergency situations, and allow other exceptions as a matter of pastoral accommodation, but only because their churches have not yet discerned an entirely consistent ethic with regard to policing, or because this may not be possible in a fallen world **(honestly unfinished pacifism)** | **3C:** Christian police officers, prison administrators, etc., are prepared to use violence in those roles (even if they are members of pacifist churches, their theology = **Lutheran Two-Kingdom Theology)** |

← *eschatological continuum (temporal)* →

center that we will find the guidance we need to respond to the challenge of policing.[16]

16. When ethicists present typologies they sometimes claim that they are only presenting a descriptive tool. But then their bias or agenda usually sneaks in and shows itself by how they arrange their presentation, often with the final type turning out to be conceptually superior insofar as it solves the problems of all the others.

That vocational center is the one that Jeremiah urged upon the Hebrew exiles in Babylon (Jeremiah 29). They should not be afraid to engage the societies in which they live (building houses, planting gardens, and raising families, as Jeremiah put it). But neither should they forget that they were exiles who must remember their true homeland and know how to pick God's voice out from among the cacophony of turbulent events and false prophets around them. For their own welfare/peace/*shalom* was inseparable from the *shalom* of their host city, and their calling was to seek the *shalom* of that city during the interim of their exile. Interim was their in-between place in time; exile placed them in their social geography as "both/and" resident aliens. As the stories in the book of Daniel would later illustrate, the vocations of some might thus be to work as civil servants aiding in the governance of Babylon—but they could only do so faithfully to their God if they kept their primary loyalty clear and were prepared to resist any idolatrous demands that Babylon might make. As children of Abraham, this was a way to continue living out the blessing by which God had called them to be a people, while simultaneously blessing other families of the earth.

For followers of Jesus, this way of engaging the world also continues to unfold the meaning of "suffering service" in ordinary life. It embeds and relates us to those who find their security somewhere other than in the cross of Jesus Christ, alternately opening opportunities to respond in service to the needs of others or creating tensions, if not conflict. And if we are honest we must also admit that in the "not yet" of our own lives, we are still struggling and learning to find our security

---

In presenting my chart and commentary, I make no such claim of objectivity. My approach, after all, was something of the reverse. Long theological reflection had already led me to the conviction that Christians need to hold the "already" and the "not yet" of God's Reign in tension, and that Yoder's "duality without dualism" captures the best impulses of both dualism and monism without their respective problems. Laying out this chart became a way of testing the explanatory power of these two sets of variables. I hope that my notion of "pivoting" from the vocational center (2B) makes clear that I am not trying to pigeonhole my fellow pacifists into any one category or type. While signaling my suspicion that problems will arise when Christians attempt prematurely to avoid any possible tension (both the temporal tension along one axis or the spatial tension along the other), I certainly see all of the modes of pacifism marked by the cross that is formed by the central column and central row of the chart as legitimate.

fully in Jesus and his creative way of nonviolence as well. Thus, often we work and serve cooperatively among those who are quicker to call the police than we, or may even do so on our behalf. Thus, sometimes we fail or simply run out of time to find creative responses to crime and violence ourselves. Thus, a few within Christian pacifist communities even wonder whether in the "not yet" interim of an imperfect world, they might be called to work in policing roles themselves. Fortunately, the vocational framework that has emerged from our analysis of salvation history, and that we have identified with the mandate of Jeremiah, allows us to respond flexibly to our neighbors yet faithfully to our Lord:

*The messianic pacifism of a community of witness* (1B): Whatever else Christians do as they engage the world should find its ground and guidance in the life of the Christian community itself. Following the lead of peace church theologian John Howard Yoder, we call this pacifism "messianic" not because we harbor illusions of grandeur but because we follow one who charted a path toward human redemption and social transformation precisely as an unexpected kind of messiah who renounced grand imperial schemes. The most basic work of Christian social ethics is simply to be the church—reconciled and recovering sinners being shaped into a new community. This shaping and this newness then demonstrate to the world that surprising, creative, and life-giving ways of responding to conflicts and threats are *already* possible. Furthermore, as Dave Jackson points out, Christian communities that encourage simpler lifestyles with fewer possessions, and that live in close proximity among themselves and practice reconciliation with their neighbors, may also be deterring crime and reducing its very causes.[17]

For Christians who stress this church-based mode of pacifist witness not only as faithful members of their church but in their vocational choices, the priority with regard to policing is to retrieve and further develop the church's own ways of governing its own community life, resolving conflicts, protecting the innocent, and guiding violators back into healthy patterns of life. To take up these tasks in nonviolent ways is to exercise the police function, call it that or not. The reason to recognize these practices *as* nonviolent policing is to take back that very

17. Jackson, *Dial 911*, 79–83.

word and thus make explicit connections as we witness to the world that there are alternatives to violence. Besides, nothing else that Christian social activists do to influence public policy in the wider world will have integrity if Christians do not begin with themselves and their own communal life. As the Apostle Paul told the Corinthians, we can hardly expect to judge the world if we do not have our own mechanisms to deal with conflicts and avoid society's criminal justice systems (1 Cor 6:1–8).

One example is particularly vivid for me because it took place on the day that my wife was ordained as a Mennonite pastor. Apparently at random, a lone fundamentalist protester who considered himself a prophet calling more liberal Christian churches to repent showed up in front of the church that very morning. Practicing their usual hospitality, church members surprised the protester by inviting him to join them for the morning, before he called down condemnation. But when he realized that the church was about to ordain a woman, he disrupted with a shout of "Abomination!" Unsure of what he would do next—disrupt further? charge the pulpit? draw a concealed weapon?—a half dozen men and one woman surrounded the protester, quietly engaged his attention, and kept him distracted. The service proceeded with only one or two more disruptions, and afterward, church members continued engaging him in conversation until he peacefully left. Though the morning had been tense and bizarre, the congregation had witnessed to the very qualities that were as much a cause for celebration that morning as was my wife's ordination.[18]

*The pacifism of Diaspora Christianity* (2B). Because God calls and sends the Christian community to witness to God's Kingdom in the world as it is, however, the Diaspora zone between already and not yet is the one where we find ourselves pivoting to other legitimate modes of Christian pacifism. Here we find ourselves engaging the world like the young Hebrew men in the book of Daniel, cooperating in some ways but not others. For even without becoming civil servants in the manner of the ancient Hebrews in Babylon, the church's own commitment to

18. For a news report on this incident, see Groff, "Protester Sparks Look at Safety Practices." For another example of what may arguably be considered nonviolent policing by the Christian community itself, but which made it possible not to call upon standard forms of policing, see Alexis-Baker, "Gospel or a Glock?," 38.

service in the world—even through its own ministries and programs—
will often be enough to take it into Diaspora mode. Faithfulness to
God's mission presents more rather than fewer difficult situations that
require case-by-case discernment. Consider, for example, the following:

- Just to be a modestly evangelistic congregation that is inviting, baptizing, and forming new Christians, or calling older
  Christians back into lives of active discipleship, will mean it
  finds itself welcoming people who have never imagined that
  they could dispense with police protection. Even if it has an
  unmistakable identity as a peace church, such a congregation
  will surely want to give people time to grow into pacifist commitment and practice.

- Despite the creative response of my wife's congregation to the
  disruptive protester at her ordination, that incident still prompted anxieties among many congregants, particularly those with
  young children. "What if he *had* been armed?" people wondered. Though no one wanted to overreact, they remembered
  news only a few months before from a neighboring state, in
  which a disgruntled parishioner had shot a pastor and others.
  Leaders of my wife's congregation decided that pastoral responsibility required them to anticipate procedures in the event that
  they ever face another such incident, so that they could handle
  the crisis redemptively and nonviolently yet anticipate when, if
  ever, to call the police.[19]

- Pastoral responsibility has required still other congregations to
  think through security procedures that allow them to practice
  inclusivity and hospitality toward men released from prison after incarceration for sex offenses, while insuring the protection
  of children and other vulnerable members. Accountability and
  accompaniment are basic here, and constitute further examples
  by which the church must learn to practice the police function
  within the church community itself. But such work hardly alle-

19. Groff, "Protester Sparks Look at Safety Practices."

viates and in fact accentuates the need for cooperation with the social welfare and criminal justice systems of the state.[20]

- Imagine another congregation whose outreach ministry in an area with gang violence leads it to start a neighborhood youth group. Leaders from the church may be committed to suffering harm in the event of an altercation rather than calling the police on their own behalf. But now families without that same commitment are entrusting their children to the church's responsibility for a few hours every week. They would be remiss not to anticipate how they will relate to the police. And if the police in their area are practicing relatively enlightened strategies of "community policing," they might even want to cooperate proactively, given the interest they share with the police in preventive approaches to socioeconomic issues that otherwise lead to violence.

The greater the justice and creative conflict resolution that the larger society is practicing, perhaps, the less these cases will present excruciating ethical dilemmas. But that is where the practical implications of Christian hope arise. How optimistic or indeed hopeful should we be about the prospects for thoroughgoing social change in the wider society, changes of the sort that might allow for less and less violent forms of policing? How much energy, time, and resources ought Christians invest in such hope? Grounded in Jeremiah's mandate to seek the *shalom* of the cities in which we find ourselves, even if we are never entirely at home, Christian pacifists may pivot in at least two other directions:

*Progressive pacifism* (2A). Because this is God's world, we should never give up on our hope for extending nonviolent responses to conflict and injustice progressively into more and more spheres of life. That a holy Hindu, Mahatma Gandhi, did so much to develop Jesus' Sermon on the Mount into politically practicable strategies is evidence that this is possible, and that Christians should be ashamed for their failures to trust in Jesus' way and the Spirit's creativity enough to do so themselves. In any case, Christian participation in coalition with broader social

20. For a fuller discussion of these challenges, see Penner, "How Inclusive Is the Inclusive Church?," in *At Peace and Unafraid*, 195–210.

movements—or, as in the case of Martin Luther King Jr., Christian leadership—have become the classic way of practicing this mode of pacifism. But meanwhile, neither historic peace churches nor broader peace movements have done more than begin to imagine and explore prospects for nonviolent policing. They must.

The restorative justice movement is a start; peace church practitioners have played a leading role in formulating alternatives to criminal justice procedures that are often dehumanizing for victims as well as offenders. Likewise we should recognize that activists doing community organizing in order to empower local neighborhoods to solve their own problems in the face of *both* gang violence *and* police brutality are nurturing localized, grassroots, non-state alternatives to standard forms of policing. Whether those schooled in either of these strategies should sometimes play a role in police reform, or whether current power structures will ever do more than co-opt efforts to develop nonviolent or less-violent forms of official policing, is a matter for debate and discernment among pacifists. The uncontested point should be this: Those who are most hopeful and optimistic about the prospect of broad social transformation and the creation of nonviolent cultures are going to have to take up the challenge of institutionalizing nonviolent forms of policing in society at large. They cannot merely critique war and police brutality from the prophetic margin without anticipating the challenge of nonviolent governance.

*Modified versions of two-kingdom theology* (2C). Even those who are not particularly optimistic about reforming social systems as a whole may remain convinced of the biblical call to do justice, release captives, and advocate for the poor and vulnerable. And so they may work, issue by issue, for somewhat less injustice and less violence within systems that they cannot imagine will ever cease to rely on police forces that have recourse to lethal violence. Their pessimism about whether this situation can ever fundamentally change is not so much Manichaean as agnostic. Yet by working *against* the system from *within* the system out of Christian love of neighbor, they are functionally dualistic. No longer keeping a hands-off attitude toward the state, they will certainly not be giving the state a blank check in the name of Romans 13 either. Theirs will be a two-kingdom theology that is less stark, however, than that of the Anabaptists and Mennonites who first used that framework to articulate Christian pacifism.

Pioneers in this mode of Christian pacifism—and to this inadvertent approach to policing—were the conscientious objectors who did alternative service in mental hospitals beginning in World War II. Appalled at the treatment of the mentally ill, they first helped prompt reform by exposing the conditions there. In some cases they then went on to contribute to reform as hospital administrators with responsibility for human beings under lock and key. Even private, church-run institutions must conduct their work in cooperation with state regulators, and so we can see this work as implicating pacifists in the structures of governance and policing, however benign and reform-minded.

Similar but even more freighted has been the work of historic peace church members who are lawyers and politicians. Imagine a Christian lawyer who began with idealistic motivations to work for the common good and promote justice. Years "fighting city hall" leave her jaded or cynical, and she knows she is cooperating with a system that depends upon the threat of violent force or even death. Yet she keeps at it, in order at least to blunt injustices, defend the poor, and come to the aid of immigrants. Now what if her sense of vocation leads her into politics? What if she is transparent about her membership in a pacifist church, yet despite a general distrust of pacifists she manages to win office? Indirectly, at least, she will have some role in supervising the police or relying on them to enforce her policies or laws. Again, other pacifists may contest the validity of such a vocation, but the point here is not to resolve that debate. Rather, it is to insist that faithfulness will require her to justify her vocation by pivoting from and being accountable to a Christian community that knows itself to be living and serving in Diaspora.[21]

*Honestly unfinished pacifism* (3B). Whether because the fallenness of the "fallen world" too often feels intractable even to those who live

---

21. On the need for and practice of this sort of vocational testing, see Yoder, *Christian Witness to the State*, 36, 55–57; Yoder, "Biblical Mandate for Evangelical Social Action," in *For the Nations*, 184–89; Yoder, "Binding and Loosing," in *Royal Priesthood*, 323–58; and my own appropriation of Yoder's thought in *Just Policing, Not War*, 83–84, 99–106.

in Christian hope, or because history is unfinished for the people of God themselves, we must admit that pacifists do not always have fully satisfying answers to the challenges that prompt some to call the police. Those challenges may even lead a few to see state-based forms of policing as a Christian vocation. To honestly practice the truthfulness that Jesus called for in the Sermon on the Mount may thus require a mode of pacifism that recognizes itself as unfinished. As Dave Jackson demonstrated in his 1981 book *Dial 911: Peaceful Christians and Urban Violence*, on the experiences of Reba Place Fellowship in Evanston, Illinois, such honesty actually helps prevent a slide into more and more fearful and security-obsessed responses to crime.[22]

Sometimes, we simply do not have the time or training to find creative responses to violence and its threat. Only the most spiteful opponent of pacifism or the most ideological proponent of pacifism would blame the Amish woman who dialed 911 in order to stop a worse massacre in Nickel Mines, Pennsylvania, for inconsistency. Justice-minded pacifists who are also feminists have done their churches a crucial service by insisting that women in abusive situations ought not refrain from calling the police. Even amid his trenchant criticism of the police, Christian anarchist Andy Alexis-Baker has admitted that some sexual predators and serial killers simply must be locked up[23] and has anticipated last-resort situations in which ordinary Christians might have to call the police.[24]

If peace churches are to be places of grace and forgiveness, they must have pastoral ways to support those who have "not yet" found creative alternatives to calling the police or practicing nonviolent policing

22. Jackson opened his book confessing that "we've not found the answer to crime and violence to be that simple," i.e., a simple choice between reaching for a gun, turning the other cheek, and dialing 911 to call the police. But his book then offered a series of experiences and tentative guidelines precisely as an alternative to an endless arms race of electronic alarms, guard dogs, martial arts, and arming oneself with guns. Jackson, *Dial 911*, 11–12.

23. Schlabach and Alexis-Baker, "Wrestling with Faithfulness in Peacemaking: Just Policing," Workshop, Peace Among the Peoples (Associated Mennonite Biblical Seminary, Elkhart, Indiana, 2010).

24. Alexis-Baker, "Gospel or a Glock?," 23–24, 36–40.

even in less-than-dire circumstances.[25] The goal of this mode of pacifism is not to rationalize Christian resort to violence, however. This is what distinguishes it from just war traditions. Rather, the goal of its very honesty is to elicit a holy dissatisfaction that recommits us to renewed work for nonviolent alternatives in all of the other modes of Christian pacifism we have outlined. A Christian or a congregation that regretfully calls the police, for example, will go on to do all it can to relate redemptively to offenders—whether by seeking mediated settlements, or by appealing for reduced sentences, or by visiting the offenders in prison. Jackson's *Dial 911* is replete with moving examples, beginning with a story that leads from a botched burglary to a hasty decision to call the police to a developing relationship through letters and prison visits.[26]

## Conclusion

Perhaps all of the answers that authors in this book are offering turn on "ecclesiology." In other words, perhaps all of them depend on how Christians see themselves situated as a people in the world, and how they hear God calling them to participate in its redemption. The challenge of policing thus presses upon Christians and Christian communities a deeper but no less urgent question of vocation: How will we discern God's call as Christian communities in our times and places? Recognizing that the church will live always in Diaspora until the coming of the fullness of God's Kingdom explains why Christian pacifists are likely to continue responding to the challenge of policing in diverse ways, befitting the flexibility they need to live faithfully in Diaspora. Grappling with God's call to seek the *shalom* of every Babylon in which

25. In this same spirit of generosity, Christian pacifists should recognize the force of arguments by Christians of other traditions. The vocationally centered theological framework developed here not only identifies the border zones where debate with their positions is likely to occur, it also offers a constructive and fair way to carry out such debate and discernment. For if it allots only two zones to positions that start to verge away from pacifism (3A and 3C), this may befit the claim of just war traditions that any justifiable use of violence will be exceptional. Thus, the biblical and theological arguments that have elicited the chart above place the burden of proof where it belongs.

26. Jackson, *Dial 911*, 17–29.

we find ourselves itself constitutes faithfulness for a Diaspora people. Yet faithfulness will express itself according to a diverse agenda:

- Those who rightly insist that the first task of Christians is to practice the politics of Jesus the Messiah within the life of the church itself must retrieve and develop the church's own practices of nonviolent policing. Believing that the witness of the Christian community is its greatest contribution to just social change makes this task more rather than less urgent.

- Those who are hopeful that society at large or even humanity as a whole can learn to resolve its conflicts peacefully must develop less and less violent forms of policing as positive alternatives to current policies and practices. They cannot be satisfied merely to critique society's current forms of policing as unjust, violent, or oppressive.

- Those who feel called to work within the system for social justice, but who are less optimistic about society's potential to make any more than piecemeal improvements, must take special care to keep their loyalty to Jesus Christ primary and their accountability to the Christian community active. Only then will they recognize when to work within legal, political, and governmental systems, and when they must conscientiously object, blow a whistle, or resign in order to keep their bearings.

- Any of these, as well as ordinary Christians whose mere life and work in the world forces the question of policing upon them, will sometimes have to admit that they do "not yet" know how to do without the protection of currently constituted police forces. Their moral response will be honesty, confession, and a holy dissatisfaction that does not rationalize but instead renews their search for better and more Christ-like responses.

- But all of these, always, will recognize themselves as Jeremiah's exiles, called to discern our vocations amid the both/and social location of resident aliens, living between the already and the not yet of God's Kingdom.

Thus may we "go in peace, to love and serve the Lord."

# 6

What about Those Men and Women Who Gave
Up Their Lives so that You and I Could Be Free?
On Killing for Freedom

Justin Bronson Barringer

But they have conquered him by the blood of the Lamb and by the word of
their testimony, for they did not cling to life even in the face of death.

—REVELATION 12:11

So if the Son sets you free, you will be free indeed.

—JOHN 8:36

## Introduction

I AM THE PRODUCT of a military family, several generations in fact.
When I was in sixth grade I lived on an Air Force base in Alaska. While
I was sleeping one Saturday night I heard a loud blast, an explosion
that woke me up. Monday morning at school I learned that the boom
came from an AWACS jet that went down during a training mission.

Tragically, a few of my classmates lost their dads in the crash. In more recent times family and friends have shared with me their close encounters with IEDs and rocket-propelled grenades in Afghanistan and Iraq. One of my friends from college lost her new husband in an attack only a few months after they were married, leaving her to raise a little girl on her own. I share this because everything that follows comes from a place of internal struggle and even reluctance due to the dissonance between my faith commitments to peace and reconciliation and my experiences with and affection for folks who have risked—and often lost—so much.[1]

I respect and admire the courage it takes to be a soldier and the personal sacrifices they make for civic freedoms.[2] I am, however, convinced that Christians cannot and should not put their faith in any form of civic freedom. We have a truer freedom in Christ that is real, present, and lasting. Furthermore, we must recognize that while temporal civic freedom is a worthwhile venture, often one worth dying for, it is not worth killing for.

Disciples of Jesus speak and live their convictions not because of those who have fought (and often killed) for their civic freedom. Rather, disciples must speak and act because we are surrounded by a great cloud of witnesses, living and dead, who have sought Jesus and his Kingdom above all else, speaking up even and especially when their lives were on the line. In other words, Christians claim loyalty and identity that come from a different group of ancestors and therefore understand freedom not primarily as civic freedom, but as freedom in Christ. Rather than pointing to "founding fathers" and revolutionary warriors, we point to apostles, prophets, and martyrs as our inspiration and reason for speaking truth. We look to those, namely Jesus of Nazareth, who willingly gave up their lives (while refusing to harm their enemies) so that the

1. Many people have helped me work through my dissonance and come to a place of bold, yet hopefully compassionate and thoughtful moral reasoning. I would especially like to thank Christine Pohl, James Thobaben, Leanne Zeck, Jimmy McCarty, Karyn Kiser-Hansson, and Danae Casteel for their insightful comments on various drafts of this essay.

2. I will use the term "civic freedoms" to refer to the liberties that kingdoms of the world seek to, or at least claim to, protect (usually through coercion, violence, or the threat of violence).

whole universe may be reconciled to its creator and we may all experience enduring freedom that starts here and now.

This is not an exercise in trying to prove a point or be right in the abstract about a very real issue. Rather, it is an attempt to call each of us to a deeper place of seeking the Kingdom first and trusting that God will provide the rest. These witnesses, these martyrs, help us to trust more in Jesus, and they likewise urge us to give our lives more fully to him, so that we too may join in his suffering and conform to his death. It is then that we will be set free in the resurrection life of Christ!

The more I read, pray, and meditate, the more I know that I simply cannot, in good conscience, buy into the idea that my rights, my salvation, my provision, or my freedom come from anywhere other than the Living God. My freedom—my true freedom—does not exist because of armies or governments, policies or soldiers. When people ask where my freedom comes from, I can only respond, "The Crucified and Risen Christ!" This freedom, true freedom, was bought by dying, but never by killing.

## Assumptions Behind the Question

The question—What about those men and women who gave up their lives so that you and I could be free?—seems to be an attempt to shame the one to whom it is directed as one who dishonors soldiers. This is a charge that I personally reject as someone who has an immense respect for those who willingly sacrifice so much. Furthermore, the question seems to be an attempt to avoid the difficult teachings of Jesus by redirecting the conversation to a place that tries to put the advocate for nonviolence on the defensive. This is problematic for Christians because we must first deal with the person and teachings of Jesus before we can rightly reflect on our contemporary situation. Proper consideration of Jesus should lead us to a place where we boast not in our soldiers, but in the cross of Christ alone (Gal 6:14).

It is pertinent to name and address some of the assumptions behind the question before moving on to a more in-depth response to the question itself. The primary assumption is that advocates of Christian nonviolence depend on freedom of speech and freedom of religion to speak and live our convictions. For one committed to the Gospel, this is simply not the case.

I have been greatly privileged in my life to live and work overseas. I lived in two countries in particular where civic and religious freedoms were greatly restricted. In one it was illegal to proselytize anyone under a certain age away from the national religious sect. The other has long been particularly hostile to religious folks and even required me to sign a contract essentially declaring that I would keep any faith convictions to myself under threat of possible imprisonment or deportation. Admittedly, there was virtually no risk that I would be tortured or killed for speaking up, but I certainly could not have relied on my legal rights had I been caught sharing the Gospel.

I did regularly share the Gospel, even emphasizing its subversive, otherworldly Kingdom elements, although I was told that we were being watched by the government and was even scolded by another American Christian for being so open about Jesus' message of supreme Lordship and what that requires of us in terms of our relationship with the powers that be. He told me that if I kept speaking in this way I would lose my respectability and be kicked out of the country. Again, I admit that deportation, or even imprisonment, would not be a great price for me to pay, but the point still stands that I am striving, and quite often failing, to declare Jesus' message of subversive hospitality, enemy love, and reconciliation regardless of my temporal circumstance. One need not have the protection of a government or the guarantee of free speech in order to share God's truths.

One might respond, "Okay, one doesn't *need* it, but isn't it still a good worth defending?" It may be that a guaranteed freedom of speech and religion are indeed good, but I argue that Christians defending them, especially with violence, is not.

Stanley Hauerwas writes, "Freedom of religion is a temptation, albeit a subtle one. It tempts us as Christians to believe that we have been rendered safe by legal mechanisms. It is subtle because we believe our task as Christians is to support the ethos necessary to maintaining the mechanism. As a result, we lose the critical skills formed by the gospel to know when we have voluntarily qualified our loyalty to God in the

name of the state."[3] In other words, when we give in to the temptation
to defend our civic freedoms, we clearly compromise our allegiance and
undermine the mission and witness of the church.

This becomes even clearer when we consider what might happen if the church actually played its properly subversive, upside-down
Kingdom role in society. Again, we turn to Hauerwas on this point:

> The illusion has been created that we live in a noncoer-
> cive society because it is one where 'the people' rule. If
> the church challenged that assumption, then I think we
> would find that our society might well think us mad. In
> particular, I suspect Christians would find our society less
> than willing to acknowledge the church's freedom once the
> church makes clear that her freedom comes from faithful-
> ness to God and as a result can never be given or taken
> away by the state.[4]

We can appreciate our civic freedom and even take advantage of it, but
we must always do so tentatively lest we allow it to deceive us into believing it is worth disobeying the clear commands of Christ about loving our enemy, even those who stand as enemies of all types of freedom.

A second assumption, which directly follows the first, is that moves
toward civic freedom can only be made and then protected through violence (which of course relies on the myth that they are worth killing for
in the first place). I will briefly recount the story of Andre Trocmé and
his companions in Le Chambon who rescued Jews during the Nazi occupation of France. They serve as but one example among many of folks
who refused to use violence yet protected the lives of countless humans
and subverted the oppressive powers of the Nazis in small but significant ways as they made moves toward freedom for their Jewish friends.

Trocmé was dedicated to nonviolence[5] and is credited with leading
one of the most successful efforts to rescue Jews and resist the Nazis
during the whole of the Third Reich's murderous campaign. Like most

3. Hauerwas, *After Christendom?*, 71.

4. Ibid., 92.

5. This is not only evidenced in the story of Andre Trocmé's life, but in his own
account of his theology in the book *Jesus and the Nonviolent Revolution*.

proponents of nonviolence, Trocmé was harshly criticized for his refusal to kill because many believed, as they still do, that some evil people
can only be responded to with violence. In one encounter while he was
in prison, Trocmé was accosted by another inmate, who declared, "A
revolution by nonviolence and nonlying—that might work with decent
people, but with skunks? . . .To succeed, you've got to be a skunk with
the skunks. You can't survive otherwise, let alone *do* something."[6]

It is this logic that the devil has been using since Cain killed Abel,
but Trocmé knew better because Trocmé knew Jesus. "Jesus was for
Trocmé the embodied forgiveness of sins, and staying close to Jesus
meant always being ready to forgive your enemies instead of torturing
and killing them. Trocmé could not bear to separate himself from Jesus
by ignoring the precious quality of human life that God had demonstrated in the birth, the life, and the crucifixion of His son."[7] Trocmé and
his companions took dead seriously, often quite literally, the command
of Paul, "Do not be overcome by evil, but overcome evil with good"
(Rom 12:21).

Though Trocmé had deep convictions that a commitment to nonviolence was fundamentally a Christian duty, regardless of its effectiveness or practicality,[8] he also believed that it could indeed be a productive
means of protecting others and preventing more violence. Trocmé believed that "only nonviolence could allow Le Chambon to resist the will
of Vichy and the will of the Germans without massacre . . . [Because]
nonviolence was disarming, and in the face of the overwhelming power
that surrounded Le Chambon during most of the first four years of
the 1940s, it was a course of action dictated by practical benevolence
toward one's fellow human beings."[9] Trocmé's story demonstrates that
faithfulness to the nonviolent way of Jesus trumps effectiveness, yet in
some instances it may be the best tool one has in an attempt to protect
innocent lives and resist even the most heinous evils.

A third assumption revolves around seeing the situation of war,
even wars for "good" causes, in its fullness. People often assume that

6. Hallie, *Lest Innocent Blood Be Shed*, 42.

7. Ibid., 34.

8. See Robert Brimlow's essay on this point.

9. Hallie, *Lest Innocent Blood Be Shed*, 162.

those who sacrifice for our civic freedom committed no wrongs while at war. When people pose the question about the noble men and women who have sacrificed their lives for my freedom and yours, they almost inevitably leave out the fact that many of these very same men and women participated in killing other human beings. Yet, as the famous American general George Patton clearly and profoundly articulated, "The object of war is not to die for your country. It is to make the other poor dumb bastard die for his."[10] When I bring this up in conversation, one of two things typically happens: either the other person gets mad and refuses even to discuss this reality, or he or she immediately begins justifying military action with dismissive statements like, "Well, some things are just worth killing for." It seems, though, that for Christians at least, in the light of Christ's nonviolent witness there is nothing for which disciples ought to be willing to kill.

Justification for war is not always stated in terms of civic freedom. For millennia, governments have been justifying their violent actions by promising peace and prosperity to their citizens. One famous example is what the Roman Empire called the *Pax Romana*, or Roman Peace, which they protected by one of the world's most powerful and often brutal militaries. (This legacy still lives on today, as some American missiles are still called "peacekeepers" and were almost named "peacemakers"!) But Jesus came preaching a different message; it was, in fact, he who was Lord—not Caesar or any government or military power—the only One capable of bringing real peace, prosperity, and freedom. It wasn't the might of the world's militaries but the meekness of the slaughtered Lamb that bought our freedom. It is only he who is worthy to open the scrolls, the deed to all of creation. It is Jesus who is King of kings and Lord of lords, the Prince of peace!

So, in whom do you put your trust to bring you peace? Those who assume dependence on civic freedom, upheld and promoted through violence, to speak their convictions; those who believe violence is the only or even the best option for helping the oppressed; and those who assume that dying for freedom in the midst of warfare does not often also entail killing may want to seriously meditate on that question, as we all should.

10. D'Este, *Patton*, 1.

## The Myth (or Demonic Lie) of Individual Freedom

Now we turn to a fourth assumption, one that needs special attention because it has proven to have a powerful, negative impact on the church in a variety of realms. There is, in a very real sense, a way in which the idea of individual freedom and personal liberties is a myth. This type of freedom is ultimately false and deceptive, and points us not to God, who demands our lives, but to Satan, who tells us that our lives are ours to do with what we please. This deception goes so far as to have people believing that they can even be free from God. The biblical narrative expresses the reality that our only choice is to whom we will be enslaved. In some sense we do not have the choice to be free,[11] yet when we go to God as slaves[12] God welcomes us as his children.

Satan's ultimate deception is that we can and should be able to do whatever we want, that freedom is about us getting our way. This deception surrounds war, convincing many that we can gain temporary freedom. But it is only through the means of the enemy—that is violence, deceit, and dehumanizing enemies—that we do so.

C. S. Lewis, in his classic work *The Great Divorce*, describes hell as a place where people are determined to have their own way. As they try to create and protect their freedom to do as they please, they grow further and further apart from each other and from God until they are so trapped in their own illusory reality that they are eternally confined in a prison of loneliness, one of their own making. However, God in his divine honesty tells us that freedom is not something we can choose; we can only choose to be slaves. It is in choosing to be slaves to God, rather than choosing to believe the devil's lies, that we can earn or choose or

11. This is not an argument about the free agency of the individual as it pertains to discussions on free will. Rather, it is an attempt to paint a picture of the reality that God in God's full honesty demands everything of us so that God can liberate us in mind, body, and soul, whereas Satan lies to us and says we can free ourselves from the demands of any external force.

12. Interestingly, as Craig Keener notes in *The IVP Background Commentary: New Testament*, 713, "Although ancient society was very status-conscious and associated power with greatness, Peter identifies Christ with unjustly treated slaves."

fight for freedom, that we are set free by Christ—set free for freedom's sake so that we may have life, and life to the fullest.[13]

Lewis suggests that hell is the deception that we can be free of each other, at least those with whom we disagree, and from God. Was this not the deception in the garden? The serpent offered Adam and Eve the chance to be free from God's rule, to have their own way and govern their own affairs. Ever since then, people have been fighting for some version of this illusive and elusive freedom. However, Christians must recognize the captive state of every human, and instead of fighting for a false freedom, we should be dying, sometimes literally, to spread the news of the bondage that sets us free as we take up our crosses to make this point the predominant reality in our lives.[14] It is when we are slaves to Christ that we are truly free, and that freedom transcends circumstance. John Donne expresses this paradox beautifully in one of his Holy Sonnets: "Take me to you, imprison me, for I, / Except you enthrall me, never shall be free."[15]

I saw a skit several years ago in which a young man was building walls around himself. An older man approached and asked what was going on. The young man replied, "I am building these walls around myself so I can be free from everyone telling me what to do. This one is to keep my parents out, and that one over there is for my teachers, and I have one for my classmates and even one for God, too." The other man offered to help build the walls. The skit ended with the two enclosed in a self-made prison, one that was supposed to provide freedom. The young man turns to the other man and introduces himself; the older man replies, "Hi, my name is Satan." It seems that too many of us are fighting for our "right" to create our own hell. This is not to say that humans do not have a choice in their destiny. Quite the contrary, God is

13. Paul and other New Testament writers regularly use the language of freedom to discuss relationship with Christ, but this must be viewed in light of Paul's self-designation as a slave of Christ (*doulos Christou*).

14. A distinction must be made between giving up one's own freedom and potentially sacrificing the freedom of others, but I will not deal with that here because it is covered in other essays in this book.

15. John Donne, "Batter My Heart, Three-Person'd God," in Harmon, *The Classic Hundred Poems*, 33. Donne was a poet and priest who lived and wrote during the sixteenth and seventeenth centuries.

clear that we can choose God and is likewise totally forthcoming about the expectations God has for God's people. Godly freedom is an assault on the harmful notions of Western, über-indivualized civic freedom because popular understandings of freedom, along with war and oppression, undermine the *shalom* God intends for his world. These popular notions of freedom stand in contradiction to the freedom we have to be in the community of Christ, which is freedom to serve God and one another (Galatians 5).

Scholar William Cavanaugh, in his assessment of the nation-state's role in keeping the common good, asserts that governments simply cannot provide godly freedom because they must hold in tension their attempts to protect freedom and the common good. He says about the necessary failure of such attempts by earthly powers, "The result is not the common good, but an—ultimately—tragic attempt to ward off social conflict by keeping individuals apart."[16] Simply put, the only way we can have freedom through worldly means is to be isolated from each other, often by killing our enemies, and this is ultimately hell itself.

Furthermore, I would argue that life together is the way Christians combat the aforementioned myth of total individual freedom and the hell to which it leads. The "peacekeepers" of the world maintain peace by keeping people in conflict apart, often through violence, but the peacemakers of God's Kingdom do so through the ministry of reconciliation (2 Cor 5:18–19) in which we bring warring parties together in hopes that, as God reconciled us to God's Self while we were still God's enemies (Rom 5:10), God will use us to reconcile others to God and one another. Instead of separating God's Self from God's enemies, God became one of us that God might befriend us (Matt 11:9) and thus reconcile us to God. Violence has no power to do this, but self-sacrificial love destroys the gates of the hells we have created for ourselves and frees the captives so that we may run into the arms of God and be eternally bound to Christ!

## True Freedom

Let me now turn my attention to the type of freedom described in the Bible. Christian freedom, true freedom, the freedom that is para-

16. Cavanaugh, "Killing for the Telephone Company," 255.

doxically only possible by being bound to Christ, does not come from having an American address or passport or living in a Western-style democracy, and it is not about protecting our rights. It comes from being a citizen of God's now-but-not-yet Kingdom, and it is about giving up our rights, even our right to life, so that others may be drawn into the love of Christ and forever fettered there. Though this freedom is quite different from the way we generally understand freedom, it is quite real and to be experienced here and now. It is the freedom to live our lives as God would have us do, regardless of what obstacles we face. Let us briefly explore what characterizes this kind of freedom.

First Peter describes the kind of freedom that God has in mind for all people, and expects of all Christians. It is a freedom found only in Christ, and it transcends circumstance. It is true freedom! Peter reminds us that we, as a community, have been called by God to be "a chosen people, a royal priesthood, a holy nation, a people belonging to God, that [we] may declare the praises of him who called [us] out of darkness into his wonderful light"(1 Pet 2:9). This provides the foundation for the kind of freedom Peter will go on to address.

We are free not because of our passport or geographic location; we are free because we have been chosen by God and now live in God's light. Peter declares that we are "aliens and strangers in the world" (1 Pet 2:11) and thus have no particular loyalty to any given country or government; rather, we are told to submit to all authorities as a way to declare that we have no allegiance to any particular worldly ruler. By allowing all authorities to subjugate us, we bear witness to Christ, who was crucified unjustly by the powers, yet rose again to bring about the impending and ultimate defeat.

We therefore know that we can submit temporarily, so long as in our submission we do not sin against God, because ultimately we will be raised to new life under the just and loving rule of the Almighty. Our submission to governments is, therefore, to bear witness to Jesus and his Kingdom. Because Peter says that we obey for the Lord's sake, there are parameters within the command. One cannot submit, by obeying for the Lord's sake, to anything that is contrary to the expressed will of this very Lord. In other words, at the moment when an authority's demands on us conflict with our duty to this Lord and his Kingdom (as is the case in waging war), we speak the truth in love, refusing to sin and accepting the consequences of our actions. True freedom means we are free to subordinate ourselves to earthly authorities precisely because we are free to disobey them when their demands are contrary to God's will.

Interestingly, Peter contrasts his statements about submitting to human institutions with an almost contradictory command to "live as free men," which he then defines as those who "live as servants of God" (1 Pet 2:16). Perhaps the most disturbing yet compelling statement Peter makes in regards to the kind of freedom we have in Christ is this: "Slaves, submit yourselves to your masters with all respect, not only to those who are good and considerate, but also to those who are harsh" (1 Pet 2:18). I am not of the mind that Peter, nor any of the other New Testament writers, was a proponent of slavery, yet Peter uses this real-life example to illustrate that even those in the worst forms of oppression can have dignity if their hope is in Christ.

He goes on to say, "For it is commendable if a man bears up under the pain of unjust suffering because he is conscious of God" (1 Pet 2:19). For Peter, true freedom is found in Christ and most clearly demonstrated in the lives of those who suffer unjustly for his sake. I don't want to romanticize suffering, especially suffering for suffering's sake, as this has nothing to do with Christian discipleship. However, suffering specifically for the sake of Christ—that is, joining Christ through faith, even in his suffering, precisely for the sake of freeing the oppressed—we can also hope to join him in his resurrection (Phil 3:9–11).

It is not those who are willing to do wrong whom God commends: "But if you suffer for doing good and you endure it, this is commendable before God" (1 Pet 2:20). Therefore, followers of Christ do not need the protection of any army or legal system because it is in suffering unjustly that we most distinctly bear witness to the slaughtered and risen Lamb! There is a danger in stating things this way because often language like this has been used to justify or even glorify the suffering of the oppressed. My challenge is that you and I embrace this suffering as a way of joining in solidarity with the oppressed to bring attention to their plight and use nonviolent action, rather than military aggression and violence, to change things and to promote freedom, both temporal and eternal.

This is a call for you and I to be willing to suffer, to actively engage in service to others, and to join them to help them out of their suffering, not to be apathetic and let others suffer unjustly. In this we mirror Christ: "To this you were called, because Christ suffered for you, leaving you an example, that you should follow in his steps" (1 Pet 2:21). We are not called to the comfort and security of the temporal freedoms that we may find in certain places in this world. As Joel Green writes, "Christians should expect to be treated as those who are powerless . . . knowing, however, that their appropriate conduct would have a redemptive effect akin to that of Jesus."[17] We are called to the great adventure[18] of following Christ wherever he may lead, even and especially when it will cost us the most!

A brief caveat is necessary here. It is not my intention to trivialize or dismiss the reality of earthly oppression or suffering. Quite the contrary, it is precisely because oppression is so real and such an important issue in our world that Christians must approach it with sound moral reasoning and an ongoing commitment to combat it wherever it exists. However, rather than doing so by employing violence, we Christians are to make ourselves like human shields on the battlefield. When someone is being oppressed, abused, mistreated, or is facing political/religious persecution, we are supposed to step in and take the blow. This is how Christians respond to abuses of civic freedom. We don't glibly critique the use of violence to protect civil rights; we sacrifice, even our lives, so that the poor, outcast, and oppressed can experience freedom, both the temporary civic freedoms of this world and the eternal freedom continuing into the next. We aim to promote and protect freedom of all godly sorts not by taking up a gun, but by taking up our cross as mediators of reconciliation, willing to die (but never kill) for the rights of others!

For a relevant and inspiring example, one need look no further than Martin Luther King Jr. and other champions of the civil rights movement, who constantly put themselves in harm's way to counter injustice and oppression. King was dedicated to the Christian values

17. Green, *1 Peter*, 72.

18. For an account on what is meant here (and later in the essay) by "adventure," see Hauwerwas and Willimon's *Resident Aliens*, specifically 49–68.

of seeking justice and refusing to do violence. He serves as evidence that the two need not be mutually exclusive. We find another example in Gandhi, who, though not a disciple of Jesus, was among those who inspired King; in fact, King quoted Gandhi, saying, "Rivers of blood may have to flow before we gain our freedom, but it must be our blood," and later, "if going to jail is necessary, [the nonviolent resister] enters it 'as a bridegroom enters a bride's chamber.'"[19]

Biblical freedom, as we see exemplified in the life of King, is first and foremost the freedom to serve God and to speak truth while we give ourselves up, as Jesus did, for those who are suffering the most. That is true freedom, the kind of freedom I will now briefly elaborate on to elucidate God's call on the lives of followers of Jesus Christ.

*True freedom* is not having the right to say whatever you want without consequences; it is being able to say what is right regardless of the consequences. Soldiers on battlefields might protect our right to free speech, but the faithful throughout the church's history have retold the story of Jesus in virtually every context, and no threat of imprisonment, torture, or death was able to shut their mouths. They took Jesus at his word and refused to fear those who could only harm their bodies, because they put their faith in the One who could destroy their souls (Matt 10:28).

*True freedom* is not being able to gather and worship without the threat of being arrested; it is assembling with your brothers and sisters to worship God even if it means your life is at risk. The earliest church members knew this.[20] They met in caves and tombs and backrooms to praise God, and even when they were caught and threatened with gruesome torture and death, many of them stayed faithful and even considered their own martyrdom as a blessing from God. Hebrews 11 briefly recounts the heroic, loving courage of these early martyrs. "Others were tortured and refused to be released, so that they might gain a better resurrection. Some faced jeers and flogging, while still others were

---

19. Miller, *Voice of Deliverance*, 89.

20. It is not that being able to meet without threat of persecution is a bad thing; it is that using freedom of religion as a reason to kill that is unacceptable for Christians. Nor is suffering necessarily a good thing, but it is something that Christians are necessarily called to embrace when it comes as a result of their faithfulness to Christ.

chained and put in prison. They were stoned; they were sawed in two; they were put to death by the sword. They went about in sheepskins and goatskins, destitute, persecuted and mistreated—the world was not worthy of them. They wandered in deserts and mountains, and in caves and holes in the ground" (Heb 11:35b–38). These women and men were heralded by the Scriptures themselves as people for whom the world was unworthy.

*True freedom* is not won or lost in Congress; it is won on the streets and in homes when we feed the poor, clothe the naked, and give shelter to the homeless. Ultimate freedom in this life is choosing to not live for oneself, but to live for God and others. This is the example set for us by Jesus, who prayed in the garden, "not my will, but yours be done" (Luke 22:42), and even in his last moments he was focused not on himself but on the very people who had nailed him to a cross. Paradoxically, it is when we choose to quit living for ourselves that we are free to live. "The more [one] demonstrates [a] willingness to serve, the more [one] experiences true freedom" (James 1:25, 2:12).[21] This is the truth about each person of the Trinity, each one graciously deferring to the others; the Father gives glory to the Son, and the Spirit testifies to the Son while the Son submits to the Father and leaves earth to allow for the ministry of the Spirit.

*True freedom* does not come from having the loudest voice; it comes from quietly taking up one's cross and following Jesus. Contrary to the cries of those political pundits and religious leaders who would have us believe that we must win the culture wars—or actual wars, for that matter—by asserting our power over "those heathens" with whom we disagree, lest we lose our right to "preach God's word," followers of Christ instead believe it when Jesus says that it is the meek who will inherit the earth (Matt 5:5). It has been said by some that the one who complains the loudest gets the "biggest crown," but in Jesus' upside-down Kingdom the least shall be made the greatest (Luke 9:48).

*True freedom* does not come from an army, government, or document; it comes from the risen Christ. Jesus sealed the freedom of every Christian with the gift of the Holy Spirit after his resurrection and as-

21. Kistemaker, *New Testament Commentary: Exposition of the Epistles of Peter and of the Epistle of Jude*, 102.

cension. He holds our lives in his hands, and we are told that nothing, not even the demons of hell, can separate us from the love of God (Rom 8:38–39)! There is no such thing as faith *and* freedom, because faith in Christ *is* freedom.

*True freedom* wasn't paid for by the lives of thousands of men and women on battlefields; it was purchased by a man dying on a cross and rising to new life. While there may be times when it is appropriate to acknowledge and lament the lives lost in war and even to celebrate the privileges we have, there is no more important ceremony than the Eucharist, whereby we acknowledge and lament the price Christ paid for our freedom and abundant life and celebrate his resurrection. It is for freedom's sake the Christ has set us free (Gal 5:1) so let us always rejoice in this beautiful reality!

It is this freedom to which we are called, this freedom for which we live and die—but never kill. The clear witness of the whole of the New Testament declares two important truths on this point. First, violence is not the way that Christians bring about change in the world, but by being faithful to Christ and bearing witness to him, we become change agents. Second, nowhere in the New Testament is freedom ever spoken of in terms of civic freedom;[22] rather, it is consistently depicted in terms of one's commitment to the will of the Father, which of course is epitomized in Jesus himself.

## Regaining a Sense of Biblical Freedom

I have asserted that fighting for civic freedom is not the place of the Christian and have established a framework for understanding the kind of freedom Scripture describes. Nevertheless, it seems odd, at least

22. Though many worthwhile insights can be drawn from the Old Testament as well, I have decided for the sake of brevity to focus only on the New Testament in this essay. One might ask about the freedom often mentioned in the OT, which was clearly civic freedom. Two responses are necessary. First, it seems clear that the civic freedom of the OT is but a shadow of the fuller freedom in Christ, and second, the civic freedom in the OT was not won by the might of Israel's military, but by God's own hand. Admittedly, there is an example in the NT where Paul invokes certain rights he has as a Roman citizen in one instance, but this is a far cry from relying on this as a lifestyle or being willing to kill for these sorts of freedoms.

initially, that Paul so readily used military language to describe many facets of the Christian life. In order to appreciate Paul's use of military language to describe the Christian life, it is first useful to name the many virtues Christians can learn from soldiers and then examine the ways in which these qualities should inform the Christian life and help us regain a sense of biblical freedom.

There are few moments in life more moving than watching soldiers come home from a tour overseas and rush through the terminal to be greeted by the fanfare of family and friends. The most powerful and poignant moment is when the soldier is first embraced by his or her loved ones. Tears roll down each face and spouses and children look up at their brave hero with so much admiration coupled with pure relief that their beloved is safely with them again. When I think about these moments, I cannot help wondering what it would look like if the church greeted missionaries and nonviolent peacemakers with the same enthusiasm. I also wonder if this will be the kind of scene with which we are greeted in heaven.

In those airport moments, I can see that it is no mistake that Paul often uses military metaphors to describe the Christian life. Soldiers are expected to be courageous, disciplined, loyal, and willing to sacrifice, and so are Christians. But we must note that Paul always turns these metaphors on their head a bit as he clarifies what it means for each of us to be soldiers in the Lord's Army. Two examples of Paul's use of military language will serve to demonstrate his reappropriation of worldly terms to describe Jesus' otherworldly Kingdom. First, Paul describes the armor that Christians should wear in his letter to the Ephesians. Paul describes the armor of God by using each piece of a typical soldier's attire metaphorically to illustrate fundamental virtues of Christian discipleship like truth, righteousness, and peace,[23] as well as attesting to God's rightful place as the bringer of salvation and the provider of God's Word. It is God, then, as Paul suggests, who truly defeats the enemy, and thus it is simply our job to stand in faithfulness, praying to the One who makes us more than conquerors that the Spirit will make us fearless to

23. I wonder if there is a significance to the armor including the shoes of peace? How does one walk peacefully in a violent world? The Gospel is brought through the means of peace—it is the feet of the soldier that carried them forward.

declare his Gospel to the world (Eph 6:11–20). This is how we fight; it is how we enact positive change against oppressive, even violent rulers of all kinds.

Paul revisits the military language in his second letter to Timothy as he affirms the Christian duty to persevere rather than fight for our rights. He tells Timothy to "endure hardship with us like a good soldier of Christ Jesus" (2 Tim 2:3). Here again, we see the authority of Christ over the life of the Christian as Paul reminds Timothy, and subsequently us, that it is faithfulness to Christ and following his lead that is the duty of the disciple. We are to have a single-minded devotion to Christ and his way of living in the world, his way of fighting so that we may "please [our] commanding officer" (2 Tim 2:3).

Devotion to the way of Christ means that we do not take up worldly weapons of violence and power; we simply do as Christ did by laying down our lives rather than trusting in our own competency to "make things right." Jesus, our commanding officer, did not win his battle by letting Peter and the others fight off the Roman guard, nor by calling legions of angels to destroy his enemies. No, he went quietly to his death, knowing that there was the joy of his resurrection to follow (Heb 12:2). "And having disarmed the powers and authorities, he made a public spectacle of them, triumphing over them by the cross" (Col 2:15)—this is exactly the way we are called to triumph, by taking up our crosses and following the way of the crucified and risen messiah (Matt 16:24)! We don't fight; we pray. We don't kill; we lay down our own lives.

As Gerhard Lohfink notes, early church leaders understood this well.[24] He describes Tertullian and Origen's belief that war was incompatible with Christian life, particularly Origen's grasp on the biblical reality that Paul describes in Ephesians 6:12. Origen knew that because our battle is not with flesh and blood but demonic systems and dark spiritual forces that we fight not with weapons forged by human hands, but with the godly armor Paul exhorts disciples—soldiers of Christ—to put on in order to withstand the attacks of the devil. Origen further ex-

24. Shane Claiborne and Chris Haw's *Jesus for President* is a good place to start investigating what the earliest church leaders had to say about Christians, nation building, and war, specifically the section that begins on p. 141. For a more thorough examination, Michael G. Long's *Christian Peace and Nonviolence* is a particularly helpful resource.

plains the kind of battle Christians are supposed to be fighting when he asserts, "We who by our prayers destroy all daemons which stir up wars, violate oaths, and disturb the peace, are of more help to the emperors than those who seem to be doing the fighting."[25]

Then what, you may ask, do soldiers specifically have to teach the church? Well, those who object to my position on the grounds of a desire to honor those who have given up their lives for others provide some clarity here. It is a lesson that Jesus himself both preached and exemplified. Jesus said, "Greater love has no one than this, that he lay down his life for his friends" (John 15:13). The church needs to regain this sense of adventurous and costly friendship with people who desperately need to know that they are loved enough that disciples of Christ would die for them. While we can learn a great deal about courage and sacrifice from soldiers, we Christians must not allow ourselves to be caught in schemes of violence, especially in this world's wars. As I have already mentioned, our battle is not against flesh and blood, but against the powers and principalities, and the only way to fight this war is by taking up our crosses of nonviolent suffering and joining Jesus in making a spectacle of the violent and oppressive powers by way of dying to ourselves and this world of violence. This is the consistent witness of the New Testament (which, by the way, never mentions civic freedom as a Christian value).

I pray that my conviction that Jesus is the Prince of Peace will be enough to carry me through if a time comes when I have to put my life on the line for his sake. I hope that I demonstrate my freedom by joining Christ in the terrifying yet liberating adventure of taking up my cross and following him. The church, for the sake of our witness, must regain the courage to nonviolently venture out in faith into dens of lions, fiery furnaces, and up to the hills on which we will be crucified. As the body of Christ, this is something we must do together. The church must reimagine ways to make heroes out of those who give all, in life and death, for the sake of the Gospel. We need to regain the notion that being part of the church should be the adventure of a lifetime. We cannot continue to be lulled into a state of complacency as we protect the status quo, nor can we misappropriate our zeal to violent causes.

25. Lohfink, *Jesus and Community*, 170.

Instead, we must rejoin the revolution of Jesus' church as we bombard the gates of hell, knowing they cannot prevail.

Organizations like Christian Peacemaker Teams (CPT) have served this function, but unfortunately they have been ignored or even rebuked by many church folk over the years. CPT serves by placing "teams at the invitation of local peacemaking communities that are confronting situations of lethal conflict. These teams seek to follow God's Spirit as it works through local peacemakers who risk injury and death by waging nonviolent direct action to confront systems of violence and oppression."[26] Their work stems from a profoundly moving, and hopefully convicting, question: "What would happen if Christians devoted the same discipline and self-sacrifice to nonviolent peacemaking that armies devote to war?"[27] I know one thing for sure: if Christians took this question seriously and responded appropriately, we would certainly please our commanding officer, who once said, "Blessed are the peacemakers, for they will be called sons of God" (Matt 5:9).

## Problems with Idolatrous Nationalism and Militarism

Along with the list of difficulties already mentioned regarding Christian involvement in war, there is one more important biblical theme that needs to be addressed. That is the idolatry of blind nationalism and militarism that sometimes prevails in church decisions even to the point of being pervasive. As Lee Camp puts it, "Nationalism and patriotism are self-centeredness writ large, community habits that prepare us to do 'whatever is necessary,' as our politicians put it these days, to 'preserve our cherished way of life.'"[28]

Somehow, no matter what the war is really about, governments have a knack for making them seem not only worthwhile but also honorable and good. History provides an example of this sort of eschewing of the truth; in the name of making war seem honorable and good, the

26. For more on the work of Christian Peacemaker Teams, visit their Web site: http://cpt.org. Specifically, check out the books written by CPT team members under the resources section.

27. Ibid.

28. Camp, *Mere Discipleship*, 160.

church's first conscientious objector was turned into the patron saint of soldiers and war! It was this great example of Christ-like courage, St. Martin of Tours, who famously said, "I am a soldier of Christ. I cannot fight."[29] Though he refused to fight and kill, St. Martin has now been co-opted by the powers as a war hero who supposedly blesses soldiers and fighting. Various governments have unfortunately followed the church's lead in this regard and made St. Martin's feast day a day to celebrate veterans of war.

The recent American wars in the Middle East, particularly the war in Iraq, exemplify the reality that virtually all wars are perverted in a variety of ways to appear as if they are right and good and holy. My friend Tripp York asks this penetrating question: "When Jesus demands that we love our enemies and our leaders demand that we kill them, whom do we obey?"[30] Though a multiplicity of church leaders and Christian scholars came out against the war,[31] Christians, instead of looking to God and the church[32] for their authority, hearkened to the calls to eradicate terrorism and succumbed to the idolatrous call to defend their freedom and their nation. The so-called war on terror became the motivator for many Christians, in a sense becoming their god—a god who, unlike Christ, demands violent and often deadly force to protect its place in the world. Sadly, too many Christians ignored the warnings of church leaders and instead bought into the cult of the American military, bowing down before its idols of power, greed, and violence, all in the name of this ever-elusive notion of freedom. If Jesus is Lord of our lives, then we follow his way of living in the world and we reject all forms of idolatry, whether love of money, nationalism, or militarism, and instead we worship the only One who has the power to free us, even from ourselves.

29. Kurlansky, *Non-Violence*, 26.

30. York, *Third Way Allegiance*, 62.

31. This link provides the names of one hundred prominent Christian theologians and ethicists, both just war theorists and pacifists, who spoke out against a preemptive attack on Iraq: http://archive.sojo.net/index.cfm?action=action.ethicists_statement.

32. Sadly, much of the church, particularly local pastors, did not speak out against the war. And many who did spoke out too late.

### My Personal Struggle

This country affords many opportunities (and yes, freedoms)—from job opportunities to the fact that I am unlikely to be beaten or imprisoned for my beliefs—that I would not have in many other places on Earth. Moreover, I understand the convictions of the many men and women who died for what they believed in. I admire people who are willing to live and die for their convictions, people who believe in the ideals of liberty, justice, and freedom. Because I have friends and family who have lost loved ones in war, I am sensitive to the complex emotional framework involved and the feelings I may hurt in writing this. There is no doubt that this issue is extremely personal to many and will strike a nerve, particularly with veterans and those who have lost loved ones in the military. However, my conviction regarding this point is so strong that I have to write this. I cannot back down, even if it costs me friendships. Like Peter before the Sanhedrin, I simply cannot stay quiet about the peaceable Kingdom of Jesus and the freedom that only comes from being bound by his nail-scarred hands.

### Conclusion

"The real temptation for 'good' people like us is not the crude, the crass, and the carnal. The refined temptation, with which Jesus himself was tried, is that of egocentric altruism. It is to claim oneself to be the incarnation of a good and righteous cause for which others might rightly be made to suffer. It is stating one's self-justification in the form of duty to others."[33] So for all those who have given up their lives on my behalf, I say thank you for your courage and sacrifice, but to those of you willing to kill—for my freedom or any other reason—I simply ask that you please not kill for me.[34]

33. Yoder, *What Would You Do?*, 42.

34. Or anyone else, for that matter. But we, of course, must be willing to suffer and die on behalf of the other, even our enemies!

# 7

## Does God Expect Nations to Turn the Other Cheek?

Gregory A. Boyd

PACIFISM IS COMMONLY THOUGHT to entail the political conviction that governments should always refrain from violence. The majority of people dismiss this conviction as impractical if not dangerously naïve. If decent governments adopt a "turn the other cheek" policy toward evildoers, they reason, evildoers will win. Had America adopted this stance toward the Nazis, for example, it seems likely that Jews would have been exterminated and a good portion of the world would have come under Nazi rule. Similarly, if America adopted a pacifistic stance today, it seems evident that Islamic extremists like Al Qaeda would quickly rule and Christianity would be outlawed. Since God obviously would not want this, many Christians conclude, we simply cannot interpret the New Testament's instructions to love enemies and refrain from violence to refer to evil nationalistic enemies like Hitler or terrorists. They must rather have been referring to personal and/or less threatening enemies.

In this essay I will argue against this perspective and instead contend that the New Testament's instructions for disciples of Jesus to love their enemies and to refrain from violence are unconditional. Thus they apply to enemies like Hitler and Islamic extremists as much as they do to anyone else.[1] At the same time, I will argue that the distinctive kind of pacifism taught by Jesus and the authors of the New Testament does not commit one to the conviction that *governments* should unconditionally refrain from violence. There is, I contend, a world of difference between the enemy-loving nonviolence practiced by citizens of the kingdom of God—what I will call "kingdom pacifism"—and the view that governments should always refrain from violence—what I will call "political pacifism."[2] By getting clear on the distinction between these two kinds of pacifism and by showing that the first does not entail the second, we are able to bypass one of the main reasons people give for dismissing the pacifistic interpretation of the New Testament—viz. they believe it entails a dangerously naïve political stance.

### Who Are the Enemies We Are to Love?

Let's begin by investigating whether or not there are any compelling exegetical or historical grounds for concluding that the New Testament's teachings on loving enemies and refraining from violence do not apply to national enemies like Hitler and Al Qaeda. As challenging as it may be for some to accept, I am convinced there are none. Indeed, it is evident to me that evil nationalistic enemies like Hitler and Al Qaeda were

1. Due to space limitations, this essay will focus exclusively on the alleged naiveté of the pacifist response to threatening *national* enemies (e.g., Hitler, terrorists) and leave it to others to respond to the alleged naiveté of the pacifist response to threatening *personal* enemies. I should also note that it is not my intent in this essay to provide anything like a comprehensive defense of the pacifistic interpretation of the New Testament. Several of the best defenses I know of are Hays, *Moral Vision of the New Testament*, 317–46; Trzyna, *Blessed Are the Pacifists*; Yoder, *Original Revolution*; Hornus, *It Is Not Lawful for Me to Fight*; and Russell, *Overcoming Evil God's Way*.

2. My distinction between "kingdom pacifism" and "political pacifism" bears some resemblance (but is not identical) to the distinction that is sometimes made between "absolute pacifism," on the one hand, and "personal" and/or "vocational" pacifism, on the other. See, e.g., Kemp, "Personal Pacifism," 21–38. What sets the kingdom pacifist apart, I will argue, is that his or her primary motivation for embracing nonviolence is not ethical, political, or in any other way utilitarian. It is rather rooted in the Lordship of Christ and the transforming experience of the Holy Spirit. For an excellent discussion on issues surrounding the distinctiveness of Christian (or "kingdom") pacifism from a perspective that is close to my own, see Hauerwas, "Explaining Christian Nonviolence," in *Performing the Faith*, 169–83.

precisely the kinds of enemies Jesus and the New Testament authors had in mind when they instructed Christians to respond to their enemies in loving and nonviolent ways (e.g., Matt 5:38–48; Luke 6:27–36; Rom 12:14–21; 1 Pet 3:9, 14–18).

It is important to bear in mind that at the time in which Jesus ministered and in which the early church was birthed, Palestine was ruled by Rome. The very fact that idolatrous and immoral pagans ruled them and occupied their God-given land was theologically offensive to most orthodox Jews. To make matters worse, however, Roman rule was often unjust and violently oppressive.[3] Peasant Palestinians had few rights over and against their rulers, and the few they had were impossible to enforce. It wasn't uncommon for Jews to lose their land, property, and/or freedom because they could not meet their enormous tax obligations. Nor was it uncommon for Jews to witness compatriots being imprisoned, beaten, and/or crucified for an alleged crime, often without a fair trial. To say that most Jews loathed this situation is to make a massive understatement. In fact, it wouldn't be going too far to compare the animosity that many Palestinian Jews felt toward their Roman oppressors to the animosity felt by most Americans toward Al Qaeda and other terrorist groups after 9/11—except that in the case of first-century Jews, the terrorists weren't simply *threatening* their country; they were already *ruling* it.

In this light, imagine that Al Qaeda had somehow managed to conquer America and that we were now under violently enforced Sharia law. If in this context a respected American teacher were to teach American audiences to love their enemies, can we for a moment suppose the audience wouldn't understand members of Al Qaeda to be included among those they were being taught to love? Obviously, this would be the first group most Americans in this context would associate with the word "enemy." Yet, this imagined scenario isn't all that different from the situation that Jesus' Jewish audiences were in. For a Jewish teacher to talk about "enemies" to Palestinian Jews in the first century was to speak first and foremost about Romans.

3. Rome's famous "incentive-deterrence" policy made for exceptionally brutal and oppressive outcomes when the "deterrent" side of the equation was brought into play. See, e.g., Hengel, *Crucifixion*.

This perspective takes on additional force when we consider that Jesus explicitly taught that his followers were to forfeit their right to decide whom they would and would not love. Just as God causes the sun to shine and the rain to fall on the just and the unjust, Jesus taught, so his followers are to love others (Matt 5:45; cf. Luke 6:35). We are to love *indiscriminately*, in other words, and this rules out any possibility that there could be certain kinds of enemies we are permitted to *not* love and do good to, let alone permitted to engage in violence against.[4]

The perspective is further confirmed by the simple fact that disciples are commanded to imitate Jesus. "Whoever claims to live in him," John writes, "must live as Jesus did" (1 John 2:6, cf. John 13:15; Eph 5:1–2). This command includes Jesus' nonviolent response to enemies, including his response to Pilate and other nationalistic enemies when on trial (1 Pet 2:20–21, cf. 3:9, 14–18).[5] Consider the implications of this. By any just war criteria, Jesus would have been justified in resorting to violence and encouraging his followers to do the same. Yet, Jesus refused to use power readily available to violently protect himself and rebuked a disciple who resorted to violence (Matt 26:51–53; Luke

4. It's important to notice that both Jesus and Paul associate loving enemies with *acting kindly* towards them (Luke 6:27–35; Rom 12:14, 17–20). This fact stands against Augustine's highly influential concept of "benevolent severity," which permitted Christians to engage in violence against enemies while claiming to love them. (See Augustine, *Against Faustus*, 22.76.79; *Letters* 47.5; 138.2.13–15; 189.4). On Augustine's attempt to combine the New Testament teaching on *agape*-love with Cicero's just war theory, see F. H. Russell, "Love and Hate in Medieval Warfare," 108–24; Stevenson, *Christian Love and Just War*. It's worth noting that Augustine was the first to use Jesus' parable of the dinner party (Luke 14:16–24) to justify religious coercion (i.e., "*compel* them to come in"). Augustine thus offered the Christian tradition a ready proof text by which to justify religious persecution for centuries to come. See Drake, "Lions into Lambs." See also Weaver, "Unjust Lies, Just Wars?" There were, of course, antecedents to Augustine's formalization, largely traceable to the effects of the merger of church and state that began with Constantine. See MacMullen, *Christianizing the Roman Empire (A.D. 100–400)*, 86–101.

5. Related to this, followers of Jesus are told to expect to carry a cross and suffer like Christ (Luke 14:27–33; 2 Cor 1:5; 4:10; Phil 1:20; Col 1:24; 1 Pet 4:12–16). On the centrality of suffering in the New Testament's understanding of discipleship, see Allen, *Cruciform Church*, and Gorman, *Cruciformity*. For a brilliant statement on the inseparability of confessing Jesus as Lord and living under his Lordship, see Hauerwas, *Peaceable Kingdom*, 72–87.

22:50–51; John 18:10–11). Most remarkably, Jesus later appealed to the nonviolence of his followers as proof to Pilate that his "kingdom" was "not of this world" (John 18:36). As the pre-Constantinian church almost uniformly recognized, Jesus' decision to die at the hands of enemies rather than to engage in justified violence against them was not merely something he *did for us*: it's also an example he *gave to us*, and it's an example which, by its very nature, admits of no exceptions.[6]

As I interpret it, Eph 6:10–12 provides still further confirmation of the view that there are no legitimate conditions or qualifications on the command to love enemies and refrain from violence. In this passage Paul encourages followers of Jesus to "be strong in the Lord" and to "take your stand against the devil's scheme."[7] Paul then explains: "[f]or our struggle [*palē*] is not against flesh and blood, but against rulers . . . authorities . . . powers of this dark world . . . [and] spiritual forces of evil in the heavenly realms." Among other things, Paul is here teaching us that we are never to regard "flesh and blood" (viz. a fellow human) to be an enemy. It doesn't matter if this human happens to be a soldier in an army our country is fighting or simply a mean-spirited coworker. As soldiers in Christ's army (2 Tim 2:3–4), we are to remember that our warfare and our enemies are entirely different from the warfare and enemies of the world (2 Cor 10:3–5). The enemies we are called and empowered to wrestle against are spiritual forces of evil, and one of the primary ways we do this is by refusing to consider any human our

---

6. Until recently it was widely accepted that the pre-Constantinian church was pacifistic. For several defenses of this view, see Bainton, *Christian Attitudes toward War and Peace*, and Driver, *How Christians Made Peace with War*. This view has been questioned by Helgeland, Daly, and Burns in *Christians and the Military*, as well as Leithart in *Defending Constantine*, 255–78. I think it must be conceded that some earlier assessments of the early church's commitment to nonviolence were not sufficiently nuanced. Yet it remains true that the pre-Constantinian church was *for the most part* committed to unconditional nonviolence. For thoughtful assessments supporting this claim, see Swift, *Early Fathers on War and Military Service*; Hunter, "Decade of Research on Early Christians and Military Service"; Brock, *Varieties of Pacifism*, 5–8.

7. Whether Paul or a disciple of Paul's is the actual author of Ephesians is inconsequential to the point we are making. The same applies to subsequent references in this essay to disputed canonical works attributed to Paul.

enemy, choosing instead to love them, bless them, do good to them, pray for them, and if need be, die for them.[8]

If my assessment of the New Testament's teaching has been correct thus far, it means that American followers of Jesus are not allowed to regard enemies of America—such as Al Qaeda—as their "enemies." Nor are we permitted to ever participate in violence against them. To the contrary, we are called and empowered to love and bless them, even as they seek to harm us and/or others we care about. And this is precisely how we take our stand against the forces of evil that ultimately lie behind all the hatred and violence in the world.

## The Foolishness of This Teaching

I am aware that this teaching strikes many people as foolish, if not offensive. Indeed, it's been my experience that in America, where it has commonly been assumed that one of the church's primary jobs is to bless and pray for the military, there are few more effective ways to thin out a crowd—especially a conservative Christian crowd!—than to preach this message with conviction. Ironically, the apparent foolishness of this teaching provides further confirmation that it is, in fact, correct. If disciples love only those whom it makes sense to love, Jesus taught, there is nothing distinctly godly and rewarding about our love. When we go beyond, and even against, the conditional kind of love that people normally extend to others and instead choose to love and bless even our worst "enemies," we reflect God's indiscriminate love in a distinctive way and thus enjoy a unique reward (Matt 5:46; Luke 6:32–33).[9] The logic of this teaching renders illegitimate any commonsense conditioning of our commitment to love enemies and to practice nonviolence. To the contrary, we only uniquely reflect and benefit from God's love to the extent that our love is *not* conditioned by commonsense considerations.

8. On loving enemies as a form of spiritual warfare, see Boyd, "Kingdom as a Political-Spiritual Revolution"; Boyd, *Myth of a Christian Religion*.

9. We ought not think of the "reward" that Jesus and New Testament authors speak of along the lines of a trophy, but rather as a natural consequence of cultivating a certain kind of relationship with Christ and a certain kind of life. For an excellent study on the generally organic nature of punishment and reward in the New Testament, see Travis, *Christ and the Judgment of God*.

Our love, in other words, is *supposed to* look foolish, if not outright offensive.

This is precisely what we should expect if we believe that Jesus Christ is the perfect revelation of God's essence (Heb 1:3). Nothing could defy common sense and appear more foolish and offensive than the proclamation that the omnipotent God, out of love, became a human and died a God-forsaken death on a cross (1 Cor 1:18, 21–23)! Yet, if this is in fact what God is like, then it follows that we most profoundly reflect God's character when we also love in foolish and offensive ways. Moreover, this undoubtedly explains why Jesus made loving enemies and refraining from violence the precondition for being considered a child of God. "[L]ove your enemies and do good to them," Jesus said, and "[t]*hen* your reward will be great, and you will be children of the Most High, because he is kind to the ungrateful and wicked" (Luke 6:35, emphasis added; cf. Matt 5:44–45). It also explains why Jesus cited his disciples' nonviolence as the proof that his kingdom was "not of this world," as we noted above. When we imitate Jesus' foolish-looking love and nonviolence, we most unambiguously reflect the self-sacrificial character of God and manifest his uniquely beautiful kingdom. To the extent that we fail to reflect this, however, we look no different from the common sense–driven world.

## The Two Radically Distinct Kingdoms

Having established that disciples of Christ are to love and refrain from violence unconditionally, we now need to consider whether or not this commitment entails that we should encourage governments to uncon-ditionally "turn the other cheek" to their enemies. Is it appropriate, for example, for kingdom pacifists to protest America's involvement in any particular war by carrying signs or wearing shirts with slogans like, "Who Would Jesus Bomb?" or "Jesus said Love Your Enemies, not Kill Them!"? Though many pacifists will disagree with me, I will now argue that associating Jesus with war protests represents a potentially harmful confusion of categories. Embracing kingdom pacifism does not entail that one also embraces political pacifism.

In my opinion, Christians who believe that governments should embrace Jesus' teaching on nonviolence are giving insufficient weight to the all-important New Testament distinction between the *kingdom of God* and the *kingdom of the world*.[10] The first is comprised of people who have submitted to the reign of God, have been placed in Christ and filled with God's Spirit, and are thus in the process of being transformed into the likeness of Christ. The second is comprised of people who have not yet submitted to God's reign and who are thus yet living as though they were lords of their own lives.

In a wide variety of ways, this foundational distinction is reflected throughout the New Testament. One thinks, for example, of the distinction between those who are "in Christ" in contrast to those who are yet "in the world"; those who "walk in the Spirit" in contrast to those who yet "walk in the flesh"; those who are "being saved" in contrast to those who are still "perishing"; those who are "dead in sin" in contrast to those who have been "made alive by the Spirit"; and those who "walk in the light" in contrast to those who yet "dwell in darkness." While each of these contrasting concepts communicates a slightly different message, they each reflect a distinction that frames the entire New Testament. Though no human is ever in a position to judge another's standing with God, it's evident that, from the perspective of the New Testament, citizens of the kingdom of God enjoy a transforming relationship with God through Christ that is not available to people outside of Christ.

It is crucial that we keep the distinction between these two kingdoms in mind when interpreting the New Testament's imperatives. As Jacques Ellul has argued, we misunderstand the New Testament's imperatives if we interpret them as attempting to espouse a universal

---

10. In Luke 4:5–7 and Rev 11:15, the governments of the world are depicted as a single kingdom under the reign of Satan. Moreover, with Vernard Eller, Jacques Ellul, William Stringfellow, and others, I understand "Babylon" in Revelation (esp. ch. 13) to be symbolic not only of Rome but also of all the world's political power insofar as it manifests Satan's oppressive rule (which, for John, it *always* does, to some degree or other [Rev 14:18; 18:3, 23; 20:8]). It is for this reason that we can speak of the kingdom of the world in the singular. See Eller, *Most Revealing Book of the Bible*, 153–58; Ellul, *Anarchy*, 71–74; Ellul, *Violence*, 2; Stringfellow, *Ethic for Christians and Other Aliens in a Strange Land*, esp. 13–37.

ethics.[11] The fact of the matter is that neither Jesus nor the authors of the New Testament reflect the slightest interest in motivating people to behave ethically as an end in and of itself. What they are rather interested in is proclaiming, displaying, and advancing the reign of God. They are interested in motivating disciples to think and behave in a certain way not because they want people to be "good," but because they want them to cultivate lives that conform to, and thus proclaim and advance, the kingdom of God. The motivation they offer is not that the world would be a better place if everyone lived in the way they prescribe, but that only the way of living they prescribe conforms to the loving, self-sacrificial character of God revealed in Christ.

From this it should be clear that, far from providing behavioral instructions that were intended to be adhered to by people *in general*, the distinctive pacifistic instructions of Jesus and the New Testament authors are predicated on an understanding and experience of God and his reign that is *not* shared by all. While non-Christians obviously are capable of loving enemies and practicing nonviolence, the ability and motivation of followers of Jesus to act in this way, according to the New Testament, is inextricably bound to their faith in Christ, their transforming experience of the Spirit, and their call to bear witness to a distinctive kingdom that is "not from this world."

When we abstract the New Testament's prescribed *practice* of nonviolence from its *theological foundation*, what we have is something fundamentally different from the pacifism of the New Testament. Yes, we still have the injunction to love enemies and abstain from violence, but the motivation and meaning of this behavior is completely different. Hence, I argue, there is a world of difference between kingdom pacifism and political pacifism, and embracing the first does not entail that one embraces the second. In fact, without denying that it is always good when governments postpone resorting to violence, I will now contend that the New Testament in general argues *against* political pacifism.

11. See, e.g., *Ethics of Freedom; Subversion of Christianity; Anarchy and Christianity.*

## Human Governments, Sin, and the Devil

There are several closely related sets of considerations that strongly suggest that God doesn't expect governments to conform to the same standard of love and nonviolence he expects of disciples of Jesus. To begin, Paul repeatedly expressed the conviction that people are unable to consistently think and act in conformity to God's will unless they belong to Christ and are being transformed by the Holy Spirit (e.g., 1 Cor 12:3; Rom 8:5–16). Indeed, outside of Christ, Paul taught, we are all dead in sin (Eph 2:1, 5; Col 2:13). It's hardly surprising, therefore, that Paul displayed no interest whatsoever in influencing or judging the behavior of people outside the church (e.g., 1 Cor 5:12).[12]

Along similar lines, it's highly significant that neither Jesus nor any New Testament author reflected the slightest interest in the politics of their day. Outside of the simple instructions to pray for peace, to not stir up trouble, to respect and submit to authorities, and to pay our taxes, we're told absolutely nothing (Rom 13:1; 1 Thess 4:11–12; 1 Tim 2:1–2; Titus 3:1–2; 1 Pet 2:17). And even these activities are encouraged not on the grounds that we owe anything *to government* but on the grounds that our singular allegiance is *to God*.[13] This complete lack of political

---

12. There are several plausible ways of resolving the apparent tension between the affirmation that one cannot consistently and fully conform to Christ without the transforming power of the Holy Spirit, on the one hand, and the acknowledgement that non-Christians are capable of loving and responding nonviolently to their enemies. In my own view, this capacity bears witness to God's "prevenient grace," viz. the presence of the Spirit throughout the world working to draw *all* people into God's reign as much as possible, given the constraints of their situation (see, e.g., Acts 17:24–28). On prevenient grace, see Crofford, *Streams of Mercy*; Pinnock, *Flame of Love*, 185–214.

13. While Jesus' instruction to give to Caesar what bears his image (Matt 22:15–22) has been used by some to argue that Christians have an allegiance to "God and State," it arguably suggests the exact opposite: viz. God alone has authority over what bears his image, and we who bear his image him are to have him alone as our Lord. See Ellul, *Anarchy*, 59–61. On the biblical foundation for the anarchist conviction that those who are subject to God's reign are not subject to any earthly ruler, see Ellul, *Anarchy*, 45–85. For several broader assessments of the biblical basis and rationale for Christian anarchism, see Eller, *Christian Anarchy*; York, *Purple Crown*; Christoyannopoulos, *Christian Anarchism*, as well as the excellent little monograph by David Black, *Christian Archy*.

interest is all the more significant when we consider that the era in which Jesus ministered and in which the church was birthed was politically intense, especially for Palestinian Jews. A variety of conflicting perspectives on an assortment of political issues were hotly debated, and people continually tried to lure Jesus into these debates. Yet, displaying remarkable wisdom, Jesus uniformly transformed these kingdom-of-the-world questions into kingdom-of-God questions and turned them back on his audience (Matt 22:15–22; Luke 12:13–15).[14]

This lack of political interest reflects the truth that the kingdom that Jesus inaugurated is not merely an improved version—or even the *best* version—of the world's political systems. It is, rather, a kingdom that is "not from this world" (John 18:36). It reflects a completely different character and operates with a completely different set of presuppositions than all versions of the kingdom of the world.

For example, God's original plan was for humans to exercise loving dominion over animals and the earth, *not over each other* (Gen 1:26–28; cf. Matt 20:25–28). God alone was to be our king—a reality that is now being recaptured in the "one new humanity" being formed under Christ (Eph 2:14–16). Scripture suggests that we crave the security of human rulers only because we are fallen and rebelliously refuse to put all our trust in God. As Yahweh made clear to Samuel, the decision to embrace a human as king is a decision to reject God as king (1 Sam 8:7). While certain political regimes are obviously more humane and just than others, all are predicated on a rebellious mistrust of God. In diametric opposition to this, the kingdom that Jesus inaugurated is predicated on people's willingness to place their total trust in God and to swear their total allegiance to him (Matt 6:24). Indeed, it is only because God is our only master and lord and only because we place our total trust in him that we can deny our own self-preservationist instinct and "turn the other cheek" toward life-threatening enemies. Having already lost our life, we no longer feel the need to cling to it (Matt 10:39; 16:25).

Not only are the governments of the world predicated on human rebellion, however, they are in the New Testament uniformly depicted as under Satan's authority! When the devil tempted Jesus by offering

14. See Boyd, "Political-Spiritual Revolution," 29–32; Boyd, *Myth of a Christian Nation*, 57–64.

him all the power and authority of the governments of the world, Jesus didn't dispute the devil's claim to own all this and to be able to give it to whomever he wanted (Luke 4:5–7). Similarly, all the governments of the world are depicted in Revelation as belonging to the empire of the deceiver and the destroyer, a point that is strongly reinforced by passages that speak of Satan as the "ruler of the world," "the god of this age," and "the principal power of the air" who controls the "whole world."[15]

Given this intensely pessimistic view of government, it's hard to imagine Jesus, Paul, or any other leader in the early church hoping to persuade Caesar to lay down his sword and "turn the other cheek" in the face of threatening enemies. To the contrary, the New Testament assumes that unredeemed people naturally seek to acquire and exercise as much power over others as they can. Indeed, the only reason Jesus bothered to draw attention to the way pagans "lord over one another" was to make the point that his disciples are to do *the opposite* (Matt 20:25–28; cf. Matt 18:4; 19:30; 20:16; 23:11; Phil 2:3–5). While all forms of government exercise power *over* their subjects, citizens of the kingdom of God are to exercise power *under* others. That is, we are to influence others— including our enemies—by loving and sacrificially serving them.[16] The New Testament's insistence on loving enemies and "turning the other cheek" is inseparable from this more general call and empowerment to manifest a radically unique kingdom that is "not of this world."

## God's Use of Sword-Wielding Governments

The intrinsically violent nature of human governments is strongly captured by Paul in Romans 13. Now, at first glance, it might appear that this passage contradicts those passages that depict earthly government as rooted in rebellion and as ruled by Satan, for in this chapter Paul en-

15. John 12:32; 14:31; 16:11; 2 Cor 4:4; Eph 2:2; 1 John 5:19; Rev 11:15; 13; 14:18; 18:3, 23; 20:8. On the remarkable authority ascribed to Satan over government and nature in the New Testament, see Boyd, *God at War*.

16. Hence, as is suggested by passages such as Rom 12:19–21 and 1 Pet 3:14–16, our refusal to return evil for evil is meant both for our benefit and for the benefit our "enemy." By refusing to use force, we keep ourselves from being defined by an aggressor's hatred and violence, and we open up the possibility that they will become convicted of their evil and turn from it.

courages disciples to submit to "governing authorities" on the grounds that they have all been "established" by God to uphold the good and punish wrongdoers with the power of the sword (13:2–4). We need not imagine a contradiction, however, for the term that is translated "established" (*tassō*) doesn't imply that God *exhaustively controls* and/or *approves* of the governments he uses (as though God controlled and approved of rulers like Hitler, Mussolini, and Stalin!). The term rather has the connotation of putting something in its proper place, the way a librarian files books.[17] Hence, Paul is simply affirming that God makes the best use possible of governments *as he finds them.* Since these governments rely on the power of the sword, God steers their sword-wielding activity to justly punish wrongdoers.

We see Paul's teaching on God's use of governments illustrated throughout the Old Testament. As a means of punishing Israel, for example, Yahweh sometimes withdrew his protection and allowed nations like Assyria, Babylon, and Persia to serve as his "rod" as they carried out their violent intentions against his people. Yet, though he used these nations for his sovereign purposes, it is clear that Yahweh didn't *make* these nations violent or *force* them to come against Israel against their will. Indeed, once he was through making use of their violence, God sometimes turned around and punished these nations for being the kind of nation he could use in this fashion and/or for being even more violent than he expected (e.g., Isa 10:6–19; Zech 1:15; cf. Jer 12:14; 55:55–56).[18] In this light it's evident that the sheer fact that God makes just use of sword-wielding governments does not imply that he approves of them in the sense that their willingness to engage in violence conforms to his ideal will. For the same reason, it is clear that there is no contradiction between affirming that God uses the world's governments as he finds them and as he sees fit, on the one hand, while acknowledging that these

17. This analogy is from Yoder, *Politics of Jesus*, 203. For a survey of other Anabaptist/anarchist responses to Romans 13, see Christoyannopoulos, *Christian Anarchism*, 181–214.

18. On several occasions Terrence Fretheim has drawn insightful conclusions from this fact. See "'I Was Only a Little Angry,'" "God and Violence in the Old Testament," and most recently, *Creation Untamed*, 56–57, 110–12.

governments are ruled by Satan (and, beneath him, by earthly rulers), on the other.

What is most significant about Romans 13 for our present purposes, however, is that in the course of affirming that God uses governments Paul *assumes* that these governments will continue to wield the sword. This is precisely why God uses them as "agents of wrath" against wrongdoers (Rom 13:4). Were these governments capable of "turning the other cheek," they could hardly be used for this purpose. Then again, given the fallen condition of the world, it's hard to imagine how any government could remain in power for any length of time were it inclined to "turn the other cheek."[19]

Some non-pacifists attempt to turn this argument around by contending that, since God is willing to make use of sword-wielding governments to preserve law and order, Christians are free, if not in some cases obligated, to participate in their governments' sword-wielding activity.[20] Among other challenges, this interpretation is contradicted by the passage itself once we read it in context. It's important to notice that Romans 13 continues a train of thought that Paul began in Romans 12.[21] Reflecting the same view as Jesus, here Paul instructs disciples to (among other things) "bless those who persecute you"(v. 14); to "not repay anyone evil for evil" (v. 17); and especially to "never avenge yourselves, but leave room for the wrath of God; for it is written, 'Vengeance [*ekdikēsis*] is mine, I will repay, says the Lord'" (v. 19). Leaving vengeance to God, we are to feed our enemies when they are hungry and give them water when they are thirsty (v. 20). Instead of being "overcome by evil," Paul concludes, we are to "overcome evil with good" (v. 21).

Immediately following this, we find Paul instructing disciples to submit to government on the grounds that government is God's instrument of vengeance (*ekdikos*) (13:1–4). This is the very same vengeance that Paul just forbade disciples to exercise and to instead leave to God (12:19). The clear implication is that, far from permitting (let alone

19. That the establishment and maintenance of nations and governments is inherently violent is a frequent theme in Ellul's work; see esp. his *Violence* and *Political Illusion*.

20. See, e.g., Colson, *God and Government*, esp. chs. 7 and 20.

21. See Yoder, *Politics of Jesus*, 197–200.

encouraging!) disciples to participate in government's sword-wielding activity, Paul is here *contrasting* government's sword-wielding activity as an agent of God's vengeance with the distinctive calling of disciples to be agents of mercy. *Of course* governments will use the sword, Paul is saying, and we can rest assured that God is continually at work to bring about as much justice by means of this violence as possible. But this is not an activity that we who follow Jesus should ever engage in. Our distinctive call and empowerment is to do what no government could ever be expected to do: namely, imitate Jesus by loving and blessing our enemies.

For all these reasons I am persuaded that embracing the enemy-loving nonviolence of Jesus does not commit one to the conviction that governments should unilaterally and unconditionally turn the other cheek. Kingdom pacifism, in other words, does not entail political pacifism. For all we know, there are wrongdoers whom God is seeking to punish through a government's willingness to use violence. Yet, like the Levite priests of the Old Testament, we who are God's royal priesthood within the new covenant are not permitted to participate in this violent activity (1 Pet 2:9; Rev 1:6; cf. Num 1:45–53). We are rather empowered to be ambassadors of a kingdom that is not of this world. And, as Jesus made clear, our refusal to fight is one of the surest proofs of this fact (John 18:36).

## The Nonviolent Christian in a Violent State

I will conclude by briefly addressing two objections to the view I've advocated in this essay. First, going back to Celsus in the second century, some have argued that it's hypocritical for Christians to benefit from state-sponsored violence when we ourselves are unwilling to participate in it.[22] In response, I admit that it would be hypocritical if pacifist Christians *encouraged* others to be willing to kill for their country. But there is nothing hypocritical about a follower of Jesus (or anybody else) confessing that their faith forbids them to engage in violence while perhaps benefiting from the fact that the faith of others does not. This lack of duplicity is particularly evident in those cases where Christian paci-

22. For Origen's response to this charge, see *Against Celsus*, VIII, 73.

fists openly encourage all individuals—including soldiers—to adopt their faith and therefore their unconditional stance against violence.[23]

Not only this, but as Origen pointed out to Celsus, while pacifistic followers of Jesus are unable to help provide security for their country by participating in violence, we contribute (or at least *should* contribute) to the security and over all well-being of our country in a multitude of other ways. For example, we make distinct contributions by praying for our leaders and by praying for and striving for peace. So, too, our willingness to sacrificially serve people in need also provides a distinctive contribution to our nation's well-being.[24] As Origen argued, there is no reason that our unwillingness to participate in one particularly visible way of contributing to our country should delegitimize all the other ways in which we willingly contribute.

A second possible objection to the view I've defended in this essay is based on the fact that Jesus calls us not only to be nonviolent, but also to be "peacemakers" (Matt 5:9; cf. 1 Pet 3:11). How can we be peacemakers in international conflicts or in regional conflicts around the globe, some may wonder, if we aren't trying to influence governments to assume a policy of nonviolence? Three things may be said in response.

First, as has already been suggested, one distinctive way followers of Jesus can and should work as peacemakers is through prayer. As Walter Wink has noted, prayer confronts the principalities and powers that fuel hostility and should thus be considered a form of "social

23. Kemp ("Personal Pacifism," 26–27) imagines a "nearly inconsistent triad" in Origen's belief that (*a*) everyone should become Christian; (*b*) no Christian should participate in violence; (*c*) non-Christians are morally justified in participating in violence to defend their community. The apparent tension disappears, however, once one realizes Christian pacifism isn't rooted in, or motivated by, ethics.

24. When almost everyone else (including doctors) would flee regions when plagues broke out in the ancient world, Christians were known for their willingness to remain behind to care for the sick, often sacrificing their own lives in the process. According to Rodney Stark, this consistent demonstration of love for strangers was one of the reasons the early church grew at such a phenomenal pace, despite frequent persecutions; see *Rise of Christianity*, esp. chs. 4 and 5. On the multitude of ways the church can and should contribute to the common good (without thereby losing her distinctive calling and identity), see Hauerwas' response to the charge of being "sectarian" in Hauerwas, "Why the 'Sectarian Temptation' Is a Misrepresentation: A Response to James Gustafson," in *Hauerwas Reader*, 90–110.

action."[25] Second, even aside from prayer, followers of Jesus don't need to go through governmental structures to become peacemakers in a particular regional conflict. Though it is frequently risky, if a believer is called to be a peacemaker in the midst of a particular regional conflict, they can simply join others with a similar calling, travel to the region, and "get in the way" of violence.[26]

Finally, to acknowledge that governments are not called to "turn the other cheek" is not to say that we shouldn't try to influence them to explore all possible peaceful solutions before resorting to violence. Of course we should. Yet, we must always bear in mind that the motivation of a follower of Jesus for embracing nonviolence is altogether different from the motivation a government might have for doing so. Without denying that governments can be motivated by humanitarian concerns, all governments ultimately act out of the self-interest of those in power and (hopefully) of the citizens they govern. Hence, if one hopes to persuade any particular government to forgo violence in any particular conflict, he or she must demonstrate to those in power that finding a peaceful solution is in their own political and national self-interest.[27]

Now, when it comes to forging these kinds of self-interested, utilitarian arguments, there is no reason to think that pacifist Christians would have any advantage over just war Christians, or even that Christians in general would have any advantage over non-Christians. In fact, as we noted earlier, there is no biblical or logical reason that anyone, pacifist or otherwise, should assume at the start that it *is* always in a government's self-interest to keep exploring peaceful options. The argument for refraining from violence must be made on a case-by-case basis. Even when a strong utilitarian argument for peace can be made, however, it's vital that Christian pacifists understand that this motivation for nonviolence is not only *different from* the kingdom's motivation

25. Wink, *Engaging the Powers*, 317.

26. The motto to "get in the way" of violence is from Christian Peacemaking Teams (www.cpt.org), one of a number of organizations that train and support people in this often dangerous peacemaking activity. Two other such organizations are *Witness for Peace* (www.witnessforpeace.org) and *Peace Brigades* (www.peacebrigades.org).

27. For several examples, see Ackerman and DuVall, *A Force More Powerful*; Lakey, "Nonviolent Action as the Sword that Heals"; Lakey, *Powerful Peacemaking*; Zunes et al., eds., *Nonviolent Social Movements*; Wink, *Engaging the Powers*.

for nonviolence; it is actually *antithetical* to it. For we who follow Jesus are empowered not only to turn the other cheek but also to genuinely love our enemies, precisely because we daily *crucify* our own self-interest. And we embrace this way of life not because it has been proven to work, but because this alone reflects the character of God and bears witness to his reign.[28]

For all these reasons I argue that kingdom pacifism does not entail political pacifism. Acknowledging this distinction allows us to overcome the objection that kingdom pacifism entails a dangerously naive political position, which in turn will help some take more seriously the New Testament's teaching that *disciples of Jesus* are called to unconditionally love all enemies and refrain from all violence.

28. See Hauerwas and Willimon, *Resident Aliens*, 85–86.

# 8

## What about War and Violence in the Old Testament?

Ingrid E. Lilly

ONE OF THE MOST frequent critiques of the Old Testament is that its angry God sanctions and even instigates religious warfare. In the next breath, the critic often points to the Crusades as a concrete example of how Christians acted on this biblical sanctioning. Indeed, in the following excerpts of a Crusade speech, we see countless allusions to Old Testament ideas:

> [we will fight] a race from the kingdom of the Persians, an accursed race . . . They destroy the altars, after having defiled them with their uncleanness . . . and the holy places which are now treated with ignominy and irreverently polluted with the filth of the unclean . . . [Crusaders,] wrest that land from the wicked race, and subject it to yourselves. That land which, as the Scripture says, 'floweth with milk and honey' was given by God into the power of the children of Israel. Jerusalem is the center of the earth . . . [l]et this one cry be raised by all the soldiers of God: 'It

is the will of God! It is the will of God!' [*Deus vult! Deus vult!*][1]

The quoted rhetoric sounds just like that of Deuteronomy, Joshua, or Ezekiel, except that it is from a speech of Pope Urban II to support the Christian invasion of Jerusalem in the late eleventh century CE.[2] It should be pointed out that the biblical allusions are taken out of context and thus often mean something totally different from their use in the Bible. Nevertheless, scriptural ideas and themes were woven into a powerful and compelling argument for religious warfare. In other words, the critics are right: the Old Testament does contain material that sanctions and can instigate religious warfare.

It is tempting to ignore the violent material in the Old Testament and focus instead on the visions for peace that also populate its pages. Surely, we can point to the small child who tends to the dangerous lion in Isaiah 11, or the ideal of ecological harmony in Genesis 2, or the creation of a new heart in Ezekiel 36. Such passages evoke humanity's highest aspirations for peace and justice. Indeed, these are the passages that largely populate the Revised Common Lectionary, used by Catholic and mainline Protestant denominations as a guide for worship readings.[3] Hence, in an important sense, many churches do tacitly ignore the violence in the Old Testament.

Nevertheless, most Christians come up against the problem of violence in the Old Testament at some point in their lives. And, unfortunately, easy answers are not ready at hand. In what follows, I will present one way to read and understand biblical violence that also affirms a deep and important pacifist stance towards the world. Thus, I will challenge the way the Crusaders and other Christians have used the

1. Urban II's speech at Clermont in 1095, according to the version of Robert the Monk, found in Robinson, ed., *Readings in European History,* 1:312–16.

2. The allusions to Old Testament passages include, but are not limited to: Jerusalem as the center of the earth (Ezek 5:5), the land promised uniquely to Israel (Gen 12:1–7; Deut 1:21), a negative view of ethnic others (Neh 13:2; Ezek 44:6–9), enemies who destroy the altar (Psalm 74), treatment of unclean people who defile altars (Num 19:20), and fighting inhabitants for the promised land (Joshua).

3. The same is true of Jewish *haftorah* readings, which include sections of Joshua, but none from the "conquest" passages.

Bible to justify militancy and violent actions. This essay is an invitation to read the Bible with maturity, wisdom, and a moral commitment to growing in Christian faith. Because the Old Testament contains a vast amount of material, we will focus our discussion on warfare. A discussion of military conflict and warfare in ancient Israel and its texts will serve as a necessary point of departure.

## Warfare in Ancient Israel

The Old Testament is not a peaceful text. Perhaps more importantly, ancient Israel did not enjoy peaceful times. Israel engaged in warfare and theologized about that warfare. Israel suffered from warfare and theologized about that suffering. Israel grew up and developed as a culture and nation in the context of empires whose strategies for domination certainly included warfare. Hence, the Old Testament literature engages the full spectrum of attitudes and experiences related to war.

At every stage, Israelites engaged in war. In fact, the first reference to "Israel" in the archeological record actually reports an Egyptian military campaign in which "Israel is laid waste and his seed is no more."[4] While the claim on the part of the Egyptian stele is characteristically exaggerated, it shows that the annihilation of peoples, the destruction of even their "seed," was a mark of national success in the ancient world. Hence, it is important to remember that war and bragging about victory was a very common mode of arbitration and domination in the ancient Near East. The larger Near Eastern kingdoms erected countless stellae to brag about their military victories and orchestrated frequent public processions to proclaim their military dominance over smaller neighboring peoples.[5] In this sense, Israel was most often the vulnerable party, enduring threat of invasion, forced migration, and/or enslavement.

The earliest Israelite society was tribal in nature. From the book of Judges, we learn that tribes would unite in mutual interest to fight over highly contested land.[6] Such tribal military coalitions continued

4. Merneptah stele, 1209 BCE.

5. For more, see Holloway, *Aššur is King! Aššur is King!*.

6. Even the story in Genesis 14 of Abram's involvement in a legendary local war points to tribal coalitions.

through the rise of the Israelite kingdom. For example, Saul is depicted as a great unifier of vulnerable tribes against the Philistines, by far the largest local power of his day. Saul sent out a call to each clan/tribe interested in land protection, and his charismatic leadership earned him the trust of the people as their first king.

Arguably, the state of Israel emerged because of unity achieved through warfare. According to the narratives in 1 and 2 Samuel, David was able to unify the tribes of Israel in large part because of his military successes: "Saul has slayed his thousands, David his ten thousands" (1 Sam 18:7). Then, Solomon is credited with creating a standing national army to avoid the fits and starts of tribal politics. Once Israel instituted the monarchy, military activity continued apace, with frequent land contests to the north and east of Israel. State oppression led to the division of Israel into two kingdoms. Finally, the two kingdoms of Israel and Judah participated in revolts, resistance, and treaty-making with the larger international powers of the day. Both kingdoms ultimately fell—the North to the Assyrians, and the South to the Babylonians—as a result of political resistance and military revolt. In all of these military events, Israelites were both aggressors and victims of war.

A large portion of the books of the Old Testament can be connected to this history of warfare. For example, the book of Lamentations contains poetry written in response to the Babylonian military invasion and destruction of Jerusalem. Nahum celebrates the destruction of Assyria's capital, Nineveh. Genesis 14 tells of Abraham's military activity and command over 318 men trained for war. The book of Ruth relates the exceptional story of a "good" Moabite, one from a kingdom that otherwise appears in ethnic and military conflict with Israel at various points. Jeremiah was imprisoned for high treason as a political dissident for his preaching on the Babylonian invasion of Jerusalem. The book of Exodus is about a divine war with Egypt and life for Hebrew slaves as refugees. Judges repeatedly describes how God raised up military heroes to fight on behalf of the Israelite tribes. Deuteronomy includes instruction on how to engage in warfare. Isaiah was involved in the royal decisions about military activity. This list could go on. Perhaps most importantly, the Hebrew writers were rarely free from the threat of invasion or occupation by the large empires of the day. Indeed, Israel's literature and theologies were forged in the crucible of international politics and threats of war.

The prophetic books contain some of the most scrupulous commentary on this history of warfare. Israel's prophets paid close attention to international politics. While their rhetoric was frequently abrasive and vitriolic, many of the prophets articulated something akin to pacifist positions to the rulers of their day. For example, Isaiah counseled both Ahaz and Hezekiah to avoid international military engagement, insisting that trusting the Lord was the only real source of strength. Similarly, Jeremiah condemned contemporary efforts to revolt against the Babylonians. Jeremiah believed the city's only future lay in peaceful submission, although he understood that this would not ultimately be Jerusalem's fate.[7]

## Joshua's Conquest: Theological Genocide

By far, the most theologically troubling case of Israelite warfare is the literary description of the wars of Joshua. The book purports to relate the military events of Israel's origins in the promised land. The character of Joshua, Israel's military commander, orchestrates battle after battle to conquer the land of Canaan for Israelite seizure. This conquest narrative includes such elements as divine sanction (e.g., Josh 10:8; 11:6), divine participation in war (e.g., ch. 10), and the consecration of human warriors to Yahweh's service. Further, Joshua's military strategies included adherence to the Israelite concept of *herem*, or total ban (cf. Deut 7:16–26). By this principle, a victorious Israel destroyed everything that breathes, a perfect genocide of Canaanite peoples (cf. Joshua 10–11, especially).

Many people use the term *holy war* to refer to the conquest described in Joshua. Holy war presupposes that war itself is sacred and that the pursuit of war is a divine calling of worship or mission. Scholarship suggests that this sacred, cultic understanding of war only emerged as a later theological reflection on war or even simply as a liter-

---

7. Indeed, Jeremiah repeatedly told Zedekiah, the last Davidic king in Jerusalem, that the city would be destroyed by God if the king incited revolt (cf. Jeremiah 27).

ary construct.[8] Indeed, the conquest narrative in the book of Joshua is a carefully shaped work of literature.[9] This fact is all the more evident after years of historical and archeological work that call its historical accuracy into question.[10] So it seems that the dominant form of warfare in ancient Israel did not follow the holy war schema. Indeed, Israel likely did not practice holy war on the scale that the book of Joshua suggests. Nevertheless, the rhetoric of holy war in the book of Joshua is still troubling and will be discussed further below.

Instead of using the term holy war, many have come to call Israel's dominant attitude towards war a "Yahweh war," which involved a particular notion of Yahweh's power.[11] Yahweh's power in warfare seems to have been conceived in at least three ways. First, it is clear that oracular assurance was sought before battle, yielding statements such as, "I will deliver you, and give the Midianites into your hand" (Judg 7:7). Second, Israelites experienced power during battle that they ascribed to divine assistance. So for example, in Judges 7, Gideon attacks the enemy with a deliberately small number of Israelite soldiers, hence revealing the Lord's power in victory.[12] Third, Israelites praised God after war.

8. Gerhard von Rad presented a robust description of what he called "holy war" in the Old Testament in *Holy War in Ancient Israel*. Subsequent studies challenged von Rad's ideal type and refined the religious dimensions of warfare in ancient Israel. See Smend, *Yahweh War and Tribal Confederation*; de Vaux, *Ancient Israel*, esp. 262; and Norman K. Gottwald, "Holy War," in Crim, ed., *Interpreter's Dictionary of the Bible, Supplementary Volume*, 942–44.

9. For an example of such an argument, see Rowlett, *Joshua and the Rhetoric of Violence*.

10. Of the numerous excavated cities that were destroyed according to Joshua's account, few were even walled cities, and only two show evidence of destruction. Moreover, around the time that Joshua's wars would have occurred, the two cities that feature most prominently in Joshua's account, Jericho and Ai, had laid in waste for over three hundred and twelve hundred years, respectively. For a good discussion of the archeological evidence, see ch. 3 in Finkelstein and Silberman, *Bible Unearthed*, 73–83, and especially their bibliography about the conquest on pages 360–62.

11. In Num 21:14, we hear of an otherwise unknown ancient work called the "Book of the Wars of Yahweh."

12. By modern standards, the power of their military strategy would be credited for the victory. Every soldier in Gideon's small company, under cover of night, encircled the enemy camp, blew trumpets, held torches, and made a clamor that frightened the encamped enemy into confusion and retreat.

They sang victory songs after trouncing enemies and praised their deity for his power. For example, Exod 15:21, Miriam's song, celebrates the abrupt end of Egyptian pursuit by ascribing it to Yahweh's power over the sea. In each of these features, the Israelites turned to Yahweh for his power to protect, vindicate, or release them from military conflict. This is still a militant Yahwism, but it does not go so far as to sanction militant human agents for a divine murderous purpose. Regardless of how humans act, battles are won and lost according to Yahweh's power.

## The Violent God: Yahweh Wars

The distinction between holy war and Yahweh war is the type of distinction that grounds one pacifist's attempt to make sense of warfare in the Bible. In his book *Yahweh Is a Warrior: The Theology of Warfare in Ancient Israel*, Millard C. Lind argues that the Old Testament does not advocate for human agency in warfare. The implication of the Yahweh war is that Yahweh's power is the only real human defense. Humans should therefore not seek out or even engage in military activity.[13] Lind's proposal successfully identifies a dominant strand of theology in the Old Testament that teaches trust in the power of Yahweh. For many pacifists, this theological conclusion is sufficient.

However, one major issue persists even after Lind's thoughtful case for pacifism: Yahweh is characterized as a god of war. In the case of Joshua's conquest, Yahweh is credited with annihilating whole people groups. Further, the literary perspective offered in Joshua's account comes very close to describing the conquest as a divinely ordained mission. This portrait of God has troubled Christians throughout the centuries. Famously, the second-century theologian Marcion of Sinope rejected the Old Testament and its God. Marcion believed that Yahweh was a lesser deity who was responsible for creating evil. Consequently, he believed that the deity of the New Testament was the only true god. Even though Marcionism was rejected by the early church, modern readers often adopt similar critiques of the Old Testament, *de facto*.

To understand the violent characterizations of Yahweh, we turn to the rich cultural background of Yahweh. Some of the oldest litera-

13. Lind, *Yahweh Is a Warrior*.

ture in the Old Testament is poetry that characterizes God as a divine warrior.[14] For example, in Deuteronomy 33, Yahweh is depicted as marching from his mountain abode flanked by his holy military entourage. Yahweh shares many characteristics with ancient Near Eastern/ Canaanite deities. In fact, Psalm 29 praises Yahweh in terms so reminiscent of Canaanite hymns to Baal that most agree that the psalm was appropriated for Yahwistic worship from Canaanite sources.[15] The images portray Yahweh as a force of nature, stripping trees and shattering forests with fire. Elsewhere, Yahweh's violent power presents as hail, fire, thunder, rain, and earthquakes.

Viewing Yahweh in his ancient Canaanite context does not erase his violent attributes. However, it serves as a reminder that conceptions of God cannot be divorced from the cultures that produced them. Modern interpreters largely subscribe to scientific understandings of weather and no longer attribute changes in environment to the supernatural. Similarly, Christian thought abandoned the anthropomorphic idea of God marching from a mountain, for instance. The characterization of Yahweh as a divine warrior is subject to similar shifts in how we conceptualize the divine. These same shifts go for war as well. Where the Israelites would attribute their victory to Yahweh's power, today we would hail our military strategies.[16]

It is also important to remember that many of Yahweh's benevolent characteristics respond to human conditions of vulnerability to warfare and violence. Hence we find the images of God as a Protector, a Deliverer, or a Shepherd.[17] These aspects of God's character are operative, for example, in the story of the exodus. This national Israelite story of origins portrayed a liberating God concerned for the oppression and

14. Cross, *Canaanite Myth and Hebrew Epic*; Miller, *Divine Warrior in Early Israel*.

15. See summary discussion of the evidence and scholarly positions in Day, *Yahweh and the Gods and Goddesses of Canaan*, 95–98.

16. The story of Gideon in Judges 7, mentioned above, is clearly a victory of Israel's strategy. See note 12.

17. Thomas Römer proposes a view of Yahweh along similar lines. He sees God as mixture of wrath and mercy in reaction to different experiences. He tries to emphasize the way in which the Bible presents oppositions in God's character in order to refute the violent depiction of God. See Römer, *Dieu obscur*. See also Murphy and Hampton, *Forgiveness and Mercy*.

mistreatment of the Hebrew slaves.[18] Yahweh goes to war with the power of the Egyptian state. Hence, the exodus story, along with the Joshua conquest narrative, can be seen as subversive political texts, constructing Yahweh as more powerful than the greatest empires and cultures of the ancient world. In these respects, both books ask readers to eradicate their enslavements to political or cultural powers by turning to an even greater supernatural power.[19] Israel developed rich theological traditions because of her engagement with the issues raised by human warfare. In this sense, warfare prompted Israel to see God's capacity to defend and protect, to reverse oppression, to empower refugees, and to free humans from their bondage to the powers of the world. These are extremely important aspects of God's relationship to humanity.

Despite the very positive conclusions one can draw from the warfare of Yahweh, we cannot leave the problem of Yahweh as a god of war. The Joshua conquest still describes the slaughter of innocent Canaanites with divine power and sanction. And Israel's Yahweh wars still model the celebration of enemy destruction. It is possible to view God's militancy as directed towards spiritual battles or political causes. I am sympathetic with this interpretive decision. However, Joshua's slaughter of innocent Canaanites, even if only a literary fiction, stains that attempt at pacifism for me. While we have made some headway, it remains difficult to square an ethic of peace with the military institutions and violent the-

18. The exodus story is another very complex composition filled with provocations, powers, and problems with respect to warfare. For an example of these difficulties, see Robert Allen Warrior, "Canaanites, Cowboys, and Indians," in Jobling and Pippin et al., eds., *The Postmodern Bible Reader*, 188–94.

19. In the case of Joshua's conquest, we should view the text as a narrative of Israelite identity. Many scholars have pointed out that the text was likely crafted by a fairly weak and unstable Israelite state using the rhetorical strategies for intimidation and control used by the dominant militaristic Assyrian empire. These strategies for generating national pride were aimed at wresting people from affiliation with the broader Canaanite culture. In this sense, Joshua is politically subversive towards Assyrian imperial power and the normative culture of Canaan. Lori L. Rowlett is a nice example of a scholar who argues along these lines. She states that "those who produced the text used the rhetoric of warfare and nationalism as an encouragement and a threat, aimed at their own population, to submit voluntarily to the central authority of a government struggling to organize itself and create its own ideological framework of inclusion." Rowlett, *Joshua and the Rhetoric of Violence*.

ologies of ancient Israel. Theological genocide, even in concept, remains abhorrent. We are still wrestling with the case for pacifism in light of Old Testament material.

## War and Peace: The Bible's Polyphonic Theologies

The beginning of my own personal solution to this problem involves my impression and position on how to read the Bible. This impression is formed after having contemplated the types of contradictions that we just saw in God's character above. Indeed, the Old Testament literature is highly diverse. It does not present one pristine and systematic theology. On the contrary, the variety of literature produces something of a polyphony of theologies. This should be expected. The number of authors in the Old Testament suggests that it is a community document, almost like a Wikipedia article. Biblical stories had to be collected, compiled, and shaped into the forms we know today. Further, the large expanse of time over which the literature was produced captures many different instances in Israel's religious traditions. This means that the Old Testament is theology on the move, in creation, in process. Such development and dialogue is often called the traditioning process. As a consequence of the traditioning process, the Old Testament preserves a range of ideas that can even at times be contradictory.

I'd like to show what I mean by contradictions. One of the best examples comes in comparing the account of David's census in 2 Samuel and 1 Chronicles. In 2 Sam 24:1, the text states that in his anger, the Lord incited David to conduct the census. By contrast, 1 Chron 21:1 credits Satan for David's inspiration. Obviously, these are two very different theological interpretations of the same plot. We can chalk that up to different authors or different time periods with different vantage points on David's career. But the fact remains, the Old Testament preserves a polyphony of theologies that can directly contradict one another.

A similar polyphony emerges when comparing two passages about the same war. In Num 21:21–26, Israel is attacked by the Amorites. The text provides a straightforward account of Israel's victory and subsequent occupation of new territory. By contrast, the same battle is recounted in Deut 2:26–37, but with numerous references to Yahweh's guiding role and other religious practices. In fact, Deuteronomy's version includes original material of a grossly more violent nature: Israel destroyed every man, woman, and child, leaving no survivors. These two accounts of the same battle demonstrate that Israelite literature about war was not univocal. In fact, Joshua's conquest narrative is not Israel's only account of its origins in the promised land. A different presentation of events occurs in Judges 1–2. The text describes how Israelite tribes settled *alongside* Canaanites, explicitly stating that the original inhabitants were *not* driven out of the land. The Judges text is summoned for what scholars call the "Peaceful Infiltration" model of Israelite origins. This model is largely preferred over Joshua's conquest model, in terms of historical probability. Further, some note the theological polyphony created by the two accounts. For example, Moshe Weinfeld suggests that the Judges version was a later interpretation, written as a corrective to the Joshua story.[20] In this way of thinking, one can appeal to inner-biblical dialogue and interpretation to mitigate or even refute the dominance of Joshua's theology.

So the Bible does not present a univocal position about warfare. One final example perhaps best underscores this point. The prophets Isaiah and Micah preached to Israel's soldiers to abandon warfare and become farmers. In presenting this powerful pacifist vision for Israel, each echoes the other:

> they shall beat their swords into plowshares, and their spears into pruning hooks; nation shall not lift up sword against nation, neither shall they learn war any more (Isa 2:4; Mic 4:3).

While these two prophets envision a radical transformation of soldiers into pastoralists for an existence free of war, the prophet Joel screams in the opposite direction:

> Beat your plowshares into swords, and your pruning hooks into spears; let the weakling say, "I am a warrior." (3:10)

20. He calls it the first midrash on the Joshua narrative. Weinfeld, *Promise of the Land*, 121–55. For a similar conclusion about the editorial layers within the book of Joshua that exhibit uneasiness with Israel's traditions of warfare, see Stone, "Ethical and Apologetic Tendencies in the Redaction of the Book of Joshua."

Joel's battle cry to weakened farmers emboldens them for war; quite the opposite intention of Micah and Isaiah's use of the same image.

## Reading the Old Testament for Moral Formation

Pointing out that the Old Testament preserves a polyphony of ideas about war does not erase the violence in books like Joshua. However, it does affirm that questions about tradition were built into the text itself. Israelites told their stories orally, and, with a long editorial process, many voices weighed in on Israel's religious traditions. Many of these voices are antithetical to the theology of the book of Joshua. For example, Isaiah and Micah's call to lay down weapons flies in the face of Joshua's triumphant militancy.

Through the polyphony in the Old Testament, we read into a conversation that models a critique of Joshua's theology. Through such a critical reading, Joshua stands as an example of how humans can erect divine sanction for national interests. Indeed, the book portrays a nation and its claim to a contested land. To watch the book of Joshua march through that land, with the cold slaughter of Canaanites, we see how religion can dull our most vital moral desires. Slaying the Canaanites is no triumph of religion, but an example of religion's darkest capacities for evil.[21] I am personally moved to repentance for the religious heritage in the biblical text. Further, I am moved to rebuke the ongoing use of religion to justify aggression, violence, injustice, and war; as one reads in Proverbs, "the one who rebukes boldly makes peace" (10:10).

To read the Old Testament is to engage human society in all of its aspects. In this engagement, we are morally sharpened by what Gerd Lüdemann calls the "unholy in Scripture," or what Phyllis Trible identifies as "texts of terror."[22] If we were to ignore the difficulty of Old Testament texts, we would lose the opportunity to confront some of the

21. Israel's prophets frequently excoriated the people for the wrong use of religion. Whether preaching against false prophets, or renouncing Israelite religion, these authors remind us that religion is sometimes not what God desires. For example, Amos spoke on behalf of God in no uncertain terms: "I hate, I reject your festivals; I reject your religious assemblies" (Amos 5:21).

22. Lüdemann, *Unholy in Holy Scripture*; Trible, *Texts of Terror*.

most powerful forces that affect human life and religious piety. To read the difficulties produces moral reflection and the vitality of theological inquiry. Following the threads of violence in the Bible awakens the dullness of religious complicity. To morally confront Joshua is to seize the opportunity to dismantle the assertion of human power with divine backing in reckless and hapless blood feuds.

Warfare, as we know from the Old Testament, is nothing new. Look around at today's world and see revolt, imperial invasion, forced exiles, state oppression, mass graves, and farmers taking up swords. Sadly, the role of religion in modern warfare and violence still holds sway. The Old Testament is as relevant as ever. And the need for insightful and reflective moral agents is a perennial calling. Hence, reading all of the Bible, including the most difficult parts, gives me hope that Christians can develop mature reading strategies and deeper moral capacities for confronting a text and, indeed, a world of warfare.

## A Moral Compass for Christians

The preceding discussion demonstrated the polyphony of Old Testament theologies and the way in which they open up a critical discussion of a text like Joshua. The difficult texts about war and violence are not erased from the sacred canon of the Old Testament. Hence, I suggested that their value lies in the moral formation they offer through reflection and discernment. They help us understand and confront a world in which violence does frequently dominate human relations. We can see more clearly for having delved into the issues more deeply.

One question is likely to linger: given the polyphony of the Old Testament text, why become a pacifist? Why read against the Joshua narrative? Why be morally formed by Micah and Isaiah's eradication of swords, and not Joel's war cry?

One might start with the larger themes of the Old Testament itself. First, the Torah of Moses (the first five books of the Old Testament) is a covenant code between humans and God. It forges a special relationship of human love and praise for God and the reciprocal divine protection and concern for humans. One of the most significant sections of the covenant of Moses is the ethical and sacral guidelines for life. These guidelines embody Israel's sense of the good society and the right honor of God. They include the Ten Commandments. Jesus distilled these guidelines into the great commandment: "Love the Lord your God and your neighbor as yourself." In other words, the Torah of Moses is a story and a set of guidelines for how to love God and the other. This torah (or instruction) envisions a model community centered on worship.

Second, the books that describe Israel's rise to statehood are often critical of the national project. Indeed, God himself indicates that statehood and kingship were not his vision; they were a concession to the people's desires for security and power. Remember, it was the logic of statehood that motivated the embellishments to the Joshua conquest story to begin with. Joshua's conquest was the story of the origin of the state and its right to the land. Hence, God's disappointment with Israel for establishing a monarchy includes an implicit disappointment with its national propaganda.

The critical stance towards the Israelite monarchy continued with the prophets. The prophets critique and condemn Israel's injustice and perverted religion. The prophets critique human failure to honor God and establish *shalom* (peace) in society. In a sense, the prophets critique the state for betraying the two great commandments: not loving God (perverted religion) and not loving neighbor (injustice).[23]

The foundation for a moral compass *does* exist in the Old Testament itself, as indicated through the two examples of the Torah: God's disappointment with the monarchy, and the prophets' critique. However, the most important source of moral formation for Christians is found in Jesus himself; he forms the basis of our moral character. His teachings and example provide us with a compass that makes sense of our moral universe. His sacrificial path guides us through death, through violence, and through the warfare of ultimate concern. He taught us how to love our neighbor and challenged us to see a neighbor in our impossible enemies. He asked us to take up our cross and hence travel into the

---

23. It is striking, then, that the prophets actually used the holy war rhetoric found in Joshua against the Israelite state. They essentially use Joshua's theology against Israel. The Joshua conquest, which erected and sanctioned the state, is then used against the Israelite state; the prophets preach that God will judge Israel through foreign conquest and destruction.

tough spots of the world with a vision of peace. With Christ's impossible triumph over violence, we can be peace in the world. And yet, with the Old Testament as our heritage, we can be that peace with greater understanding and insight into human longing and desire, human power and influence, and human nature and society.

# 9

## What about Romans 13: "Let Every Soul Be Subject"?[1]

Lee C. Camp

WHILE TEACHING A CHRISTIAN ethics class and introducing the issue of war making, I simply raised the question of whether Christians may legitimately engage in the practice. One of my students, a veteran of the first Iraq War, raised his hand and, regarding his experience, said, "I did not want to be there and I did not like being there. But I went, because it was my duty to go and defend our nation."

Such a stance is often justified by a commonsensical appeal to Romans 13: Be subject to the powers that be, which exist to be a terror to those who do evil. Given this teaching, war making may be justified for the Christian when it is engaged in service to a just cause.

My assignment in this essay first entails the assumption that the Gospel requires non-retaliatory love of enemies, which excludes the possibility of a Christian's legitimate participation in war. But if that be the case, what then of Romans 13, in which the Apostle Paul did indeed admonish disciples of Jesus to "be subject" to the rulers and powers that exist for the purpose of punishing the wicked? Here I raise three

---

1. My thanks to Britt Norvell, who assisted in research for this essay.

significant considerations that may serve a rightful interpretation of Romans 13, given the starting assumption that discipleship requires non-retaliatory, suffering love.

## Context: The Christian Vocation

First, the immediate context of Romans 13 must be noted. Chapter 12 begins a new section in Paul's address to the Roman Christians, and it highlights first and foremost *the Christian vocation* within the work God inaugurated in Jesus:

> I appeal to you therefore, brothers and sisters, by the mercies of God, to present your bodies as a living sacrifice, holy and acceptable to God, which is your spiritual worship. Do not be conformed to this world, but be transformed by the renewing of your minds, so that you may discern what is the will of God—what is good and acceptable and perfect. (12:1–2)

To rightly make sense of the New Testament, we must continually hold before ourselves the fundamental claim of the New Testament: namely that the new *aeon* had broken in. *Aeon* is the Greek word often translated into English as either "age" or "world," and the New Testament speaks often of this "present *aeon*." But the Good News is that the new *aeon*, the kingdom of God, has broken into the midst of human history. The "present *aeon*" has not yet passed away, and it is as if the two are now overlapping. But the call of discipleship is to live according to the New, even while the old is yet languishing but sure to be defeated. Jesus in his death set us "free from the present evil *aeon*" (Gal 1:4). Thus Romans 12 begins with the admonition, "Do not be conformed to this *aeon*." This makes sense only when we realize, in the language of the Pauline writings, that a "new creation" has begun with the work of Christ (2 Cor 5:17). There is now a "new humanity" that transcends the alienation between Jew and Gentile (Eph 2:15). The work of Christ overcomes the alienating force of varied sociological markers: "neither Jew nor Greek, bond nor free, male nor female" (Gal 3:28).

Just as important as this claim—that the Kingdom of God has broken in, and will ultimately be made consummate and destroy all the enemies of the Reign of God, including that final enemy, Death—is a correlating claim for that community of people we call "church." If the Kingdom of God has broken in, and will ultimately triumph, then the church is to *live proleptically* according to the now-present-and-coming Kingdom. To *live proleptically* means to live *now* according to something that is still yet in the future, that is, a future reality so sure to come to pass that we live according to that reality even now. In the case of war and peace, we are so confident that the peaceable Kingdom of God will finally triumph over war, hostility, and death-dealing that we live *now* according to that coming reality. We do not refuse to fight wars because we naively assume that, simply and immediately, all will lay down their weapons. Instead, we lay down our arms because the peaceable Kingdom of God, which is characterized by beating swords into plowshares and spears into pruning hooks, has been inaugurated in Jesus's ministry, death, burial, resurrection, and ascension. That inaugural event, moreover, poured out, upon all who will receive the gift, the power of the Holy Spirit, which makes possible such peaceable living in the midst of a warring and maddening world. Finally, the resurrection of Jesus guarantees the triumph of God's Kingdom over all the ruptures in God's good creation, ultimately defeating Death itself.

It was for this very reason that many of the early church fathers contended that former enemies, once divided by tongue and allegiances, no longer bear the sword against one another, but have learned the ways of peace: the Kingdom of God has broken into human history, and while the nations still make war, the people of God embodies a new alternative. The mission of the church is to serve as an outpost of the coming peaceable Kingdom, putting away our former ways of war making.[2]

Thus this central issue of *vocation* is of utmost importance: the church is called to embody the way of the peaceable Kingdom of God. Romans 12 makes clear that Christian discipleship, then, requires such behavior as this:

2. See Driver, *How Christians Made Peace with War*, 20–22. See also discussion in Camp, *Who Is My Enemy?*, ch. 7.

> Bless those who persecute you; bless and do not curse them
> . . . Do not repay anyone evil for evil, but take thought for
> what is noble in the sight of all. If it is possible, so far as
> it depends on you, live peaceably with all. Beloved, never
> avenge yourselves, but leave room for the wrath of God;
> for it is written, "Vengeance is mine, I will repay, says the
> Lord." No, "if your enemies are hungry, feed them; if they
> are thirsty, give them something to drink; for by doing this
> you will heap burning coals on their heads." Do not be
> overcome by evil, but overcome evil with good. (12:14–21)

In continuity with the work of Christ, the church embodies the
way of the peaceable Kingdom in response to those who do evil. Thus,
as already noted, Paul begins the chapter by admonishing the Roman
believers to have their minds "transformed." Instead of living in conformity to "this *aeon*," they are to live according to the New. To live
according to the Reign of God requires nothing less than a conversion
of one's habits, thoughts, and behaviors.

This way of life, it must be noted, is itself an "embodied" existence.
The Apostle Paul is not merely describing an "attitude" (though, as
noted, such love certainly entails a change of one's entire self, including
one's "mind" and attitudes). He is not merely describing how disciples
should conduct their personal relationships, or their inner spirituality.
This is an embodied reality: "present your *bodies* as a living sacrifice"
(12:1; emphasis added).

This embodied reality is important to note because many, following the lead of Martin Luther, have imposed a dualism upon the pages
of the New Testament, and upon the text of Romans 12–13, which cannot be maintained. Luther, for example, insisted that Romans 12, with
its emphasis upon love of enemies, "serves the guidance and peace of
the inner man and his concerns," while Romans 13 "serves that of the
outward man and his concerns."[3]

Luther no doubt would have judged the Nazis who arose four centuries later on German soil to be an arrogant and demonic manifestation of power. But the inherent social conservatism in Luther's ethic,
and the dualism in his theology, plowed the field in which the Nazis's

3. Luther, *Commentary on the Epistle to the Romans*, 164.

dualism would later flower: The "German Christians" who early on saw themselves as allied with Hitler's quest asserted that they "profess an affirmative and typical faith in Christ, corresponding to the German spirit of Luther and to a heroic piety." They believed that this supposedly "typical" faith stood in continuity with seeing "in race, folk, and nation, orders of existence grounded and entrusted to us by God. God's law for us is that we look to the preservation of these orders." Consequently, a Christian mission rightly proclaims, "'Keep your race pure,' and tells us that faith in Christ does not destroy one's race but deepens and sanctifies it." Thus, "we also demand," their "guiding principles" continue, "that the nation be protected against the unfit and the inferior." Even a "mission to the Jews" that makes room for the entrance of "alien blood into our body politic" must be rejected, with its danger of "racial camouflage and bastardization."[4]

But Luther's dualism is never assumed in the New Testament. The biblical texts never divide human reality into "spiritual" and "secular" spaces.[5] The Gospel is not a call merely to a new spirituality or piety separable from the real stuff of life, from human history and bodies and the sociocultural matrix. The Gospel is a call to embody the New Reality, with its reconciling, suffering love, right in the midst of the old: a call to be a toehold for the New, perhaps sometimes while hanging precipitously on the craggy face of the old.

Indeed, Romans 12 employs an extended "body" metaphor: the church is a body comprising different gifts and capacities. The "body of Christ" is in fact Paul's favorite metaphor for the church: the church continues to enflesh the mission and ministry of Christ in the world.[6] Both in this context and elsewhere, Paul maintains that the "body of Christ" is called to a new unity made possible in the work of Christ.

4. "The Guiding Principles of the Faith Movement of the 'German Christians,' June 6, 1932," in Cochrane, *The Church's Confession under Hitler*, 222–23.

5. Even when Paul uses a dichotomy of "flesh" and "spirit," he does not thereby mean embodied versus disembodied realities, but an embodied life driven by *mere fleshly concerns* versus a life driven by the Spirit of God.

6. Cf. conversation on this in Philip H. Towner, "Romans 13:1–7 and Paul's Missiological Perspective: A Call to Political Quietism or Transformation?," in Soderlund and Wright, eds., *Romans and the People of God*, 152ff.

In this regard, it must be observed that the modern nation-state stands, in practical terms, as one of the greatest enemies of the unity of the church: the nation-state alone has demanded that Christians living within its borders kill Christians who happen to live behind the borders of another nation-state. But our baptism grants us a new citizenship in the Kingdom of God. Consequently it will not suffice to simply cite "our duty" to the powers as justification for killing brothers and sisters in Christ on the other side of a political dispute. It is this factual rupturing of the unity of the body of Christ that is so very often overlooked in many conversations about Christians and war making.

Back to Romans 12: it must be reiterated that the love of enemies required there is no utopian idealism, which refuses to face the facts of the reality of wickedness in human history. Indeed, the "way of the cross" presupposes that the old has not yet been consummately defeated. It *has* been defeated, a defeat guaranteed by the resurrection. But the demonic powers and fallen realities still lurk about. Death has not yet been finally defeated as it shall be. In the meanwhile, we do good to our enemies, and overcome evil with good, and do not presume to take vengeance upon those who do evil. That is God's prerogative, to do in God's way and in God's time.

It is all this that sets the context for the claims of Rom 13:1–7.

## Specific Teaching: The Vocation of the Governing Authorities

This vocation of the church—to embody the peaceable way of the Kingdom of God—combined with a realism about the ongoing reality of sin in the world is what gives definition to *the vocation of the powers and governing authorities.* Given that the triumph over the power of sin is not yet final, we may expect that wickedness will still rear its ugly head, will strike and lash out. Corruption and murder and death have not yet been finally defeated, and thus we continue to see its work made manifest on the pages of history. It is precisely this reality that defines the work of the governing authorities: to channel the vengeance and wickedness back upon itself, to limit the destructive and maddening effects of violence by turning it in on itself.

As we have seen, the vocation of the church is to embody the New. But all have not received the New as Good News, and thus continue to live under bondage to the forces of death. What then? The governing authorities are "ordered" by God to have a "preservative" effect. Unlike Luther, who claimed that the governing authorities were part of the "orders of creation," Dietrich Bonhoeffer called the powers "orders of preservation." That is, they have a function of employing a sharply limited amount of violence or coercion in service to checking chaos, keeping madness at bay. As the prince or king or emperor may thus excusably employ coercion in this manner, meanwhile the church embodies the New, and proclaims the New, inviting all to come participate in the New.

Note John Howard Yoder's insight here:

> God is not said to *create* or *institute* or *ordain* the powers that be, but only to *order* them, to put them in order, sovereignly to tell them where they belong, what is their place . . . Nor is it that by ordering this realm God specifically, morally approves of what a government does. The sergeant does not produce the soldiers he drills; the librarian does not create nor approve of the book she or he catalogs and shelves. Likewise God does not take the responsibility for the existence of the rebellious "powers that be" or for their shape or identity; they already are. What the text says is that God orders them, brings them into line, providentially and permissively lines them up with divine purposes.[7]

Thus with little systematic consideration, the New Testament writers simply assume a given role for the governing authorities that may be summarized thus: the governing authorities, with their police function, serve the larger mission of the church. In parallel with Romans 13, 1 Timothy 2 and 1 Peter 2 depict the relationship between church and governing authorities in this way.

This stands in continuity with the Old Testament witness, in which the powers of the world were used in God's sovereignty for God's purposes in history. Assyria, Babylon, Egypt, and Persia are all described

---

7. Yoder, *Politics of Jesus*, 201–2. Repeatedly, Romans 13 uses cognates of the Greek verb *tasso*, which means to "order" or "fix" a thing or person.

in various ways as being the servants of God's purposes, typically employed for punishing and chastising the wicked. As Paul will claim in Romans 13, these (themselves wicked) nations are God's "ministers," in the limited sense of serving God's overarching order, in that God employs the arrogance and violence of the nations against one another, so that the earth and its creatures are not utterly destroyed.

Several notes in this regard: first, this way of putting the matter stands at odds with the assumption of Western, liberal democratic orders. In the West, it is typically assumed that "religion," whatever that means, pertains to the realm of the private; it is a compartmentalizable element of life that need not—and for many, ought not—impinge upon the realm called "public." For some secularists, "religion" is simply dispensable and unnecessary altogether, though "public" notions of "human rights" require a political order in which "religion" is "protected" as a private affair. For others, "religion" turns out to be something that is needed by democratic regimes, providing something like a moral compass or ethical ballast to a ship that would otherwise wander aimlessly. In this view, called an "instrumental view of the church," the church serves the broader, and purportedly more public, role of the nation-state. The nation-state, or democracy, is seen as the larger, more "public," and more significant player in human history. So far as *history*, so far as the "real world" is concerned, the *state* or democratic polities are seen as the *historical savior*. And the church thus serves the democracy, and not the other way around. President Eisenhower best depicted this instrumental, if not parasitic, view of the church when he said, "our form of government has no sense unless it is founded in a deeply felt religious faith, and I don't care what it is."[8]

8. Eisenhower, "Address at the Freedoms Foundation." Note that it was also the Eisenhower administration that amended the pledge of allegiance to include "under God," and that this employment of "God" also serves in an instrumental capacity: "Especially is this meaningful as we regard today's world. Over the globe, mankind has been cruelly torn by violence and brutality and, by the millions, deadened in mind and soul by a materialistic philosophy of life. Man everywhere is appalled by the prospect of atomic war. In this somber setting, this law and its effects today have profound meaning. In this way we are reaffirming the transcendence of religious faith in America's heritage and future; in this way we shall constantly strengthen those spiritual weapons which forever will be our country's most powerful resource, in

Thus the New Testament claim is, from the start, offensive to modern sensibilities. Ephesians 3 notes, for example, that the salvific wisdom of God is revealed to the powers *in the church.* "Although I am the very least of all the saints, this grace was given to me to bring to the Gentiles the news of the boundless riches of Christ, and to make everyone see what is the plan of the mystery hidden for ages in God who created all things; so that through the church the wisdom of God in its rich variety might now be made known to the rulers and authorities in the heavenly places" (Eph 3:8–10). Paul's decidedly antimodern stance in 1 Cor 2:8 further demonstrates this claim: when believers go before unbelievers to settle disputes among themselves, Paul can hardly fathom it. Why, he asks, would you take a dispute to be judged by unbelievers when it is the believers who will, in the end, judge the world? It would be better to be defrauded, he claims.[9]

We might think of it in this way: the church is putting on the stage show, while the governing authorities serve as the ushers at the show. The usher is necessary and helpful. But the artists and musicians and performers are the reason for the gathering. And it does not serve the affair at all for the artists and musicians and performers to busy themselves with ushering, for then the show cannot go on. They have a special vocation to which they must attend.[10] From the New Testament perspective, the state and governing authorities serve the mission of the church, and the church is the primary character in God's mission to the world. This claim must not and cannot be construed in a triumphalist manner, in which the church then seeks to arrogantly vaunt itself over the powers and over the peoples: for the vocation and mission of the

---

peace or in war" ("Statement by the President Upon Signing Bill").

9. Cullman, *State in the New Testament*, 56.

10. Yoder, *Discipleship as a Political Responsibility*, 44–45. Note in some comparison the provocative claim of David Lipscomb—although it is perhaps neither rhetorically expedient nor sufficiently nuanced—who, in encouraging disciples of Jesus not to go running after governmental offices and powers, conceded that human governments are indeed "ordained" by God. They are ordained to punish wickedness and keep order. But hell, Lipscomb also maintained, is ordained by God for the same purpose, and no one goes running after the job to govern hell. See Lipscomb, *Civil Government*, 30–32.

church, as we have already seen, is to embody suffering love and the peace of God's Kingdom, and to call all to participate in this Reign.

Second, for the Christian to "be subject" to the authorities cannot mean, then, "blind subjection."[11] There *is* a certain social conservatism in the text on this score: the powers that be are ordered by God to serve their role of keeping wickedness at bay through the employment of coercive force. In serving that role, Christians must not seek to overthrow governments, but should acknowledge the ordination or vocation of those powers.

But this cannot mean a blind subjection, an indiscriminate blessing of whatever the powers do. Such a position would obviously stand at odds with the overarching teaching of the entire Bible. From the prophet Nathan to the exile Daniel, from John the Baptizer to Peter the apostle, a consistent prioritization of allegiances appears: "we must obey God rather than human authorities." To the degree that the human authority requires something of us which does not stand at odds with our first and prior allegiance to Jesus as Lord, to that same degree must we yield our obedience. There is *something* that we must yield to "Caesar," but only when whatever Caesar demands has not been previously demanded by the Creator.[12]

Third, then, the powers may become "demonic," may begin to demand for themselves absolute and abject obedience. The powers may begin to assert themselves as God. Instead of serving the very limited role ordered by God, the powers too often see themselves as saviors, as being the hope and light of the world. And this terribly dangerous conceit is not a dynamic with which the New Testament is unfamiliar. Thus *Revelation 13* needs to be as much in the Christian consciousness as *Romans 13*, for in Revelation we see the full flowering of an arrogant imperial power demanding abject obedience. And—again it is important to note—that in John's depiction in Revelation, it is not those who rise up in revolutionary violence—like *Braveheart's* William Wallace ("Freedom!") or the American Patriots against the British ("Give me liberty or give me death!")—who triumph. Instead, John maintains that it is those who bear witness to the Lamb through the sword of God's

11. Barth, *Shorter Commentary on Romans*, 157–58.
12. Cf. Cullman, *State in the New Testament*, 65.

word, it is those who are martyred who triumph over the evil empire. The persecuted ones, even in the midst of their own "axis of evil," are called not to make the world turn out right by employing the means and methods of empire, but the means and methods of the Lamb of God, trusting that God is at work both in heaven and earth, to bring about the triumph of God's Kingdom.

A corollary to this claim is this: we cannot assume that God specifically ordains whatever specific government or governmental policies exist.

## What May Be Said, if Anything, to the Powers?

It is sometimes assumed that to embrace non-retaliatory love entails a withdrawal from governments. The logic runs this way: governments find their very reason for existence in the coercive use of force; if it is claimed that disciples of Jesus eschew the employment of coercive force, then disciples will have neither part nor parcel in the government. Moreover, they have no right to voice their agenda or concerns to the powers.

Here, Yoder's *The Christian Witness to the State*,[13] to which I refer the reader, proves most helpful. For the sake of argument, Yoder assumes that Christian discipleship entails the rejection of war, and the practice of suffering love. He then asks what we might say to those powers who have indeed, according to the New Testament, a police function in human society. Throughout, Yoder insists that our ultimate aim for any statesman, whom we must love as our neighbor, is to draw him or her to embrace the Lordship of Christ and the Way of Christ. But, if the statesman cannot (yet) embrace the Lordship of Christ and the Way of Christ, then we may simply ask him or her to take a step in the right direction. If the tyrannical dictator is practicing grave injustice, we might ask him, at least, to practice some common decency. If the good middle-class-morality president is embracing a way of war making that celebrates nationalism and an ass-kicking machismo, then we might call him to take the restraints of the just war tradition more seriously. Yoder

13. It is unfortunate, in my opinion, that so few of those who critique Yoder appear to know the arguments Yoder presented in this book.

calls these steps in the right direction "middle axioms": that is, we seek some middle space between, on the one hand, the place in which the statesman finds himself and, on the other, the call of Jesus to nonviolent love of enemies. Even though such steps are not a step into the fullness of the call of Christ, they will undoubtedly, notes Yoder, require great faith: as much real faith as that required by the newly recovering alcoholic not to drink one day at a time. Just because it is not yet a mature or full faith does not mean it is not faith.

Thus, the witness of the disciple of Jesus to the state entails calling the statesman toward these new steps, toward the way of the Gospel. Let me make several other important points in this regard, and in light of the agenda of this essay: First, there *is* a qualitative difference between war and policing. If policing is an excusable function of the use of coercive force for the powers, this does not lead directly to the legitimacy of warring. There are obvious differences: Policing adheres to the use of the minimal force necessary, while modern war, especially since the US Civil War and embodied in the "Powell doctrine" of overwhelming force, hits with as much force as possible in order to make resistance unsustainable. In the event of the use of mortal or fatal violence, policing typically has review policies in place, while the casualties of war, except perhaps in some instances of gross violation of civilian populations, are rarely reviewed. Policing is restricted by forms of due process and various mechanisms of oversight, which are absent in warring. Policing—and the assumption for the powers in the New Testament—is meant to preserve order and check chaos, while war creates chaos in the name of creating some new order. Thus even if one does concede the rightfulness of the powers employing police-like coercion, one is not thereby bound to conclude that there is therefore an obvious legitimacy of warring. On the other hand, there does seem to be here some space for the possibility of envisioning police-like employment of excusable force by multilateral contingencies, in which the very minimum of force is used in order to check the wickedness of a tyrant or aggressor.

Second, we must take a realistic vision of the role of the state. If we keep in mind that, prior to the final consummation of God's Kingdom, no human system or government or power shall attain the fullness of God's purposes—which is to say that Death, though it has been defeated, has not yet suffered its final defeat—then such a vision will allow us to practice a thoroughgoing realism with regard to "politics." In other words, we should not expect too much of nation-states. This is not cynicism. This is an "eschatological realism."[14]

As a corollary, we should beware of the co-option of theological terms and categories by the nation-state. In the most recent presidential election, I was struck by the manner in which both the loser, in his concession speech, and the winner, in his acceptance speech, said the same thing in effect: namely that America is the hope of the world. But such speech is not only patently absurd; it is fundamentally idolatrous. The hope, the longing of human history, is not the triumph of the United States, but the triumph of the peaceable Kingdom of God. Thus any sort of utopian or grandiose political projects may be suspect: for, living between the times, the depth of human sin continues to plague even our best intentions.

But does this mean that we should simply withdraw from any witness or work with the powers-that-be? Does this mean that we simply accept a sort of practical determinism, in which we can have no hope for any improvement or progress or worthwhile developments in contemporary political and social movements? No, it most certainly need not entail such things. A realistic assessment of the idolatrous tendencies of Western political liberalism need not lead us to some sort of legalistic withdrawal, some self-righteous stance in which we refuse to dine with Republicans or Democrats or Fascists or Communists. Instead, we focus upon particular injustices, particular questions and issues, and seek to bear witness to the will and purposes of God, and ask the ruler or governor to take a step in the right direction.

14. Eschatology is the study of the end of all things. Too often, this has meant a concern with the *timing* of the end, or the historical occurrences through which one can supposedly discern the nearing of the end. This has always been a failed and embarrassing form of inquiry. More importantly is the New Testament claim that *the end*—namely, the victory of the Kingdom of God—has already broken into human history, while the old *aeon* has not yet been fully vanquished, but most certainly shall.

## Conclusion

Romans 12 and 13, taken as a single literary unit, are of great importance for understanding both the mission of the church and, while we await the consummation of God's Kingdom, God's use of the powers-that-be. The church is called as an outpost of the coming Kingdom to embody the ways of peace and non-retaliatory love, to live not according to the old *aeon* but according to the new work of God made manifest in the merciful work of Christ.

But this calling does not naively assume that all peoples will then lay down their wickedness and embrace the way of Christ, that warring and wickedness will simply be undone. Quite to the contrary, Christian discipleship assumes that as we embody the way of Christ, we will often suffer and carry a cross akin to our Lord's. But let us not seek vengeance, nor seek to overcome evil on its own terms; rather, let us seek to overcome evil with good. The Father will bring about punishment and recompense in God's way and in God's timing.

Then Romans 13 declares that it is the "authorities" and "powers" that God uses for such ends, uses to channel vengeance back upon itself. It is as if the apostle, just after advocating what many dismiss as "idealism," advocates a most thoroughgoing "political realism." This makes sense only if we understand Christian mission: the church is called to be transformed, to live according to the way of Christ, empowered by the Spirit of God. But even until God's Kingdom triumphs, the ongoing reality of sin persists; and in the midst of the persistence of the power of sin, God's Providence employs the powers to moderate the rebellion, and keep the forces of wickedness at bay.

In the meanwhile, Romans 13 continues, we followers of Jesus are to "owe no one anything, except to love one another; for the one who loves another has fulfilled the law . . . Love does no wrong to a neighbor; therefore, love is the fulfilling of the law. Besides this, you know what time it is, how it is now the moment for you to wake from sleep. For salvation is nearer to us now than when we became believers; the night is far gone, the day is near. Let us then lay aside the works of darkness and put on the armor of light . . ." (13:8–12).

# 10

## Didn't Jesus Say He Came Not to Bring Peace, but a Sword?

Samuel Wells

JESUS OFFERS FIVE EXTENDED sermons in Matthew's Gospel,[1] and well into the second one he says these words:

> Do not think that I have come to bring peace to the earth; I have not come to bring peace, but a sword. For I have come to set a man against his father, and a daughter against her mother, and a daughter-in-law against her mother-in-law; and one's foes will be members of one's own household. Whoever loves father or mother more than me is not worthy of me; and whoever loves son or daughter more than me is not worthy of me; and whoever does not take up the cross and follow me is not worthy of me. Those who find their life will lose it, and those who lose their life for my sake will find it. (Matt 10:34–39)

These words—and, in particular, the opening sentence—seem counter-intuitive to a disciple or interpreter shaped by the nonviolent tenor of the gospels as a whole. They raise five questions: Why did Jesus come?

---

1. The five sermons are chapters 5–7, 10, 13, 18, and 23–25.

In what ways did Jesus expect his disciples to imitate him? Did he truly not bring peace? Did he truly bring a sword? What might such a statement constructively mean today? In what follows I address each of these questions in turn.[2]

## Why Did Jesus Come?

Jesus here utters the phrase "I have come to . . ." three times. He doesn't offer a list of imperative instructions; instead, he indicatively describes his mission and its effects.[3] This naturally raises the question of what his central mission was.[4] There are other places in the gospels where this question is answered in summary form: Luke 4:18–19 offers a far-reaching rendering of what a Jubilee Year might look like on political, social, economic, psychological, and interpersonal levels; John 13:1–15 offers a succinct summary of Jesus' ministry and its implications for the disciples; Matthew 25:31–46 indicates where Jesus is to be found and how disciples are to encounter him. This passage isn't a summary statement of such a kind—although the repeated "I have come to . . ." might misleadingly suggest that it is.

---

2. I am grateful to Rebekah Eklund for helping me think through the argument for this paper and offering suggestions and further references.

3. Frederick Dale Bruner points out the significance of the indicative (Bruner, *Christbook*, 487). R. T. France notes several other instances of the configuration "I have come to . . . " in Matthew: Jesus says, "Do not think that I have come to abolish the law or the prophets; I have come not to abolish but to fulfill" (5:17); "Go and learn what this means, 'I desire mercy, not sacrifice.' For I have come to call not the righteous but sinners" (9:13); "The Son of Man came not to be served but to serve, and to give his life as a ransom for many" (20:28) (France, *Gospel of Matthew*, 408).

4. France helpfully elucidates this point: "In the Fourth Gospel this sort of language represents Jesus as a preexistent figure who has 'come into the world' (John 1:9; 9:39; 18:37) from heaven (John 3:13, 31), and it is tempting to find the same implication in Matthew. In a variety of ways Matthew implies or indeed openly states that Jesus is 'God with us,' but he does not elsewhere use language which specifically states his preexistence, and the fact that the same verb ('came') introduces the distinctive ministry of John the Baptist in 11:18 and 21:32 suggests caution in reading too much into it. It conveys a sense of mission rather than a metaphysical claim" (France, *Gospel of Matthew*, 184).

The question of why Jesus came is obviously a huge one, but it can be answered in two kinds of ways. One refers to the tasks that Jesus himself sought to achieve and the character of God that he set out to display. The second refers to the forms of life he looked to make possible and that he deemed to be in keeping with the nature of God and God's reign. In simple terms, we may call the first, theology, and the second, ethics.[5]

The first, theological, kind of answer centers around reconciliation. Matthew puts it like this: "You are to name him Jesus, for he will save his people from their sins . . . and they shall name him Emmanuel, which means, 'God is with us'" (1:21, 23). Christ came to reconcile the world to God; to break down the dividing wall between Jew and Gentile and make one people; to heal the past by bringing the forgiveness of sins and to open up the future by inaugurating everlasting life; to make a final sacrifice that brought to an end all sacrifice; to be with people, even at the risk of straining the inner relations of the Trinity (Matt 27:46), to show God's utter commitment never to be except to be with us. The second, ethical, kind of answer centers around love, summarized by Matthew in 22:37–39: love for God, expressed in a life of worship and ministry; love for neighbor, embodied in costly witness alongside even the enemy, most succinctly embodied in the beatitudes (Matt 5:3–11); and love for self, based on seeing oneself as a neighbor, too.

In the light of this very brief summary, it quickly becomes clear why the statement "Do not think that I have come to bring peace to the earth; I have not come to bring peace, but a sword" is so troubling. Peace is the one thing about which there seems a consensus that Jesus came to bring: humanity's peace with God, with itself, and with the created order—a mixture of reconciliation that sets things right and love that keeps things right. Even those who are quite certain that followers of Jesus cannot rule out, and must in some circumstances embrace, the use of weapons of lethal force, invariably assume that the violence in question is a brief interruption—and ushers in a deeper manifestation—of God's original and everlasting peace.

Thus no one—neither advocates of just war, nor pacifists, nor even crusaders—truly argues that this phrase should be taken at face value.

5. Of course I don't believe ethics and theology are two discrete fields, but here I am using them as a heuristic device to exegete the text.

Almost all Christians believe Jesus came to bring peace, and not a sword.[6] The difference between pacifists and advocates of the just war lies not with whether or not Jesus came to bring a sword—all agree that he did not. The difference lies in whether one is most faithful to Christ in assuming his mission succeeded, and thus laying aside the sword oneself (the path of theological pacifism); in assuming his mission modeled an effective ethical method of addressing conflict, which followers should imitate (the path of pragmatic pacifism); or in assuming his mission's ultimate success requires disciples to lay aside its nonviolent methods, in precisely defined circumstances, in order to face up to the enemies— sin and evil—that Jesus defeated but didn't finally eradicate (the path of the just war).

All of which translates quickly into the question of how Jesus expected his disciples to imitate him.

## In What Ways Did Jesus Expect His Disciples to Imitate Him?

John Howard Yoder addresses the question of the ways disciples should, and should not, expect to follow Jesus. He does so in characteristically lapidary tones. Yoder sees in the New Testament no Franciscan glorification of barefoot mendicancy; no appeal to Jesus as an example of celibacy; no highlighting of Jesus' years as an artisan, or his rabbinic ministry, or his calling of fishermen, or his illustrations from rural life. All these absences show, by contrast, how central is the notion of participation in the suffering of Christ. "Only at one point, only on one subject—but then consistently, universally—is Jesus our example: in his

6. This is true even of those who take Jesus to mean the sword literally, such as Brandon, *Jesus and the Zealots*; see France, *Gospel of Matthew*, 408 n. 6. Stephen C. Barton argues that those who interpret the sword literally do so "against the background of the Jewish holy war tradition, a tradition kept alive at Qumran, and justified scripturally on the basis of such texts as Exodus 32:27–9 and Deut. 33: 6–11." Thus "the saying in 10:34 represents a claim by [Jesus] to be the agent of God's End-Time wrath, bringing the sword of judgment against Belial and all his followers in heaven and on earth." Although Barton concurs that Matthew is indeed drawn to apocalyptic ideas and images, he adds, "it is not clear that he [Matthew] understands missionary discipleship in conventional holy-war terms, given the priority of the love-commandment in his gospel, and the fact that mission is to Gentiles as well as to Jews" (Barton, *Discipleship and Family Ties in Mark and Matthew*, 167 n. 158).

cross."[7] And what is the cross? Yoder explains as follows: "The believer's cross is no longer any and every kind of suffering, sickness, or tension, the bearing of which is demanded. The believer's cross must be like his Lord's, the price of his social nonconformity. It is not, like sickness or catastrophe, an inexplicable, unpredictable suffering; it is the end of a path freely chosen after counting the cost. It is not . . . an inward wrestling of the sensitive soul with self and sin; it is the social reality of representing in an unwilling world the Order to come."[8]

Jesus' words, "Do not think that I have come to bring peace to the earth; I have not come to bring peace, but a sword," are part of the second of his five sermons in Matthew. This section of the sermon portrays the past, present, and future of salvation. Jesus *came* (three times, past, verses 34–35); he judges that anyone who fails to show absolute loyalty to him "*is* not worthy of me" (three times, present, verses 36–37); and then points out the consequences of these choices as disciples "will lose" or "will find" their lives (twice, future, verse 39).[9] Perhaps the chief significance of these words is not that they refer to a sword, but that they are Jesus' first mention in Matthew's Gospel of the cross. No doubt to the disciples' consternation, the cross "comes on the scene, startlingly, not only as *his* eventual fate, but as *theirs*."[10]

The important point is that it would be a mistake to interpret the statement, "Do not think that I have come to bring peace to the earth; I have not come to bring peace, but a sword," in isolation from the two elements—about separating relatives from one another, and about taking up the cross—that immediately follow it. The difficult part is that these three elements blend the theological and the ethical dimensions of Jesus' ministry mentioned above. The phrase "Do not think that I have come to bring . . ." belongs to what I have called the theological dimension—the part of Jesus' ministry unique to him, and not for imitation by his disciples. Indeed, of the two aspects of the theological dimension—the performative (what Jesus achieves) and the revelatory (what

7. Yoder, *The Politics of Jesus*, 95.

8. Ibid., 96.

9. This is pointed out by Bruner, *Christbook*, 487, who cites Joachim Gnilka, *Das Matthäusevangelium*, 1:393.

10. France, *Gospel of Matthew*, 407.

Jesus shows)—it belongs to the latter, revelatory dimension, sometimes known as apocalyptic. The same is true of the subsequent sentence ("For I have come to set a man against his father . . ."). It is only the final part of the section ("Whoever loves . . . is not worthy of me," and "Those who find their life will lose it . . .") that can be described as ethical, in other words as ways disciples are to imitate their Lord.

A simple ordering may clarify these distinctions.

### Jesus' ministry

1. Theological—what only God, in Christ, can do

   a. Performative—what Christ achieves—e.g., offering his body as the final sacrifice

   b. Revelatory/Apocalyptic—what Christ reveals or shows—e.g., the signs of the end times

2. Ethical—what disciples themselves are to do

   a. Imitation—following Christ as example—e.g., taking up the cross and voluntary suffering in the face of power

   b. Obedience—obeying Jesus' commands that are not explicitly manifested in Jesus' own life—e.g., instructions about divorce

Because Jesus' sermons are made up of many ethical instructions, and because parts of this section are indeed ethical instruction, it is easy to see how interpreters may imagine that the phrase "Do not think that I have come to bring . . ." is also ethical instruction. But this would be a mistake. The phrase belongs in the category 1b above. The material later in the section belongs to 2a ("Those who find their life . . ." clearly follows the pattern of Jesus, who lost his life and found it) and 2b ("Whoever loves father or mother more than me . . ."—although it is arguable this could also be assigned to 2a, if one considers the tensions between Jesus and his Nazareth family, e.g., Matt 12:46–50).

It is not uncommon for the contemporary interpreter to struggle with what I am calling 1b material. This is because a good deal of apocalyptic is expressed in vivid and what may seem to be exaggerated language—for example, when it comes to describing the nature and experience of hell. Much of the struggle is due to the genre of apocalyptic writing, which flourished around the time the gospels were written. It is time to look at the apocalyptic dimension of this saying in more detail.

## Not Peace?

It is almost impossible to take Jesus' words, "Do not think that I have come to bring peace to the earth; I have not come to bring peace" at face value. R. T. France explains why.

> Not only is peace a basic human aspiration, but it was understood to be the purpose of the Messiah's coming (e.g. Isa 9:6–7; Zech 9:10) and the defining characteristic of God's eschatological rule (e.g. Isa 11:6–9). Matthew will draw attention in 21:4–5 to how Jesus presented himself as the messianic king who brings peace, and his nonconfrontational style will be commented on in 12:15–21 and demonstrated in chs. 26–27 in the story of his quiet acceptance of unjust accusation and condemnation. His coming was proclaimed as the dawn of "peace on earth" (Luke 2:14), and it is "peace" which the disciples are being sent out to offer (v. 13). Peacemaking is an essential part of the good life (5:9).[11]

Nonetheless, there have been some historical interpreters who have attempted to follow through on a literal rendering of these challenging words. Ulrich Luz perceives two strands of this vision.[12] One sees Jesus as a genuine worldly revolutionary. In the view of H. S. Reimarus, Jesus set out to redeem Israel from servitude, but failed, and the disciples spiritualized his story after his death. For Ernst Bloch, Jesus announced the advent of love and the kingdom of peace, but in many cases there is less talk of loving enemies than of spiritual warfare, "and Jesus finally was correctly understood and executed as an insurgent." Jesus was not a Zealot, because he wasn't seeking to restore a Davidic kingdom; but

11. Ibid., 408.

12. Luz, *Matthew 8–20*, 109–10.

he did proclaim an eschatological exodus. The other strand, by contrast with the first, sees Jesus rejecting the external peace of the world in favor of the inner peace of the heart—the peace of one's conscience, and the peace between God and humanity, available only in the church and not in the secular political realm.[13]

Luz rejects both of these interpretations on the grounds that they pay scant attention to the immediate context of this section of Matthew's Gospel. What Luz perceives is that

> The coming of Jesus and his message of the kingdom of God are at odds with familial and societal ties. It is the disciples' greeting of *peace* that causes the split (cf. vv. 12–14).[14] And it is the rejection of the greeting of peace that seals the split with unheard-of sharpness (cf. v. 15).[15] As a result of this division the disciples are to suffer (cf. vv. 17–23; vv 38–39 after v. 37).[16] . . . The message of ultimate peace, the reversal of secular rule, and of the love of God for the underprivileged has a political dimension and evokes the resistance of all those who defend power and privileges. For them, the disciples whose life corresponds

13. This view is associated with Johannes Brenz (1499–1570). Luz adds that the allegorical interpretation, prominent in the medieval period, is that the "mother" and the "mother-in-law" of verse 35 refer to the synagogue.

14. Matt 10:12–13: "As you enter the house, greet it. If the house is worthy, let your peace come upon it; but if it is not worthy, let your peace return to you."

15. Matt 10:14–15: "If anyone will not welcome you or listen to your words, shake off the dust from your feet as you leave that house or town. Truly I tell you, it will be more tolerable for the land of Sodom and Gomorrah on the day of judgment than for that town."

16. Matt 10:17–23: "Beware of them, for they will hand you over to councils and flog you in their synagogues; and you will be dragged before governors and kings because of me, as a testimony to them and the Gentiles. When they hand you over, do not worry about how you are to speak or what you are to say; for what you are to say will be given to you at that time; for it is not you who speak, but the Spirit of your Father speaking through you. Brother will betray brother to death, and a father his child, and children will rise against parents and have them put to death; and you will be hated by all because of my name. But the one who endures to the end will be saved. When they persecute you in one town, flee to the next; for truly I tell you, you will not have gone through all the towns of Israel before the Son of Man comes."

to this message and who abandon the structures of the world are not pleasant figures.[17]

Thus we come to read Jesus as saying, "Don't think I came to bring a simple, passive, harmless peace. This gospel is going to mean a turbulent life for you, and it's going to cause profound tensions between you and even those who are closest to you."

The trouble is, Jesus doesn't say "profound tensions"; he says "a sword." What does he mean by saying not just "I have not come to bring peace," but "[I have come to bring] a sword"?

## Bringing a Sword

A sword may be used for active violence, whether defensive or aggressive. But it may also be used for cutting or dividing one tender piece of fabric, food, or flesh from another. Both are relevant in contrast to peace. The sense of the first is obvious—violent combat is clearly not peace. The sense of the second is more subtle—dividing one thing or person from another may be necessary or inevitable (one thinks, in a modern idiom, of the work of the surgeon in dividing one conjoined twin from another to save the lives of both); but it is not peace, at least peace understood as the absence of any disturbance. If we have established that Jesus is saying he came not to bring a simple, passive, harmless peace, then we may suppose this second sense is the one intended: Jesus' sword is like the surgeon's knife. It causes pain and division, but the purpose is for removing disease and bringing about healing.

The questions that arise, then, are: Is this second meaning truly in view here? And why does Jesus think a sword is apt for the circumstances he describes? Taking the first question, Luz helpfully summarizes the views of Luther and Calvin.

> Since the Reformation the distinction between "passive" and "active" sword has become important. The former is

17. Luz, *Matthew 8–20*, 112. In reference to Luke, Joel Green makes a similar connection between earlier narrative promises of peace through Jesus' ministry (Luke 1:79; 2:14; 7:50; 8:48; 10:5–6) and the way Jesus' peace brings social disapproval and opposition (Luke 2:34–35; 3:17; 7:36–50) (Green, *Gospel of Luke*, 510–11).

> meant in our text, that is, "not a sword that the disciples are to use, but the sword that is drawn and used against them." The saying is then almost always understood to express result and not purpose. Christ came not in order to bring the sword, but the coming of Christ resulted in dissensions and struggles. They are caused by the world's evil.[18]

This is fine, so long as one ignores the fact that it substitutes "Christ came not in order to bring the sword" for the text's "I came to bring a sword." France's rendering configures this paradox more successfully. He says, "The very purpose of Jesus' coming is 'not peace but a sword,' because the message of God's kingship is one which always has and always will lead to violent response from those who are threatened by it (11:12).[19] As 5:11–12 has already reminded them, this has been true in the experience of God's prophets even before Jesus came . . . ."[20] To represent Jesus is to accept a share in the way he is treated by a hostile world (vv. 24–25)."[21]

The Reformation line of interpretation inclines toward invoking Eph 6:10–17, particularly verse 17: "Take the helmet of salvation, and the sword of the Spirit, which is the word of God." I suggest that a more fruitful place to look for a precedent for the kind of sword Jesus is talking about is 1 Kings 3, where Solomon is faced with two women who each claim the same baby.

---

18. Luz, *Matthew 8–20*, 110; the quotation is from Karl Barth, *CD* 4/3.625. Luz adds, "The saying was then used to justify the spiritual battle against *heretics*. In questions of doctrine one may make no concessions for the sake of external peace."

19. Matt 11:12: "From the days of John the Baptist until now the kingdom of heaven has suffered violence, and the violent take it by force."

20. Matt 5:11–12: "Blessed are you when people revile you and persecute you and utter all kinds of evil against you falsely on my account. Rejoice and be glad, for your reward is great in heaven, for in the same way they persecuted the prophets who were before you."

21. France, *Gospel of Matthew*, 407. Matt 10:24–25: "A disciple is not above the teacher, nor a slave above the master; it is enough for the disciple to be like the teacher, and the slave like the master. If they have called the master of the house Beelzebul, how much more will they malign those of his household!"

> So the king said, "Bring me a sword," and they brought a
> sword before the king. The king said, "Divide the living
> boy in two; then give half to the one, and half to the other."
> But the woman whose son was alive said to the king—be-
> cause compassion for her son burned within her—"Please,
> my lord, give her the living boy; certainly do not kill him!"
> The other said, "It shall be neither mine nor yours; divide
> it." Then the king responded: "Give the first woman the
> living boy; do not kill him. She is his mother." (1 Kings
> 3:25–27)

The threat of violence is real: but it is a device to elicit truth and bring
about justice, and is never used. Solomon's sword therefore resembles
Jesus' eschatological judgment: it elicits truth and brings about justice,
but it can hardly be described as violent. Solomon's sword is perhaps the
only precedent for Jesus' sword that preserves the literal sense of Jesus'
words while remaining true to the tenor of Jesus' whole ministry.

Moving to the second question, Why does Jesus think a sword
is required for the circumstances he describes? The text indicates an
answer in its allusion to Mic 7:6, which states, "For the son treats the
father with contempt, the daughter rises up against her mother, the
daughter-in-law against her mother-in-law; your enemies are members
of your own household." It seems that the family threatens to be one of
the most significant obstacles to faithful discipleship. One subtle signal to this effect is the terminology employed. As Warren Carter notes,
"The verb to *love* (*philein*) is rarely used in Matthew and only to express
disapproval (6:5; 23:6, 26:48).[22] Here to *love* is to place any relationship
and obligation above Jesus."[23] Robert Tannehill continues in the same
vein: "The text contradicts our desire to think of such family divisions
as temporary and accidental, as problems which can be overcome with

---

22. Matt 6:5: "And whenever you pray, do not be like the hypocrites; for they love
to stand and pray in the synagogues and at the street corners, so that they may be seen
by others." Matt 23:6: "[The scribes and the Pharisees] love to have the place of honor
at banquets and the best seats in the synagogues." Matthew 26:48: "Now the betrayer
had given them a sign, saying, 'The one I will kiss [*phileso*] is the man; arrest him.'"

23. Carter, *Matthew and the Margins*, 243. Matthew uses another word for love
(*agapao*) in a very positive way in Matt 22:37–40, by contrast.

time or better counseling techniques."[24] The crucial point, to which Mic 7:6 gives a signal, is that the context is eschatological.[25] Stephen Barton summarizes the scholarly consensus on this point: "As it occurs here in Matthew, the [sword] metaphor has eschatological rather than political/ military connotations. The End-time divisions and familial strife tradi- tionally associated with the time before the coming of the Messiah are linked here with the coming of Jesus. There can be little doubt that they have direct associations also with the experience of Matthew's implied readers."[26]

Frederick Dale Bruner renders the intent of Jesus' words in more pastoral terms: Jesus knows, he says, that his mission is

> a rugged minority movement, a tough, divisive affair, and he prefers to make this clear rather than to give false hopes . . . The effect of this minority movement as it moves ag- gressively into the massive majority culture is bound to be friction. Jesus does not want his disciples to expect great triumphs and then, when persecution, hostility, and re- jection are their experience, to feel betrayed. "This is the way it goes," Jesus assures them; in fact, "this is the way I plan it to go." . . . Matthew's Jesus knows "that the most troublesome side of his faith is the painful difficulties it brings—the persecution by authorities, the ridicule by friends, [and now] the disapproval by families."[27]

That disapproval by families, as France emphasizes, was hugely exacer- bated by the shame of crucifixion, a punishment earmarked for slaves and rebels, involving not just cruelty but the scorn and mockery of

24. Tannehill, *Sword of His Mouth*, 143.

25. "Micah spoke of the threatening situation in his own day, but the passage was commonly understood in Jewish interpretation to refer to the woes of the messianic age" (France, *Gospel of Matthew*, 408–9).

26. Barton, *Discipleship and Family Ties in Mark and Matthew*, 176. Nonetheless, Barton offers eight examples of the sword as a synecdoche for war, all from Isaiah and Jeremiah.

27. Bruner, *Christbook*, 488. Bruner quotes Davies and Allison, *Critical and Exegetical Commentary*, 2:230. In the same spirit, we may recall Simeon's words to Mary and Joseph in the temple: "And a sword will pierce your own soul too" (Luke 2:35).

public disgrace, including both the fixing of the condemned man to the cross and also, beforehand, his procession through streets lined with jeering crowds.[28] France concludes, "It is not of course true that every loyal disciple will be a martyr, but all must recognize and accept the possibility of dying for Jesus, and many who have not faced literal execution have nonetheless known well the social stigma implied in carrying the cross behind Jesus."[29]

Thus the true meaning of the sword is that it marks a divide between the disciple's relationship to Jesus and all other relationships. Barton puts it thus: "The main point of the section is to show that persecution arises out of the disciple's relationship to Jesus and through him to the Father, that this relationship provides grounds for fearless endurance and witness, and will, in the end, bring sure reward."[30]

## A Contemporary Illustration

We have seen that Jesus did not, in his words about bringing a sword, condone violence. We have also seen that his words belong in an eschatological context that recognizes the divisive nature of his presence and insists that decisive choices need to be made between lesser, albeit generally appropriate, loves, and the one true focus of loyalty and devotion. But this is not enough if we are to feel the contemporary challenge of Jesus' words. What is also required is to offer a constructive illustration of what bringing not peace but a sword might mean today in the practice of Christian nonviolence. That is what I now attempt to do, by way of conclusion.

In his book *Blessed Are the Organized: Grassroots Democracy in America*, Jeffrey Stout argues that broad-based organizing has the potential to revitalize the languishing condition of democracy in the contemporary United States. Stout is intrigued to find, in Barack Obama, a man steeped in the thinking of community organizing and its key thinker, Saul Alinsky (1909–72), the founder of the Industrial Areas Foundation. Alinsky was a hugely influential and controversial figure,

28. France, *Gospel of Matthew*, 410.

29. Ibid., 411.

30. Barton, *Discipleship and Family Ties in Mark and Matthew*, 165.

whose methods centered on empowering hitherto voiceless groups through face-to-face meetings, isolating issues, never doing for a person what they could do for themselves, having no permanent allies and no permanent enemies, employing some trickster elements, and fundamentally holding public figures accountable. Obama's campaign speeches stressed the vigilant need to hold corporate and governmental officeholders accountable; the requirement for democratic change to come from the bottom up; and the necessity for democracy to express, rather than circumvent, the people's religious commitments. These are all insights drawn from Alinsky.

Barack Obama sought to graft the spirit of organizing into the politics of Washington, DC. As a young man, Obama was an organizer—but also went to law school. As president, he seeks to combine the roles of Martin Luther King Jr. (the activist) and Lyndon B. Johnson (the administrator). He seeks to be "both the stimulus of grassroots activism and the conduit of the democratic concerns he has aroused."[31]

But Stout bitterly criticizes Obama's actual practice as being either confused about bottom-up change or slyly manipulative. On Wall Street, health care, Afghanistan, and Guantanamo, among other issues, Obama's policies have come from the top down. Stout's critique is provocative, because it identifies precisely the kind of inclination to a bland peace that Jesus' words in Matt 10:34 should shake Christians out of.

This is how Stout describes what we might call Obama's "mission to bring peace": "He imagines himself as the representative of the people who genuinely want everyone to get along, who already identify their interests as converging in the common good. To them, he offers the hope that postpartisan amity, of the sort that his leadership style is designed to exemplify and to foster, will permit an inclusive, peaceable, and magnanimous society to emerge in the wake of the culture wars."[32]

My intuition is that many Christians recognize themselves in Stout's description. Indeed, many Christians who see themselves in a tradition of nonviolence identify with Barack Obama's magnanimity and desire to take a broad view. But Stout dismantles this equanimity in withering terms.

31. Stout, *Blessed Are the Organized*, 264.

32. Ibid., 270.

It should be clear that Obama's nice-guy pragmatism differs fundamentally from grassroots democracy . . . His approach to policy negotiations begins with depolarization and builds, very late in the game, to polarization, but only when a debate among ruling elites has already settled what exactly needs to be decided.

This approach reverses the pattern of grassroots citizens' organizations, which take care to exercise their own agency in defining the issue to be decided, proceed to a phase of polarization around the issue they have defined, and move to depolarization only when the fight is resolved. Both approaches rightly reject the permanent-polarization of the culture warriors, but do so in quite different ways. The practical effect of Obama's approach, his rhetoric to the contrary notwithstanding, is to eliminate accountability from political life. A politics of accountability presents politicians with precisely articulated choices designed to distinguish allies from opponents . . . Officeholders must answer for any grave injustices they have committed before the public can extend forgiveness to them and a process of reconciliation can be initiated. From the beginning, the new president demonstrated his reluctance even to name and renounce, let alone prosecute, the numerous high crimes and misdemeanors of the previous administration. For Obama, reconciliation comes first, before the reasons for being angry with tyrants and oligarchs have even been acknowledged. Accountability is thereby rendered a meaningless, ineffectual, afterthought. Accountability isn't always nice.[33]

Stout illustrates his argument from the 2009–10 health care debate. Obama tied his own hands. Instead of insisting that health care reform be addressed first by independent citizens' organizations, he permitted insurance executives to frame the issue by excluding a single-payer health care system and public insurance option. Stout offers similar examples from foreign affairs and economic policy.[34] In the terms of our

33. Ibid., 270–71.
34. Ibid., 272–74.

current inquiry, Obama withheld the sword of division, but at terrible cost: the peace of Obama is not a just peace.

The challenge of Stout's critique to Christians who wonder, "Why can't we all just get along?" is clear. Barack Obama becomes the epitome of a bland quest for peace—a naive ethic that believes that there can be peace without the sword of division.[35] For Stout, Obama's way of seeking peace fails to acknowledge and address the deep forces and histories of injustice and violence that hold contemporary American society in their grip. Stout proposes that the way to address this kind of opposition is to hold it accountable, making sure both allies and enemies are kept responsible for their commitments.

Stout's proposal, articulated most fully by Alinsky and illustrated by the early stages of the Obama presidency, offers a contemporary rendering of Jesus' words, "Do not think that I have come to bring peace to the earth; I have not come to bring peace, but a sword." Christians committed to theological nonviolence need to remember that "Why can't we all just get along?" is not a gospel question. Instead the question is, "How are we to walk in the footsteps of Christ in the presence of great good but also of genuine evil?" The answer is not a simple, blithe, "Peace!"

Jesus does not call for a sword of violence. That is not the way of peace. But sometimes a sword of division is called for. That is not the nature of peace, but it is sometimes the inevitable result of witnessing to the truth of Christ. To avoid division at all costs may sometimes be the substitution of a bland peace for a truer, more hard-earned one. Sometimes the sword of division is needed, that healing may more truly come.

35. As France writes of Jesus' ministry, "the way to peace is not the way of avoidance of conflict, and Jesus will be continuously engaged in robust controversy" (France, *Gospel of Matthew*, 408).

# 11

## What about the Centurion?
## A Roman Soldier's Faith and Christian Pacifism

Andy Alexis-Baker

CENTURIONS HAVE CAUSED A lot of trouble in Judeo-Christian history. They were the ones who maintained Rome's expansionist policies, and their presence throughout the empire ensured the smooth operation of its economic system. Rome was no democratic colonial power. Instead, it ruled over and extracted resources from other territories through bureaucratic systems of law and taxation. When a territory rebelled, soldiers suppressed the people, sometimes in the most brutal ways. Describing their cruelty, the Jewish chronicler Josephus wrote: "The soldiers out of the wrath and hatred they bore the Jews, nailed those they caught, one after one way, and another after another, to the crosses, by way of jest; when their multitude was so great, that room was wanting for the crosses, and crosses wanting for the bodies."[1] A few decades earlier, Roman soldiers used the same torture to execute Jesus, the son of God.[2]

1. Josephus, *Jewish Wars*, 5.451.

2. We should not assume that Roman soldiers were Romans. Rome had no legions stationed in Judea at the time of Jesus, having withdrawn their legion from Jerusalem in 30 BCE, expecting Herod to maintain order in the area. To do this, Herod, like

Although the Roman Empire would eventually fall, Roman soldiers' influence on history continued through interpretations of Matt
8:5–13.[3] There, Jesus encounters a centurion and by the end of the ex-
change declares the centurion to be a man of great faith. This text has
been successfully used to legitimate Christian participation in war making and to justify everything from the crusades to policing, wreaking
havoc on innumerable lives.

Around 400 CE, Augustine reasoned that Christians could take
up arms and go to war because Jesus "did not tell him [the centurion]
to leave the service."[4] His observation that Jesus did not reproach the
centurion for being a soldier nor tell him to leave the army has echoed
through Christian history ever since. Thomas Aquinas cited this story
along with Augustine's interpretation to justify Christians fighting in
war.[5] Martin Luther proclaimed, "The centurion's office was sangui-
nary business, and yet Jesus allowed him to keep the sword, lets him

---

all puppet rulers, raised auxiliary forces (comprised of Babylonian Jews, Idumeans,
and "barbarians" such as Gauls, Thracians, and Germans) that the emperor could
call upon in emergencies, but which normally functioned as Herod's army. Rome's
legions played a part only when situations became extremely volatile, such as during
the Jewish revolt from 66 to 70 CE. Yet even then, Jews from the area played an active
part in aiding the Romans. One scholar estimates that the Jewish contribution to the
Roman war effort was as high as 20 percent of the Roman forces at various points in
the conflict. In fact, the de facto leader of the Roman forces that crushed the Jewish
revolt was Tiberius Julius Alexander, who came from a prominent Jewish family in
Alexandria. He later rose to the level of Praetorian Prefect, a powerful position that
would be equivalent to US Secretary of State. See Roth, "Jewish Military Forces in
the Roman Service," 20; Turner, "Tiberius Julius Alexander," 61–64; and Schoenfeld,
"Sons of Israel in Caesar's Service," 116. Thus the centurion who approached Jesus
was probably not Roman, but from the surrounding provinces such as modern Syria.
I use the word "Roman" to describe the entire military apparatus whose allegiance
was to Rome.

3. There are several other places in the New Testament where centurions appear
besides Matt 8:5–13; 27:54; Mark 15:39–45; Luke 7:2–6; 23:47; Acts 10; 23:17–23;
24:23; 27:1, 6, 11, 31, 43. I will focus on Matthew's text so that the material is more
manageable. I will occasionally mention these and other stories from the New
Testament in the text and footnotes, but I will not treat them with the depth with
which I treat Matthew's text.

4. Augustine, *Reply to Faustus the Manichean*, 22.74–79.

5. Aquinas, *Summa Theologiae*, II-II 40.1.

carry on in his bloody office, and does not forbid him from engaging in war and pursuing his bloody tasks."[6] More recently, some Christians have used this story to justify participation in armed military interventions and police forces.[7] The centurion's story has subverted Christian nonviolence for nearly sixteen hundred years, as Jesus' silence on the centurion's profession has become a tacit endorsement of Christians becoming involved in state-sponsored killing. But, is this the best way to interpret this text?

## A Closer Look at Matthew's Text (Matt 8:5–13)

In Matthew's Gospel, a centurion approaches Jesus, asking him to cure the centurion's servant. When Jesus offers to go to the centurion's home to heal the young man, the centurion stops him and says, "Lord, I am not worthy to have you come under my roof; but only speak the word, and my servant will be healed. For I also am a man under authority, with soldiers under me; and I say to one, 'Go,' and he goes, and to another, 'Come,' and he comes, and to my slave, 'Do this,' and the slave does it" (Matt 8:8–9). Jesus, the text says, "was astonished" or "amazed" at the centurion's statement. Then he says to the people around him: "In no one in Israel have I found such faith. I tell you, many will come from east and west and will eat with Abraham and Isaac and Jacob in the kingdom of heaven, while the heirs of the kingdom will be thrown into the outer darkness, where there will be weeping and gnashing of teeth" (Matt 8:10–12). Many have taken Jesus' amazement and statement quoted above to be an affirmation of the centurion's occupation in the Roman military. But, there are several issues that call this interpretation into question.

### Jesus' Amazement at the Centurion

One of the questions often asked of Christian pacifists is why Jesus was so astonished at the centurion's words (Matt 8:10; Luke 7:9). Jesus'

6. Luther, *Faith and Freedom*, 122.

7. See, for example, Lepard, *Rethinking Humanitarian Intervention*, 85, and Brnjas, "What about Peter?," 12.

amazement seems entirely positive, they claim. But, this is a misreading. The underlying Greek word, *thaumázō*, does not necessarily connote positive approval. For example, in Matt 22:22 the Pharisees marvel at Jesus' crafty answer to their trick question about paying taxes to Caesar. Their "amazement" was anything but appreciative. Likewise, Pilate was greatly amazed at Jesus' silence (Matt 27:14; cf. Mark 15:5), and yet Pilate's amazement culminates in his ordering Jesus to be flogged and eventually executed.[8] In neither case does the marveling and amazement connote approval. The only other case in the Gospels where Jesus is said to marvel at other people is in Mark 6 (cf. Matt 13:53–58). Jesus had returned to his hometown and begun teaching and healing people. But the people begin to belittle Jesus as a mere carpenter, whose family they know. Jesus responds by saying that prophets generally have no honor in their own homes, and as a result, he was unable to heal many people. Mark states that Jesus "marveled because of their unbelief" (Mark 6:6). Jesus' amazement was certainly not a positive appraisal of his compatriots. Thus, we should not assume that Jesus' amazement at the centurion meant that he affirmed the centurion's statements.[9]

8. Scholarship on Jesus' interaction with Pilate has largely depoliticized the scene by making Pilate a helpless, indecisive pawn whom the Jews browbeat into condemning a man that Pilate is "amazed" with and believes to be innocent. See, for example, Bond, *Pontius Pilate in History and Interpretation*, 120–38. A minority of scholars, however, do not think Matthew's Gospel paints such a rosy picture of Pilate. For them, he is a bureaucrat who embodies Rome's self-interested focus and whose condemnation exposes the injustices of the Roman regime. See Ellul, *Anarchy and Christianity*, 65–71, and Weaver, "Power and Powerlessness," 454–66.

9. In the Gospels *thaumázō* is used more frequently to connote something negative than something positive: Negative uses are Matt 21:20; 22:22; 27:14; Mark 6:6; 15:5; Luke 4:22; 11:38; 20:26; 24:41; John 3:7; 4:27; 5:28; 7:15, 21. Positive uses are Matt 8:27; 9:33; 15:31; Mark 5:20; Luke 1:63; 2:18, 33; 5:20; 9:43; 11:14. Then there are uses that are more ambiguous: Matt 8:10; Mark 15:44; Luke 7:9; 8:25; 24:12. Similarly, outside of the Gospels *thaumázō* usually means something negative (Acts 3:12; 4:13; 13:41; Gal 1:6; 1 John 3:13; Jude 16; Rev 13:3; 17:6, 7, 8) as opposed to something positive (Acts 2:7; 7:31; 2 Thess 1:10). We could say that *thaumázō* is a kind of wonder "at the madness of existence." It does not necessarily connote joy or happiness, which according to Eberhard Jüngel is the "origin, the source, of the true thought of God, to the extent that joy is that 'existential' in which God is thinkable *for the sake of his own self*. For joy is always joy in something for its own sake." See Jüngel, *God as the Mystery of the World*, 192.

The Centurion's Faulty View of Jesus

The centurion's view of authority was based on a strict chain of command. He follows orders and gives orders. Jesus, he believed, also operates within this military-like chain of command. This was not an unusual assumption about Jesus. For example, when Jesus healed a mute man, the Pharisees charged that Jesus could only perform such powerful acts because he was a commanding officer in a chain of demonic beings (Matt 9:32–34).

However, there are numerous indications throughout Matthew's Gospel that Jesus rejects the centurion's chain-of-command type of authority. For instance, in the temptation stories (Matt 4:1–11), Jesus renounced the techniques of imperial authority. In the second temptation, the devil tempts Jesus to satisfy his hunger at the devil's command and thereby enter into the demonic chain of command that characterizes imperial power. The third temptation clearly links imperial power with demonic hierarchy. Satan claims to control "all the empires of this world" (4:8–9), which would include the Roman Empire. This scene juxtaposes demonic imperial power with God's purposes. Jesus resists the imperial structure and the temptation to enter into its chain of command. If Jesus had succumbed to these temptations, he would have become what the Pharisees and the centurion reckoned him to be: a glorified part of the demonic imperial chain of command. In rejecting the temptations, Jesus disclosed his intentions to be an unconventional "lord," one who sees authority very differently.

Jesus' view of authority became explicit when he denounced the system of "Gentile rulers" (Matt 20:17–28). After telling his disciples that he would be tortured and killed in Jerusalem—and inviting them to come along—Jesus told them: "You know that the rulers of the Gentiles lord it over them, and their great ones are tyrants over them. It will not be so among you; but whoever wishes to be great among you must be your servant, and whoever wishes to be first among you must be your slave; just as the Son of Man came not to be served but to serve, and to give his life a ransom for many" (Matt 20:26–28). In this passage, Jesus uses nearly the same Greek words that the centurion used to describe authority. The Gentiles "lord it over" (*katakyrieúō*) and "exercise authority" (*katexousiázō*), which parallels the centurion's words when he calls Jesus "lord" (*kyrie*) and states that he is under "authority" (*exousian*). Furthermore, the centurion claimed that as part of a chain of command, he could tell soldiers under him to come or go, and could say "to my slave, 'Do this,' and the slave does it" (Matt 8:9). But Jesus overturns this hierarchy by telling his disciples that they are to become servants and slaves like him, not people who command others. Thus, in Matthew, Jesus rejects the centurion's assumptions about who Jesus is, namely, one who "lords it over" others in the same way as military commanders.

When Jesus praises the faith of the centurion, therefore, he is not praising or endorsing the centurion's view of Jesus nor the centurion's hierarchical assumptions about how the social world should work. The centurion said one thing and acted another way. By coming to Jesus on behalf of his servant, the centurion upset the chain of command that he espoused. In his actions, but not his words, the centurion demonstrated a care for his servant that went beyond what his contemporaries would have expected. In fact, he did the opposite of what some people would have expected of him. For example, in *De Agricultura* 2.7, Cato—an influential Roman statesman who was active in politics in the second century BCE—counseled that overseers sell "worn-out" cattle and tools as well as any "old or sickly slave" as "superfluous." In moving beyond these utilitarian calculations and rigid social distinctions, the centurion acted better than his social world expected and his own words betrayed. In Jesus' immediate experience with some Pharisees, the centurion acted far more faithfully in breaking with such social norms.

## Jesus and the Centurion's Occupation

Yet in praising the centurion for his action that upset social norms for the sake of his servant, Jesus did not praise the centurion's occupation or approve of it. Jesus focused on something else. While talking to those who watched the scene unfold, Jesus says that "many will come from east and west and will eat with Abraham and Isaac and Jacob in the kingdom of heaven." Here Jesus alludes to last-things prophecies from the Hebrew Scriptures where the Gentiles are said to make a pilgrimage to Israel and learn peace. Jesus does not quote a single text, indicating that he had in mind a broad tradition of prophecy. This is what scholars call a "topos," which could be used in a variety of contexts. We are thus free to mine the prophetic texts that envision an ingathering of peoples.

The context of Jesus' statement is his encounter with a Gentile in Israel. While some people have heard in Jesus' words an exclusion of Jews, Jesus' inclusion of Abraham, Isaac, and Jacob, who were Jewish themselves, precludes such an interpretation. Moreover, many Jews had responded to Jesus' message even in his own lifetime, such as his disciples (and Jesus himself was Jewish!). Often the prophetic eschatological texts to which Jesus here refers envision Diaspora Jews returning home (Psalm 107; Isaiah 25–27; 49; Ezekiel 37–39). Thus, the "many" to which Jesus refers includes a wide variety of people—not least of which is marginalized people such as the centurion's slave.[10] In Mic 4:1–8, even those who are lame, such as the centurion's servant, are said to make the pilgrimage and become God's special instruments.

The Roman Empire had created social conditions in which many people did not have adequate access to the basic necessities of life. Although "all roads lead to Rome" in the metaphorical ideology of the empire, the resources were Rome's possession to dole out as it saw fit. But here, Jesus calls on the prophetic tradition in which all peoples would come to "eat" at a banquet.[11] No longer would people see each other as competitors for scarce resources that they must guard with centurions and violence. Indeed, the nations would no longer make weapons of war at all:

> In days to come the mountain of the Lord's house shall
> be established as the highest of the mountains, and shall
> be raised above the hills; all the nations shall stream to it.
> Many peoples shall come and say, "Come, let us go up to
> the mountain of the Lord, to the house of the God of Jacob;
> that he may teach us his ways and that we may walk in his
> paths." For out of Zion shall go forth instruction and the

10. See Carter, *Matthew and the Margin*, 203–4.

11. Regarding this banquet, we might see the Eucharist as a foretaste. It is worth noting that as a foretaste of that banquet the Eucharist replaces the killing of a lamb with the breaking of bread. It thus reconfigures the nonviolent banquet of the prophetic tradition to exclude violence toward nonhuman animals.

> word of the Lord from Jerusalem. He shall judge between
> the nations, and shall arbitrate for many peoples; they
> shall beat their swords into plowshares, and their spears
> into pruning hooks; nation shall not lift up sword against
> nation, neither shall they learn war any more. (Isa 2:2–4)

Isaiah presents a comprehensive vision for this peace that includes not only the Gentiles, but all of creation: "The wolf shall live with the lamb, the leopard shall lie down with the kid, the calf and the lion and the fatling together" (Isa 11:6). This amazing vision of a comprehensive peace ensues because the nations seek the Messiah: "the root of Jesse shall stand as a signal to the peoples; the nations shall inquire of him" (Isa 11:10).

The Messiah would bring about a peaceable kingdom, but not through warfare. In these visions, God "makes wars cease to the end of the earth" (Ps 46:9) and "smites the violent with the rod of his mouth and the breath of his lips will slay the wicked" (Isa 11:4). Wars will end through God's word and Spirit, not through further violence. Furthermore, the kind of Messiah that would come would not be a king in the normal sense. Riding a donkey rather than a warhorse, this "humble" Messiah would take away the weapons of the nations and Israel and "command peace to the nations" (Zech 9:10).

Furthermore, in the Gospels, Jesus taught such things as "blessed are the peacemakers" (Matt 5:9) and neither to return violence for violence nor to resist violence: "but if anyone strikes you on the right cheek, turn the other also" (Matt 5:39). In the passion narratives when Peter used his sword to injure a man trying to apprehend Jesus, Jesus told him, "Put your sword back into its place; for all who take the sword will perish by the sword. Do you think that I cannot appeal to my Father, and he will at once send me more than twelve legions of angels?" (Matt 26:52–53). Messianic expectation for the end of war and the beginning of peace, as well as Jesus' teaching and example in the Gospel narratives, point to the fact that Jesus did not approve of this soldier's occupation.

All of this is in the background of Jesus' words about the centurion. When the centurion comes to Jesus, despite his inadequate ideas of authority, he begins to participate in this process. The text does not tell us what happened to the centurion after this. Did he become a disciple of Jesus? Did he go away confirmed in his view of Jesus as a typical wonder-worker without changing his life? We do not know. But in this moment of encounter, Jesus wanted to highlight that the messianic age, which is inextricably bound up with the end of war and the beginning of peace, has begun. The point of this narrative in Matthew is to indicate that the messianic age had begun. Though Jesus was silent about the soldier's occupation in this small passage, peace pervades the passage through messianic expectation and the surrounding context of the Gospel.

### The Argument from Silence Fallacy

Augustine and those who followed him argued their case from Jesus' silence, not from what he actually says in the text. We can justify anything from such reasoning. Since Jesus did not rebuke Pilate for being a governor of an occupying force, he must have sanctioned the Roman occupation and their right to exploit weaker nations, and by extension all colonial and military expansions. Since he did not ask Zacchaeus to leave his job as a tax collector, he must have approved of Roman tax collection and their right to drain resources from an area to the wealthy elite in Rome. Since Jesus did not admonish Pilate for murdering some Galileans in the midst of their sacrifices (Luke 13:3), he sanctioned police brutality and severe repressive measures. Since Jesus did not tell the judges at his own trial that they were wrong for their irregular court proceedings, he sanctions kangaroo courts and dictatorships today. Since Jesus did not reprove the centurion for owning slaves, he therefore condones slavery, even today. These arguments from silence can make Jesus to be the advocate of whatever we want. At one moment he sanctions aggressive warfare, and at the same time he sanctions defensive military action. At another moment he sanctions police brutality and kangaroo courts, at another law and order. Arguments from silence allow Jesus to sanction nearly anything and to contradict himself. The point is that we have to base our analysis of this text on what Jesus says to the centurion, on the entire narrative that Matthew weaves, and even more broadly, on the picture that the New Testament paints of Jesus in regard to nonviolence.[12]

## Early Christian Practices

The interpretation I have offered better comports with how the earliest Christians viewed occupations within the Roman military. For example, second-century Syrian Christian Tatian said, "I don't want to be a king; I don't desire to be rich; I refuse military service."[13] Tertullian, however, was the first individual theologian to deeply examine in writing the question of whether a Christian should be employed in the military: "Is it likely we are permitted to carry a sword when our Lord said that he who takes the sword will perish by the sword? Will the son of peace who is forbidden to engage in a lawsuit espouse the deeds of war? Will a Christian, taught to turn the other cheek when struck unjustly, guard prisoners in chains, and administer torture and capital punishment?"[14] He defined the military as the "enemy" and declared that being employed as a soldier was "to leave the camp of light and enlist in the camp of darkness."[15] Tertullian's statement covered all the soldier's duties from guarding prisoners to killing them (which would preclude modern occupations in police forces or prisons). He addressed the objection that Jesus praised the Capernaum soldier's faith by stating, "Once we have embraced the faith and have been baptized, we either must immediately leave military service (as many have done); or we must resort to all kinds of excuses in order to avoid any action which is also forbidden in civilian life, lest we offend God; or, last of all, for the sake of God we must suffer the fate which a mere citizen-faith was no less ready to

---

12. Jean Lasserre develops this argument in *War and the Gospel*, 53–54. We can apply this same logic to Peter's visit to the home of Cornelius, a centurion, in Acts 10. It is an argument from silence to claim that because Peter did not reprimand the soldier he therefore approved of soldiering. But this has no more validity than to claim that James approved of prostitution because he praised the faith of Rahab (Jas 2:25).

13. Tatian, *Oration to the Greeks*, 11.1. See also 19.2 and 23.12. Translation from the Greek is mine from *Oratio adversus Græcos*, col. 829.

14. Tertullian, *Chaplet*, 11.2.

15. Ibid., 11.4.

accept."[16] Tatian and Tertullian's judgment against soldiering was widely shared in the first three hundred years of Christianity and even beyond.

Perhaps the most compelling and widespread document of the early church forbidding military service was the third-century church order, the *Apostolic Tradition*, which regulated church life. It was repeatedly copied and translated into at least four different languages across the Roman Empire and beyond. In a section providing guidance for teachers screening people for their suitability as potential catechumens, the *Apostolic Tradition* states: "A soldier in command must be told not to kill people; if he is ordered so to do, he shall not carry it out. Nor should he take the oath. If he will not agree, he should be rejected. Anyone who has the power of the sword, or who is a civil magistrate wearing the purple, should desist, or he should be rejected. If a catechumen or a believer wishes to become a soldier they should be rejected, for they have despised God."[17]

As church leaders evaluated a candidate's suitability for joining the Christian church, they asked questions about their lifestyles and occupations to determine whether the prospective catechumen was "able to hear the word."[18] The early Christians judged that those in military service who were willing to kill were not able to comprehend the gospel and conform to its demands, including martyrdom. For this reason, any Christian who attempted to enlist in the military would be excommunicated, because "they have despised God." The text makes clear that the primary issue here is killing. The *Apostolic Tradition* does, however, assume that it might be possible for a soldier-convert to remain in the military, at least for a time, and not kill. Of course, this document rubs up against the more stringent statements of Tertullian, which I quoted above. Nevertheless, the *Apostolic Tradition* clearly states that if orders were to come down for a soldier to kill, he must refuse and accept the

16. Ibid.

17. *Apostolic Tradition*, 16. This is Alistair Stewart-Sykes' translation in *On the Apostolic Tradition*, 100.

18. *Apostolic Tradition*, 15. For a study of the early Christian catechumenate, its impact on Christian belief, belonging and behavior, and how it shifted over time see Kreider, *The Change of Conversion and the Origin of Christendom*.

military's punishment of death. We should not anachronistically assume that the early church approved of Christian violence in police forces.[19]

The early Christian practice of excluding converts from military occupations lasted well past the Constantinian compromise in the early fourth century.[20] For example, in about 400 CE Paulinus of Nola wrote to a young military convert urging him to stop being a soldier because such a life is incompatible with Christian discipleship.

> Do not any longer love this world or its military service, for Scripture's authority attests that "whoever is a friend of this world is an enemy of God." He who is a soldier with the sword is the servant of death, and when he sheds his own blood or that of another, this is the reward for his service. He will be regarded as guilty of death either because of his own death or because of his sin, because a soldier in war, fighting not so much for himself as for another, is either conquered and killed, or conquers and wins a pretext for death—for he cannot be a victor unless

19. Some have interpreted early Christian interactions with soldiers to mean that the Roman military functioned as a police force and Jesus endorsed this more restrained form of state violence. This is anachronistic, however, because police forces are a modern institution. The typical Greek or Roman *polis* had neither a police force nor a standing army available to quiet disturbances, enforce contracts, or apprehend criminals; citizens themselves performed these tasks. One catches a glimpse of this arrangement in Acts 21 where Paul's presence in the temple caused some people to cry out, "Men of Israel, help . . ." This was the common cry made by anyone who had been victimized. When someone called for help in this way, everyone nearby was expected to aid the person. Thus a crowd aided the men and dragged Paul out of the temple and began to beat him. Responding to what sounded and looked like a riot, the military commander gathered some soldiers in order to quell a potentially unsettling disturbance (Acts 21:31). The authorities' response exhibits the fact that throughout the empire the military's function was to suppress riots and rebellions, not to arrest people for crime. In *Public Order in Ancient Rome*, Wilfried Nippel goes so far as to state that "we do not even know to what degree (if at all) the Roman authorities undertook prosecution of murder" (2). We should not anachronistically assume that the early church approved of Christian violence in police forces. For more on this see my articles: Alexis-Baker, "The Gospel or a Glock?"; "Community, Policing and Violence"; "Just Policing"; and "Policing and Christian Forgiveness."

20. On the "Constantinian" shift that moved Christian discipleship away from nonviolence see Yoder, *Christian Attitudes to War, Peace, and Revolution*, 42–74.

he first sheds blood. So the Lord says: "You cannot serve two masters," the one God and mammon, that is, Christ and Caesar, even though Caesar himself is now keen to be Christ's servant so that he may deserve kingship over a few peoples. For it is not some earthly king who reigns over the whole world, but Christ God, for "all things were made by Him and without Him was made nothing. He is King of kings and Lord of lords. Whatever He pleases He does in earth, in the sea, in the deeps."[21]

By the beginning of the fifth century, Paulinus' view of military occupations had become a minority viewpoint amongst Christian theologians. Yet this minority voice echoed the earlier Christian model, which did not see Jesus' interaction with the centurion at Capernaum as an excuse for Christians to become soldiers or to kill. In addition to biblical analysis, that early Christian practice and theology around the Roman military should be a guide for interpreting the centurion's story.

## Conclusion

The question of why Jesus did not call the centurion to immediately leave his post has been put to pacifists throughout Christian history. Whether the question has been meant to justify Christian participation in warfare or policing, the results have been to undermine Christian nonviolence and peacemaking. The later Christian understanding of the text has too easily led to a positive assessment of the centurion's statements without accounting for the larger context in which Jesus explicitly rejects the centurion's view of authority. Furthermore, this interpretation has missed the way in which Jesus' interaction with the centurion points to an eschatological peace in which soldiers come from east and west to "beat their swords into plowshares." However, the biblical text does not support Christians being in occupations that employ violence.

Arguing from silence to a resounding affirmation of killing, theologians have justified virtually everything with such readings. Yet this

21. Paulinus of Nola, *Letter* 24, *To Crispinianus*. The translation is from *Letters of St. Paulinus of Nola*, 73.

did not and does not have to be. Early Christian practices and interpretations of this text show that a door was and is open for us to call upon soldiers to accept the costly grace of discipleship. Why didn't Jesus call the centurion to leave his job? Tertullian answered for Christian nonviolence: "the Lord, in disarming Peter, *disarmed* every soldier."[22]

22. Tertullian, *De Idolatria*, 19.

# 12

## Didn't Jesus Overturn Tables and Chase People Out of the Temple with a Whip?

John Dear

MAHATMA GANDHI CONSIDERED JESUS the most active person of non-violence in the history of the world. He was dismayed, however, that so few Christians understood or embraced Jesus' nonviolence. "I like your Christ," he once said, "but your Christians are so unlike your Christ."

Martin Luther King Jr. considered the Hindu Gandhi the best modern disciple of this nonviolent Jesus because Gandhi so spectacularly adhered to Jesus' teachings of nonviolence, applying them even to the national and international levels, perhaps for the first time. Both Gandhi and King insisted that everything Jesus did was nonviolent, that his teachings comprised a veritable catechism of nonviolence, and that the way he faced his execution was the epitome of nonviolence. If we want to follow him, they taught, we, too, must be nonviolent.

When I speak to church congregations about the nonviolent Jesus, the question inevitably arises, "Yes, but didn't Jesus overturn tables and chase people out of the Temple with a whip? Isn't that violent?" Many remember El Greco's unhelpful painting *Christ Cleansing the Temple*, where Jesus raises his arm high into the air, his hand grasping a long whip, ready to strike a group of people, including terrified women.

In each instance, I find myself saying: El Greco was wrong. Jesus did not use violence. He never hurt anyone. He never struck anyone. He never killed anyone. He did not tolerate injustice, greed, hypocrisy, or untruth. He confronted systemic injustice head on, as his disciples Dorthy Day and Martin Luther King Jr. would later do. He gave his life for God's reign of justice and peace, but he always did so through meticulous nonviolence.

Our problem is that the nonviolent Jesus was decidedly not passive. He did not sit under a tree and practice his breathing. He walked regularly into the face of danger, spoke the truth, and demanded justice. As far as decent, law-abiding, religious people were concerned, he was nothing but trouble. He hung out with the wrong people, healed at the wrong time, visited the wrong places, and said the wrong things. His nonviolence was active, provocative, public, daring, and dangerous. Most of Jesus' actions were illegal. He committed civil disobedience on an almost daily basis. That's why I've begun to think of him as a one-man crime wave walking through the Roman Empire, beginning the process of disarmament wherever he went.

The story has become so warped for the benefit of the ruling elite that we forget that Jesus was executed by the empire as a terrorist. Indeed, he was a revolutionary, but a nonviolent revolutionary.

As far as I can tell, only four events appear in all four Gospels: the multiplication of the loaves and fishes; his street theater entrance into Jerusalem; his dramatic civil disobedience in the temple; and his execution on the cross. (The risen Jesus does not appear in Mark's Gospel; we only hear of an empty tomb.)

Mark, Matthew, and Luke present the same basic storyline. Jesus organizes the poor and disenfranchised in Galilee. Then he turns, sets his face to Jerusalem, and starts a walking campaign of nonviolence right into the temple, where he engages in peaceful civil disobedience. For this he is arrested, tried, tortured, and executed.

The Synoptic Gospels tell how Jesus turns over the tables of the money changers and the seats of those who were selling doves, and drives out those selling and buying. Mark says he did not permit anyone to carry anything through the temple area. Then he started to teach the crowds. "Is it not written," he asks in Mark, "'My house shall be called a house of prayer for all peoples'? But you have made it a den of thieves" (11:17).

There is no mention of a whip, no talk of violence, no report of anyone being hurt. The whole event probably lasted five minutes. It would have stunned the crowds, who apparently stayed to hear his message. As anyone who has engaged in nonviolent civil disobedience knows, this was a classic example of symbolic, nonviolent direct action.

And it needed to be done. The Jerusalem Temple, built by Herod Antipas at the beginning of the century, was held up as the one and only place where God dwelt. We have nothing quite like it today. It combined worship, commerce, local government, execution site, and imperial control. It would resemble some massive building in Washington, DC, containing the Pentagon, the US Capitol, the White House, Wall Street, the World Bank, Citibank, Goldman Sachs, Walmart, the National Cathedral, and the Shrine of the Immaculate Conception—all rolled into one, as God's home on earth.

The faithful were expected to pay God a visit in the temple each year, so every Passover they made the long trek to Jerusalem and paid a hefty fee to enter God's sanctuary. The population tripled to over 180,000. Over eighteen thousand lambs would be purchased and slaughtered for holy sacrifice in the temple. A heavy tax was charged for all of this commerce. In effect, the temple housed a national bank, hawked loans, tracked debts, and changed money for unclean sinners so they could pay with "holy" temple money. Special fees were added for this money changing. Women, poor people, and other outcasts had to purchase expensive doves so that they could be "purified" to offer worship. The various fees robbed the poor and did so in God's name under the watchful, greedy eye of the Roman Empire.[1]

Anyone who cared about justice or read the prophets would be outraged at such institutionalized injustice. It was only natural that Jesus took action to protest this big corporate, imperial, religious rip-off.

As commentators note, Jesus did not merely want lower prices for the poor. He did not seek to reform the temple. Through his symbolic action, he called for an end to the entire temple system. He taught a new, authentic worship of the living God. In Mark, Jesus urges his disciples

1. As commentators such as Ched Myers in *Binding the Strong Man* note.

to live in faith, pray all the time, and forgive those who have hurt them every time they pray. This simple plan was Jesus' spiritual practice for a new world beyond the temple cult. With this action, he announced that God was present within every person; present whenever two or three gathered to pray in his name; present in the hungry, sick, or imprisoned; present in the breaking of the bread and the passing of the cup; present in Spirit and in Truth.

Jesus' action and those teachings threatened and outraged the religious authorities. Their economic and political privilege would end if his teachings were adopted, so they had him killed.

Certainly, Jesus' action in the temple is the boldest political event in the entire Bible. And, it has been duly ignored and misunderstood for two thousand years. Mark's version (11:11–26) notes that Jesus first entered the temple, looked around, left, returned the next day and then took action. Only those who have undertaken civil disobedience with a steadfast commitment to nonviolence could understand that sentence: Jesus was casing the joint! He wanted to see for himself what was happening, plan his action, pray over it, and be perfectly nonviolent.

Jesus did not turn over the tables in an outburst of anger. His act was premeditated nonviolence following his initial reconnaissance. As one who has been arrested many times for acts of nonviolent civil disobedience, I understand that need to prepare oneself thoroughly if one intends to be nonviolent. This detail from Mark, for me, proves the nonviolence of Jesus in the temple.

The only mention of a "rope" or a "whip" is in John's Gospel, written decades after the Synoptics. While Mark, Matthew, and Luke tell a similar story, John changes the entire plotline. He begins the Gospel with Jesus' nonviolent direct action in the temple (John 2:13–26). Written twenty to forty years after the Synoptics, John has a completely different agenda. His Gospel describes various signs and wonders, offers a series of self-descriptive "I am" sayings, and culminates his Gospel with the dramatic raising of Lazarus from the dead. With that, he takes us to the Last Supper, where Jesus offers a lengthy reflection and teaching before his arrest.

Throughout John's Gospel, like the others, Jesus is perfectly nonviolent. Indeed, he speaks more often here than the other gospels about nonviolent love—agape—the Greek word for "unconditional, non-retaliatory, universal, sacrificial love." It's in John that Jesus announces the heart of nonviolence—"No one has greater love [agape] than this, to lay down one's life for one's friends."

John's story begins with the miraculous changing of water into wine during the wedding at Cana, a sign that all ritual, religious cleansings are now abolished and God's reign,[2] an eternal wedding banquet of agape, has begun. Jesus then suddenly appears in Jerusalem during the Passover feast to continue this work of abolishing the religious cult. He enters the temple area, "makes a whip of cords" and drives out the oxen, sheep, doves, and everyone else.

> He found in the temple area those who sold oxen, sheep and doves, as well as the money-changers seated there. He made a whip of cords and drove them all out of the temple area, with the sheep and oxen, and spilled the coins of the money-changers and overturned their tables, and to those who sold doves, he said, "Take these out of here and stop making my Father's house a marketplace." His disciples recalled the words of scripture, "Zeal for your house will consume me." At this the Judeans answered and said to him, "What sign can you show us for doing this?" Jesus answered and said to them, "Destroy this temple and in three days, I will raise it up." The Judeans said, "This temple has been under construction for forty-six years, and you will raise it up in three days?" But he was speaking about the temple of his body. Therefore, when he was raised from the dead, his disciples remembered that he had said this, and they came to believe the scripture and the word Jesus had spoken. (John 2:14–22)

Most scholars agree that John deliberately paints Jesus as a righteous prophet in the tradition of Jeremiah, who engaged in similar dramatic actions. John's readers would immediately recognize Jesus as a great prophet who comes directly out of the prophetic tradition.

2. Most scholars, such as Wes Howard-Brook in *Becoming Children of God*, present this conclusion.

My Scripture professor at the Jesuit School of Theology in Berkeley, California, told us that this reference to a "rope" or a "whip" was the only instance in the entire Bible for that particular obscure Greek word.[3] To get thousands of sheep, oxen, and doves into this enormous structure, my professor explained, cattlemen and shepherds used cords and ropes to lead animals up the high stone walkways into the building. Jesus simply took those cords, which the cattle, sheep, and oxen would have recognized, and started to drive them outside. Then he overturned the bankers' tables and launched into his speech.

But didn't he take a rope or a whip and start striking people? Some translations would have you believe so, but my Scripture professor said, "No." That would be entirely inconsistent with the Jesus portrayed throughout John's Gospel, as well as the Synoptics. Jesus was nonviolent from Cana to the cross and back to Galilee—but he was a bold revolutionary. With such spectacular nonviolence, one cannot imagine Jesus even striking the poor animals. Indeed, he was liberating them from their impending execution!

Misinterpretation of this one word has been used to justify countless massacres, crusades, wars, and even the US nuclear annihilations of Hiroshima and Nagasaki. Perhaps we want Jesus to have some trace of violence in order to justify our own violence. We desperately hope he was violent so that we can dismiss his teachings, wage war, and build nuclear weapons without any guilt.

The key lies in John's punch line: "Destroy this temple and I will raise it up in three days" (2:19). John's version has a different agenda. For John, Jesus is the new temple, and it will rise. The focus is on Jesus' resurrection. If the climactic action of Jesus' life, in John's testimony, is the raising of Lazarus, then Jesus' allusion to resurrection here at the start makes sense. As I wrote in my book *Lazarus, Come Forth!*,[4] Lazarus represents the entire human race, which Jesus calls out of the culture of war, empire, and death into the new life of resurrection. With this prophetic action in the temple, Jesus points to himself right from the start as "the Resurrection."

3. Rev. John Boyle, SJ.
4. Published by Orbis Books (2011).

Later, during his arrest, trial, torture, and execution, Jesus remains nonviolent. He forgave his killers and surrendered himself into the hands of his beloved Father. His nonviolence cannot be doubted, I submit, if we read through these shocking passion accounts. He displays no trace of violence, vengeance, retaliation, or even anger.

With this in mind, I think we are asking the wrong question. The real question is, "What does Jesus' dramatic illegal, nonviolent direct action against systemic injustice mean for us, his followers? If Jesus gave his life to confront temple injustice, what would he want his followers to do today in the face of the Pentagon, Los Alamos, the School of the Americas, or other US military institutions?"

I think Jesus expects his followers to undertake similar bold, nonviolent action. He would want us to go to our own Jerusalems, turn over the tables of injustice, and speak out for justice and peace. Not only would he expect us to be people of contemplative prayer, he would insist that we be people of creative nonviolence who resist injustice and work for God's reign of peace, come what may.

That is why Jesus' greatest followers have undertaken similar campaigns of active nonviolence and civil disobedience. Mahatma Gandhi marched to the sea, picked up the illegal salt, and announced India's revolution. Dr. King marched illegally in downtown Birmingham on Good Friday, 1963, to bring down the evil US segregation laws. Dorothy Day was repeatedly arrested in the early 1960s for refusing to go underground during New York City's nuclear air raid drills. Daniel and Philip Berrigan and seven others entered the Catonsville, Maryland, draft center in May, 1968, took hundreds of A-1 draft piles, dumped them in the parking lot and burned them with homemade napalm to protest the US war in Vietnam. Such nonviolent actions continued Jesus' campaign of nonviolent civil disobedience. All of these peacemakers were misunderstood and accused of being violent, just as Jesus was, even though they practiced meticulous nonviolence whenever they acted publicly.

Because of Jesus' nonviolent civil disobedience in the temple, I have engaged in civil disobedience actions and have been arrested over seventy-five times at US military and nuclear bases around the nation. In my first arrest, in April, 1984, I sat down in the doorways of the riverside entrance to the Pentagon. My sit-in lasted only a few minutes. I hit no one and yelled at no one. I was quickly surrounded by a dozen armed policemen and soldiers, and then arrested. (Later, a judge found me guilty but refused to put me in prison.) Still, hundreds of people gathered to watch me. One could say that like Jesus, I prevented people from coming and going. It was a peaceful, prayerful, symbolic act. As I later told the judge, I was just trying to follow the nonviolent, civilly disobedient Jesus.

The Gospels portray Jesus of Nazareth as the most active person of nonviolence in the history of the world. He taught a glorious vision of nonviolence: "Love your enemies. Blessed are the peacemakers. Put down your sword. Be as compassionate as God. Hunger and thirst for justice. Seek first God's reign and God's justice." As his followers, we are forbidden to support war, killings, executions, nuclear weapons, corporate greed, environmental destruction, or violence of any kind. More, we are sent into the culture of violence and war on a mission of prophetic peacemaking and active nonviolent resistance to evil.

If we want to follow this daring nonviolent Jesus, I suggest that we confront our own unjust institutions, even to the point of nonviolent civil disobedience, in pursuit of God's reign of justice and peace. We too may be misunderstood and persecuted, even arrested and jailed. But if we can maintain the steadfast nonviolent love of Jesus, then God's reign will breakthrough again, and we will herald the coming of a new world without war, poverty, injustice, or nuclear weapons, a whole new world of loving nonviolence. Then, we will have learned a faith, one not worth killing for, but worth living for.

# 13

## What about the Warrior Jesus in Revelation 19: "He Has Trampled Out the Vintage"?

J. Nelson Kraybill

Then I saw heaven opened, and there was a white horse! Its rider is called Faithful and True, and in righteousness he judges and makes war. His eyes are like a flame of fire, and on his head are many diadems; and he has a name inscribed that no one knows but himself. He is clothed in a robe dipped in blood, and his name is called The Word of God. And the armies of heaven, wearing fine linen, white and pure, were following him on white horses. From his mouth comes a sharp sword with which to strike down the nations, and he will rule them with a rod of iron; he will tread the wine press of the fury of the wrath of God the Almighty. On his robe and on his thigh he has a name inscribed, "King of kings and Lord of lords." (Rev 19:11–16).

WHAT ARE PERSONS WHO experience the love and forgiveness of Jesus to make of a passage in Revelation that portrays Christ armed with a sword, going into battle? For that matter, how are we to understand the entire book of Revelation, with its depictions of violence or outright vengeance?

Novelist D. H. Lawrence railed against Revelation as a "grandiose scheme . . . of flamboyant hate and a simple lust . . . for the end of the world."[1] More recently, historian James Carroll stated that "the so-called New Testament, in its dominant interpretations, puts forward a punishing, violent God." He adds that "in no text of the entire Bible is God's violence, and the violence of Christ himself, more powerfully on display than in the New Testament's denouement, the book of Revelation, also (and more tellingly) known as the Apocalypse."[2]

I wince when I read such blithe and scathing dismissals of Revelation, because I find in Revelation a Lord who is redemptive, just, and loving. To be sure, countless interpreters, from sixteenth-century reformers to the authors of the recent *Left Behind* series, have used Revelation to portray God as vindictive. While no one can miss the suffering and violence that recur throughout Revelation, it is simplistic to read Revelation as validation of divine or human violence against creatures of the earth. Rather, we should read Revelation as reassurance that God has chosen to act and redeem in the midst of a messed-up world.

## A Protest against the Civil War

The founder of the church where I am pastor[3] was John F. Funk, who was a businessman in Chicago during the US Civil War (1861–65). Funk risked his business career by visiting Confederate prisoners held at nearby Camp Douglas and by daring in 1863 to publish a booklet in which he rejected Christian participation in the "legalized murder and robbery" of warfare. "We cannot pray for the destruction of our fellow men," Funk wrote, "even though they be our enemies, for Christ says, 'Love your enemies.'"[4] Funk used the Sermon on the Mount, with its ethic of love and forgiveness, as the hermeneutical key with which to interpret other parts of the Bible.

---

1. Lawrence, *Apocalypse*, 80.
2. Carroll, *Jerusalem, Jerusalem*, 45.
3. Prairie Street Mennonite Church in Elkhart, Indiana, founded by Funk in 1871.
4. Funk, *Warfare*, 1.

## Origins of "The Battle Hymn of the Republic"

While John Funk was in Chicago arguing against war, a poet named Julia Ward Howe watched Union troops marshaling in Washington, DC. Drawing heavily from Scripture—especially the book of Revelation—she penned "The Battle Hymn of the Republic," which begins:

> Mine eyes have seen the glory of the coming of the Lord:
>
> He is trampling out the vintage where the grapes of wrath are stored;
>
> He hath loosed the fateful lightning of His terrible swift sword:
>
> His truth is marching on.

The "coming of the Lord" is a common translation of the New Testament word *parousia,* often understood in popular theology as the "second coming" of Christ in judgment. Although the Greek word *parousia* does not appear in Revelation, the certainty of Christ's imminent return is pervasive in John's vision. Violence and retributive judgment seem to attend the (imminent) appearance of Christ, who arrives on the kind of white horse that was iconic of military conquerors in the first-century Roman world: "Then I saw heaven opened, and there was a white horse! Its rider is called Faithful and True, and in righteousness he judges and makes war . . ." (19:11).

## The Sword Is the Word of God

Though not specifically named, we recognize Jesus in this passage by the titles "Faithful and True" (see 3:14), and by the symbolism that John already has attached to Christ: his eyes are like a flame of fire (1:14), and a sword issues from his mouth (1:16). If the Jesus of Revelation 19 were engaging in literal warfare, his sword would be used to hack enemies. But Christians in the first century had already established the sword as a figure of the word of God (Eph 6:17; Heb 4:12). The fact that the sword Jesus bears in Revelation comes from his mouth indicates that John of Patmos is referring to the *spoken word of God.* It was sheer divine will that ended primordial chaos and created the cosmos through God's spoken word at the beginning of time (Genesis 1). Now the sheer will of God, through Jesus the Word, will end the darkness of malevolent empire and bring in the new heaven and new earth.

This is not to suggest that evil is left unscathed in God's design. But most of what gets destroyed in Revelation 19 are *structures* of evil—political and economic systems of the Roman Empire, which in John's view had been utterly corrupted by emperor worship and unbridled greed.[5] Ultimately it is the devil, the beast (of idolatrous empire), and the false prophet (the ideology of imperialism and emperor worship) that get thrown into the lake of fire (20:10). We need feel no sympathy or regret for the demise of these spiritual forces and ideological manifestations of evil; they are not human beings!

If "nations" (*ethne*) get struck down the by rider on the white horse (19:15), we might understand this as the end of corrupt regional governing systems or the end of nationalism. It is, after all, nations (*ethne*) that have been deceived by the sorcery of Babylon (18:23). Whatever it means for Christ to strike the nations, it does not signal wholesale slaughter.[6] The blood on Christ's garment (19:13) is not that of enemies; it is his own, shed at Calvary to redeem the world.[7] Paradox imbedded in this imagery suggests something other than simple retribution: the nations (*ethne*) that get "struck down" will someday walk by the light of the new Jerusalem (21:24)! The agent of this restoration is the Lamb, whose redemptive power makes him worthy of praise. Just as Domitian added new titles to his name after conquest, Christ bears the new title "King of kings and Lord of lords" (19:16). Allegiance to Jesus displaces ("strikes down") allegiance to every other political entity that would be king or lord in our lives.

---

5. See my recent book, *Apocalypse and Allegiance*, 53–69, 139–155.

6. In 14:9–11 there are humans who appear to face eternal torment—but it is the Lamb who presides in this improbable scene! I read these verses as cathartic: John is expressing rage at the oppressors and idolaters of his world. He is right to articulate such anger in a worship setting and to let the Lamb exact punishment—the same Lamb who repeatedly loved and forgave enemies. The overall trajectory of Revelation is redemption and restoration, not retribution.

7. Note that blood is on the rider's garment *before the battle begins,* strengthening the argument that this is Jesus' own blood from the cross.

Immediately after the appearance of the equestrian Christ, we see the political/military establishment of the Roman Empire getting devoured at a ghastly banquet. Buzzards circle at the feast to eat the flesh of kings, captains, and horses with their riders (19:17–18). The military-industrial complex will end! Lest we think that this is literal human dismemberment, John later points out that even kings of the earth will enter the new Jerusalem (21:24). Kings of the earth are the worst of the rogues in Revelation, having been in bed with harlot Babylon (18:9)—and God's grace is so big that they somehow experience redemption!

## Redeeming Revelation

James Carroll reminds us in the quote already cited that *apocalypse*—the first word of Revelation in Greek—today often just means cataclysmic violence and destruction. But in John's day, *apocalypse* simply referred to the *uncovering* or *revealing* of something. What Revelation reveals is that the Roman Empire is aligned with forces of greed, death, and idolatry. More importantly, Revelation reveals that God is very much in control of the universe and has chosen to redeem a war-torn and sin-weary world through the unlikely agency of Jesus the Lamb.

Referring to Jesus as the Lamb is confessional poetry, to be taken as true but not literal; we will not get to heaven to discover that Jesus is a sheep. And because of everything we know about Jesus from elsewhere in Revelation and the rest of the New Testament, it is unlikely that we should take the warrior image of Jesus in Revelation literally. What is true about Revelation 19 is the good news that God through Christ has destroyed or soon will destroy structural, systemic, and pervasive evil in our world.

## The Lamb as Governing Image

To understand *how* God destroys evil, we must rely on the governing imagery that John of Patmos uses for Jesus—and that is the image of Jesus as the Lamb. John seems keenly aware of the paradoxical nature of the Lamb's power. We see this when John is before the throne of God, weeping because no one is worthy to open the scroll (which apparently contains God's plan for or foreknowledge of the trajectory of history). John is told not to weep, because "the Lion of the Tribe of Judah" has conquered. But when John looks up, he sees not a ferocious predator but *a Lamb standing as if it had been slaughtered* (5:6). This verse more than any other is the hermeneutical key to understanding violence in Revelation: amidst the chaos and war and destruction of our world, God has chosen to intervene in the form of a vulnerable Lamb.[8]

The word "Lamb" appears twenty-seven times, in twelve of the twenty-two chapters of Revelation. Jesus the Lamb is the "shepherd" of God's people (7:17), and the saints *follow him* wherever he goes (14:4). Christians hold citizenship in the new Jerusalem, where the Lamb is the "lamp" guiding them (21:23). If readers of Revelation still wonder whether they ever should take up weapons, even in the face of lethal persecution, John inserts this aside: "If you are to be taken captive, into captivity you go; if you kill with the sword, with the sword you must be killed. Here is a call for the endurance and faith of the saints" (13:10).

Christians are to respond to evil and suffering not with violence, but with the "faithful endurance" of unwavering loyalty to Jesus and the way of the cross. We are to be engaged enough in political, economic, and social struggles of the world that we might face death—without ever becoming agents of violence ourselves. "Take up your cross and follow," Jesus told inquirers before he went, lamb-like, to Golgotha (Mark 8:34). "I am sending you out like lambs into the midst of wolves," he told his disciples when he taught them how to take the gospel to the world (Luke 10:3). "Let the same mind be in you that was in Christ Jesus," Paul told his readers (Phil 2:5), portraying Jesus' nature as that of a slave. God will bring an end to evil, and the risen Christ is the primary agent and ethical model for the restoration of creation. From the transforming power of Dr. Martin Luther King Jr. in the 1960s to the fall of corrupt governments in the Arab Spring of 2011, we have seen fundamental change in our own era that is not based in violence.

8. For a thorough treatment of this theme, see Johns, *Lamb Christology of the Apocalypse of John*.

## License to Kill?

Revelation's imagery of the demise of evil is unsettling, with the picture of Christ in a blood-drenched robe treading out the "wine press of the fury of the wrath of God" (19:11–16). Julia Ward Howe appropriated this image as the Lord "trampling out the vintage where the grapes of wrath are stored."

Generations of Americans have heard that phrase as license for *us* to exact revenge on enemies. The "Battle Hymn of the Republic" was played on September 14, 2001, at Washington National Cathedral and at Westminster Abbey during memorial services for the victims of the September 11 attacks—the preamble to multiple wars launched by the United States and England.

Even the sacrificial death of Jesus on the cross morphs into validation of human warfare in the "Battle Hymn":

> I have read a fiery gospel writ in burnished rows of steel:
> "As ye deal with my contemners,[9] so with you my grace shall deal;
> Let the Hero, born of woman, crush the serpent the with his heel,
> Since God is marching on."
>
> In the beauty of the lilies Christ was born across the sea,
> With a glory in His bosom that transfigures you and me:
> As He died to make men holy, let us die to make men free,[10]
> While God is marching on.

## Only God and the Lamb Have Coercive Authority

Just as Julia Ward Howe had marching Union soldiers in view when she wrote "The Battle Hymn of the Republic," John of Patmos had access to

---

9. "Contemners" is an archaic word for persons who hold something or someone in contempt.

10. Today most versions of this hymn change the wording to "let us *live* to make men free."

abundant military imagery in the first-century Roman world. But Howe and John of Patmos *appropriate military imagery of their respective eras to opposite ends:* Howe uses imagery from the Bible and the Civil War to summon Christians to take up weapons in physical battle against political foes. John of Patmos subverts military imagery from the Roman Empire to say that only God and the Lamb ultimately have authority to coerce.[11]

The transforming power of God and the Lamb that we see in Revelation is of a different order than the brute force of the Roman Empire or modern equivalents. We have already noted that the sword with which Jesus "strikes down" the nations actually is God's spoken word, not a physical weapon. Most English translations of the next phrase in Rev 19:15 say that Christ will *rule* the nations with a rod of iron. But the term in question (*poimano*) is better translated as Christ will *shepherd* or *guide* the nations! How will Christ both *destroy* and *shepherd*? The very paradox of the imagery for the warrior Christ shows that this is not the ordinary use of power so common in John's day and in our own.

## Images of Warfare in John's Day

If we accept the prevailing view of modern scholars that John wrote Revelation late in the first century, it is likely that Emperor Domitian (CE 81–96) was on the throne. A Roman coin from CE 85 portrays Domitian on the obverse, crowned with the laurel wreath of victory. In a scene reminiscent of Revelation 19, the reverse of the coin shows a mounted soldier—probably the emperor himself—charging in battle.

---

11. This aligns with the ethic of the Apostle Paul, who understood that the coercive power of a legitimately functioning government was by authority *derived* from God (Rom 13:1–7). John of Patmos saw the authority exercised by the Roman Empire of his day as derived from Satan, who had usurped it from God (Rev 13:2).

*Sestertius* coin of Emperor Domitian, CE 85.
(Used by permission of Classical Numismatic Group, Inc., www.cngcoins.com).

Domitian was the younger brother of Emperor Titus (CE 79–81), whose triumphal arch commemorating victory over the Jews and destruction of Jerusalem in CE 70 still stands in Rome today. Domitian had a hard act to follow, with few obvious military achievements of his own. But in CE 83 there was a disturbance among tribes in Germany, and Domitian joined a military expedition to bring order. Josephus, eager to ingratiate himself to his Roman overlords, later described Domitian as a hero in this venture. The young emperor

> marched against the barbarians immediately; whereupon their hearts failed them at the rumor of his approach, and they submitted themselves to him with fear, and thought it a happy thing that they were brought under their old yoke again without suffering any farther mischiefs. When, therefore, Domitian had settled all the affairs of Gaul in such good order, that it would not be easily put into disorder any more, he returned to Rome with honor and glory, as having performed such exploits as were above his own age, and worthy of such a father.[12]

Contemporary Roman historian Tacitus dismissed Domitian's military exploits in Germany as a *falsum triumphum*, going so far as to

---

12. Josephus *Wars* 7.86–88. Domitian's father was Emperor Vespasian (CE 69–79), who launched the reconquest of Palestine after the Jews revolted in CE 66. Domitian's brother Titus was general in Palestine when Jerusalem fell.

say that the emperor dressed up slaves to look like German captives.[13] But Domitian made a big deal of the campaign, and added the title *Germanicus* to his name (see *GERM*[*icus*] just above Domitian's head in the illustration). The emperor portrays himself on the coin as a charging equestrian soldier with sword raised, ready to pierce a German tribesman falling under the horse's hooves.

## Revelation Subverts Roman Imperial Iconography

A conquering emperor on a charging horse was a familiar icon in John's day; the Domitian coin is one of thousands of such triumphalist icons in Roman statuary and coins. Rather than taking the figure of a warrior Christ in Revelation 19 as equivalent to Domitian charging into battle to kill German tribesmen, we might consider how John subverts and transforms this imagery.

John's Apocalypse repeatedly depicts parallel or opposing political/spiritual structures of (1) the Kingdom of God—represented by the Lamb and the new Jerusalem, and (2) the domain of evil—represented by the beast and Babylon. Parallel realities in Revelation illustrate John's dualism:

> Satan, first beast, second beast // God, Lamb, Spirit
>
> Babylon // new Jerusalem
>
> harlot // woman clothed with the sun
>
> throne of the beast // throne of God
>
> mortal wound of the beast healed // resurrection of Jesus
>
> worship of the beast // worship of the Lamb
>
> mark of the beast // seal of the living God.

In all of these we see good and evil as mirror images. Or, better said, evil is a fraudulent imitation of the good. John repeatedly states or implies that readers must choose their loyalties; they cannot belong to both realms.

13. Tacitus *Agricola* 39.

## Life Setting of John of Patmos

Such radical dualism is not an adequate framework for every nuance of ethical discernment Christians need to engage the world. But we must understand this polarized imagery as the perception and political experience of a prophet who experienced the Roman Empire as idolatrous, violent, and drunk with greed. While we cannot be certain of John's circumstances, we know that he writes from the island of Patmos, and he probably was sent there in exile. Repeated references to martyrdom and suffering (current or impending) indicate that John expected the Roman Empire soon to strike violently against the church. Perhaps a recent parallel would be the Confessing Church in Nazi Germany, where circumstances required believers to make decisive choices of loyalty. Shortly after Hitler's assumption of power in 1933, his associate Hermann Rauschning declared, "One is either a Christian or a German. You can't be both."[14]

John's familiarity with the Hebrew Scriptures, the Hebrew language, and Jewish faith make it almost certain that he was a Jew. If he wrote his vision near the end of the first century, as most scholars contend, he would have been fully aware of the catastrophic violence inflicted on Jerusalem by Rome in CE 70. John's contempt for Rome as the harlot city (Revelation 17) and his anticipation of the fall of Babylon/Rome (Revelation 18) are logical and cathartic responses of someone who saw his homeland humiliated and destroyed. His preoccupation with a *new* Jerusalem (Revelation 21–22) may even suggest that he was a survivor of the catastrophic Jewish War.

In addition to hating the oppression perpetrated by the Roman Empire (see, for example, 18:24), John also vehemently rejected any concession to emperor worship. The imperial cult so pervaded first-century politics and economics that "no one can buy or sell who does not have the mark . . . of the beast" (13:17). That is, no one could thrive politically or economically in the Roman world without somehow participating in the beastly business of acknowledging the emperor as divine.

---

14. Conway, *Nazi Persecution of the Churches, 1933–45*, 15. Rauschning renounced Nazism in 1934 and fled to the United States.

## Others Also Hated Roman Oppression

John and fellow Christians were not alone in hating what the Roman government was doing at the end of the first century. Emperor Domitian unleashed a reign of terror against all kinds of real or imagined foes in his last years, and the vitriol of Revelation may reflect this era. Pliny the Younger reports that when Domitian was assassinated in CE 96, a spasm of hatred and relief irrupted across the empire, often taken out on statues of the emperor: "It was our delight to dash those proud faces [images of Domitian] to the ground, to smite them with the sword and to savage them with the axe, as if blood and agony could follow from every blow. Our transports of joy—so long deferred—were unrestrained."[15]

Ironically, Pliny was the Roman governor in Asia Minor early in the second century who tried and executed Christians in about CE 112. Before condemning Christians, Pliny offered to set them free if they would curse Christ and put incense on an altar to the divine Caesar.[16] Pliny himself became part of the oppression and idolatry that John of Patmos, a few years earlier, hated and yearned to see end.

But instead of joining an assassination plot (as if that would have been an option!) or even smashing images of the emperor, John of Patmos assigns retribution to God alone. The whole of Revelation is worship, and we might understand John's images of punishment as the cry of a suffering and frightened person for God to act. So understood, some of the violence in Revelation might be parallel to lament psalms in the Old Testament, which call for God to destroy enemies. The critical insight for Christians, who might feel enough rage at injustice to pray for divine intervention, is that we ourselves do not take violent action. That is the prerogative of God, the God who engages the world as a Lamb and eliminates evil by his spoken word.

## Revelation as a Warning

Much of the violence of Revelation appears in three sets of seven plagues, marked by seven seals, seven trumpets, and seven bowls of wrath. Some

---

15. Pliny the Younger, *Panegyricus* 52.4–5, in *Letters and Panegyricus*, 441.

16. Pliny the Younger, *Letters* 10.96.1–4.

of the mayhem of these plagues, especially the earliest, can be credited to human malfeasance.[17] The equestrian warrior of the first seal (6:2), for example, may represent imperial conquests of the Roman Empire. But the fact that these plagues run approximately parallel to plagues visited upon Egypt at the time of Moses suggests that the suffering depicted in Revelation has a redemptive purpose.

Three times John notes his surprise that mortals suffering these woes did not repent (9:20; 16:9, 11), as if repentance was the intent of the plagues. We might view the twenty-one plagues as a protracted warning to humanity to care for the created order and turn to the Creator before it is too late. Thus the plagues may reflect God's mercy and patience, an attempt to get the attention of humanity, which is on a path that will not lead to life.

While I do not believe that John *predicted* events of the twenty-first century, the template of his vision may inform our own faithfulness to God. Should we see famine in countries of the Two-Thirds World as today's manifestation of the rider with scales announcing that wheat and barley have been priced out of the reach of the average working person by globalization (6:5–6)? If every living thing in the sea dies (16:3) from pollution in our day, might we awaken to our moral failing and honor God by caring for creation?

## A Healing of the Nations

It is not surprising that issues of violence and suffering seem paradoxical in Revelation, because they usually are morally complex in our world. But if we hone in on the governing theme of God's redemptive action through Jesus the Lamb, we find hope and guidance in this cataclysmic book. The central mandate of Revelation relates to worship and allegiance: give praise and loyalty to the Lamb rather than to the beast of empire. Belong to the new Jerusalem rather than to the corrupt values of Babylon.

Just as followers of Jesus are not to take up the sword, we also should not imagine that we ourselves bring in the kingdom of God. The church-in-mission does not save the world or even ourselves. Rather,

17. See Kraybill, *Apocalypse and Allegiance*, 102–3.

we have our eyes opened to see where God already is bringing something of the new Jerusalem into being, and then align our lives with that.

Jesus the Lamb is the one who taught us to pray, "thy kingdom come on earth as it is in heaven." This is the Lord at the center of the new Jerusalem, where we hold citizenship. The river that flows from that city waters the tree of life, whose leaves are for the healing of the nations (22:2). However much we struggle with conflicting imagery in Revelation, the Lamb of suffering love wins by the power of resurrection in the end. Our task is to worship him, follow him, and live like him. Since this is one who forgave even the Roman soldiers who crucified him, and rose again to restore and redeem the world, we can confidently say with John, "Come, Lord Jesus!"

# CONCLUSION

## A Faith Worth Dying For:
## A Tradition of Martyrs Not Heroes

Tripp York

---

The church has no arguments for its faith more convincing
than the form of Christ . . .

—DAVID BENTLEY HART

IN HIS BOOK *Dissident Discipleship*, David Augsburger discusses an
incident in which his colleague Nancey Murphy was challenged after
a presentation she gave on Christian nonviolence. The challenge came
not from a Christian critic; rather, she was approached by two Muslims.
Perplexed, they asked, "Did we hear you correctly? You are a Christian
and you believe in nonviolence?" Murphy affirmed what they heard and
explained how her Anabaptist tradition had long attempted to follow
the nonviolent path of Jesus. They continued to push her on the subject,
asking if she would kill in order to protect her loved ones. She told them
that while she would certainly die for her family and friends, she would
not kill for them. They left the conversation confused, saying, "This is

part of the Christian tradition? This is not the Christianity we know about."[1]

Augsburger's anecdote, I believe, gets to the heart of the matter. What we have attempted to do in this book is not just make a case for Christian nonviolence, but to argue that Christianity is ultimately about faithfully witnessing to Christ. To represent Christ well, we must "proclaim the gospel of peace" (Eph 6:15). The story above is just one small occasion illuminating our failure to do so. These two strangers to Christianity could not even conceive of the possibility that Christians could be anything other than violent.[2] If those outside of Christianity cannot comprehend the possibility of a peaceable Christian, then we have to at least raise the question as to whether or not we have been faithful to the Prince of Peace.

Christian ethicist Stanley Hauerwas argues that the best evidence we can provide for the existence of God is the manner in which we live.[3] Our claims about God are only as intelligible as the manner by which we embody those claims. This is truly a daunting and humbling task. For it means that God cannot be located or proven in some sort of logical analysis, no matter how carefully constructed. Rather, Jesus requires us to reveal his presence to others. We bear the burden of proof. As I said, daunting.

Nevertheless, such is our task. We are to be a light to all nations, a city on the hill proclaiming, by the manner in which we live, the good news that is Jesus. How is this done? Clearly, as the greatest practitioners throughout the tumultuous history of Christianity have revealed, there is no one way. The varied and diverse witness provided by folks ranging from Vibia Perpetua to Philip Berrigan is cause for celebration. Perhaps the one thing that can be said is that while there is no one way to be a disciple, there may be a certain form of life—a visual grammar—that denotes the peculiar path of Jesus. Our best witnesses/arguments share

---

1. Augsburger, *Dissident Discipleship*, 129. I am indebted to Chuck Seay and Meredith Wadlington for comments on an early draft of this chapter.

2. Granted, I'm sure that many Christians would make a similar argument about Islam, but this book is not about the inherent violence or nonviolence of Islam, it is about our ability to represent, faithfully, the one we call Lord.

3. Hauerwas, *With the Grain of the Universe*, 205–41.

one thing in common: they understand that those who "tout" the path of Jesus must live lives that are a reflection of the God they profess to worship.

What this means is that we are called to engage in those activities that are exemplary of the character of God. For example, if we are compelled, due to our understanding of who Jesus is, to provide aid to the poor, the needy, the stranger, the widow and the orphan, it is because we think such practices are determinative of the character of Jesus. If we believe Jesus would do such things, and if we believe Jesus commands us to do such things, then we must, if we are to be his followers, do such things. In doing so, we reveal to others our understanding of Jesus. On the other hand, if we call ourselves followers of Christ, yet we do not engage in such activities, it is because we do not imagine such practices have anything to say about the nature of God.

For some reason, when it comes to issues regarding violence, the above exercise becomes quite convoluted. Self-defense and the "necessity" of war become matters of so-called common sense by which being a Christian suddenly has nothing to do with following Jesus. Instead, we assume some other normative means by which we base our decisions.[4] If it is the case, however, that how we live is intertwined with what we claim about Jesus, then matters revolving around war, self-defense, and survival are of utmost importance. Whether or not we decide to employ violence in order to protect ourselves, our loved ones or our neighbors is certainly a matter of concern for those who claim to follow an executed criminal, killed by his enemies. For if we decide to resort to violence, then we are clearly saying something about the character of that person we profess to be the Prince of Peace. To be sure, if what I have been arguing above is true, then the fact that so many Christians throughout history have resorted to violence must certainly cast doubt on whether or not Jesus *really is* the Prince of Peace.

In this chapter, I want to flesh out the correlation between who we claim Jesus to be and how our lives either do or do not substantiate that claim. If Jesus is who we say he is then our practices and habits

4. On this particular point, there is no treatment better than John Howard Yoder's *Politics of Jesus* at revealing how embedded we are in seeking prescriptive norms of decision-making other than Jesus.

must reflect this reality. It is on this point that I find the practice of nonviolence to be nonnegotiable. In order to substantiate this claim, I will make an argument for why Christianity is a faith worth dying for and, inversely, why it is a faith *not* worth fighting for. Christianity, when necessary, produces martyrs—not heroes. To physically attempt to secure one's faith, one's life, or the lives of others, runs counter to Christianity's central declaration that Jesus is Lord. For if it is the case that our actions can either substantiate or negate our claims, then it is contradictory to insist that Jesus is Lord while simultaneously disobeying him. As it says in the Bible, anyone who professes to know Jesus yet "does not do what he commands is a liar, and there is no truth in him" (1 John 2:4). Our knowledge of Christ is not based on what we say about him; it is based on whether or not we obey him. Knowledge of Christ is predicated on obedience to Christ. What matters most is not simply *what* we claim about Jesus, but *how we embody* what we claim about Jesus. If Jesus is Lord, the question for us is, what does this look like in respect to our enemies?

### Defending Christianity with a Cross, Not a Sword

You can kill us, but you cannot hurt us.

—JUSTIN MARTYR

Approximately two and a half centuries after the death of Jesus, a young man by the name of Maximilian of Tebessa was executed for refusing military service. It was 295 CE, and Maximilian was required to fulfill his obligation to serve in the Roman army. This posed a problem for Maximilian, as it did for most Christians prior to the middle of the fourth century.[5] First, depending on the emperor, Christians were often not even allowed to live—much less serve the needs of the empire. Second, the majority of Christians would not serve in the military, for it necessitated disobedience to Jesus. Service in the military required, as it still does today, the would-be solider to swear an oath. Yet Jesus specifically demands that we not swear oaths (Matt 5:33–37). Jesus also

5. For a further account of Christians in their own voice during this period, see Michael Long's *Christian Peace and Nonviolence*, 15–34.

requires that we love our enemies, put down our swords, refuse to resist evil, and not return violence for violence (Matt 5:38–39, 43–45a; Matt 26:52; Luke 6:27–28). Though service in the Roman military did not necessarily imply that a person would have to live a violent life (as the Roman military also adjudicated a number of disagreements that were not predicated on violence—much as the modern police officer does with negotiating competing stories revolving around, for example, a traffic accident), it did assume the power of the sword as a possible mode of recourse against one's enemies. For many early Christians, the idea of killing one's enemies, when Jesus clearly demanded a different response, was unthinkable. Oftentimes the Christian's refusal to defend himself was what gave him away for being a Christian.

When asked his name by Dion, the proconsul of Africa who was recruiting new soldiers, Maximilian responded, "Why should you want to know my name? I cannot serve in the army, I am a Christian."[6] Maximilian assumed that this knowledge alone should preclude him from military service. After all, what good is a person in the military who is in the trenches praying for his adversaries rather than attempting to kill them?

Dion countered that, Christian or not, a person's highest loyalty was to Rome. Military duty was a responsibility placed on certain citizens, regardless of their religious convictions. Maximilian's civic duty, assumed Dion, was far greater than any obligation Maximilian might have to his tiny political/religious movement. Dion disregarded Maximilian's dissent and proceeded to fit him for military garb.

Maximilian interrupted the fitting process by continually stating his inability to serve. Dion ignored his pleas and informed him that if he did not serve he would be executed. Maximilian responded, "[C]ut off my head if you like, but I cannot be a solider of the world; I am a soldier of my God . . . My service is for my own Lord. I cannot engage in worldly

---

6. Water, *Encyclopedia of Christian Martyrs*, 351. *Non facio; non possum militare; Christianus sum*, can also be translated as: "I won't do it; I cannot be a soldier; I am a Christian." I expound on this particular narrative in my "Early Church Martyrdom: Witnessing For or Against the Empire?," in Budde and Scott, eds., *Witness of the Body*, 20–42.

warfare. I have already told you that I am a Christian."[7] Dion, again, told Maximilian that if he continued to refuse military service he would die. Maximilian was not intimidated by Dion's threat and explained how it was impossible for a Christian to die since they live in Christ. Dion accepted the challenge and told him he was to be beheaded. Maximilian simply responded, "Thanks be to God," and gladly accepted the gift that the church names "martyrdom."[8]

I refer to martyrdom as a gift because that is how the church has historically understood it. It cannot be sought, though it may be desired, and it cannot be forced, though many have longed for it. Such a desire is not rooted in a pathological or morbid longing for death; rather, martyrdom can only be desired as it functions as the ultimate manner by which a person can imitate Christ (which, not incidentally, happens to be *precisely* in relation to how we deal with our enemies). Those who desire to know Christ must follow Christ, and evidence that we have followed him faithfully could result in our dying like him.[9]

Martyrdom is only made possible due to the martyr's participation in the life, death, and resurrection of Jesus. Yet, this is not just a gift for the martyr, nor is it only for the church left behind. Martyrdom, inasmuch as it is an act that is obedient to the manner by which Jesus died for his enemies, functions as a gift *to* our enemies. By taking the form of Christ, the martyr presents the enemy with a revelatory experience of how Jesus deals with his adversaries. While it is true that many of us will never be martyrs, we can nevertheless practice the manner of life by

---

7. Water, *Encyclopedia of Christian Martyrs*, 352.

8. Ibid. In his book *Martyrdom and Persecution in the Early Church*, W. H. C. Frend notes that what directly led to Maximilian's execution was his refusal to swear the oath (360). To be sure, this is true. This does not, however, render insignificant the early Christian's refusal to participate in violence. If anything, it makes things more complicated for us today by requiring us to justify our willingness to swear oaths to our nation-states. Jesus says not to swear oaths or make promises. Citing something like the Pledge of Allegiance is a promise (a pledge is a promise). How does a Christian justify such disobedience?

9. This, of course, does not mean that to follow Christ we have to die like him. Though it certainly, at the very least, may demand that we inquire as to how we have escaped treatment similar to that inflicted on the one who said, "No servant is greater than his master. If they persecuted me, they will persecute you also" (John 15:20).

which such a gift has been given to others.[10] By imitating Christ, especially when it matters most (in dealing with our enemies), we present to those who would cause us harm the manner by which Christ deals with them. For if we do not treat our enemies as Christ has taught us to treat them, how will they know the one we proclaim to be Lord?

Maximilian is a faithful example of one who provides a bodily reenactment of Jesus for those who do not know him. He shows Jesus to the world. Maximilian was one of many Christians in the early church who, rather than curse, hate, or attempt to resist violent Roman laws directed against them, instead chose to love, forgive, and absorb the violence unjustly forced upon them. The first three centuries of Christianity are full of examples of people whose faithfulness to Christ required that they turn the other cheek and love those who impaled them on burning stakes. What we need to ask now is this: How did a once predominantly nonviolent movement like Christianity ever become so thoroughly entrenched in a warrior mythos? How has Jesus been so easily co-opted into a mentality by which many of his followers are willing to kill to preserve their own life, their family, or their nation? How is it possible that so many Christians, throughout history and today, are capable of killing in the name of the very one who demands that we love our enemies?

## Christianity Makes Peace with War

All human sin seems so much worse in its consequences than in its intentions.

—REINHOLD NIEBUHR

While there is certainly not enough space in this chapter to adequately address the above questions, allow me to briefly comment on at least one historical shift that has greatly altered the manner by which we read Jesus' teachings on enemies. The first three centuries of Christianity were a time when Christians were often persecuted, hunted, hated, and reviled due to their allegiance to Christ. To follow Christ meant to imitate him, and if this meant refusing to elevate the good of the nation, the

10. For more on this notion of martyrdom as gift, see the epilogue to my *Purple Crown*, 145–55.

market, or the family to the level of worship, then many of them chose Christ. Because of such an absolute commitment, many of these early Christians did not make good citizens (at least in the eyes and minds of non-Christians). In some sense, depending on how you define what it means to be a "good citizen," this may be true. Though there were a few exceptions to the rule, until the early-to-middle part of the fourth century Christians rarely exercised positions of significant authority in the empire. There was not a single bishop during this period of time who approved of Christian participation in warfare, and the basic Christian assumption that all kingdoms of the world were temporal, destined to fall, and, though God-ordained, under the power of Satan, did nothing to encourage their pagan peers to see them as champions of the empire.[11]

In their defense, many of the early Christians did think it significant to seek the peace of the city (Jer 29:7). They understood that the temporal good was still a good. They also prayed for the empire and its leaders—even when these leaders were their enemies. They imagined themselves loyal to the empire inasmuch as they refused to allow the empire to think it was the highest good. They refused to burn incense, to eat sacrificial meat, and to consider their leaders as representatives of salvation (as is so tempting in modern democracies). They also refused to carry the sword. It is easy to see why they were viewed as enemies of Rome. This is why, of course, this period is often referred to as the golden age of martyrdom. Mixed allegiances were not allowed. Any person not willing to defend, protect, and kill for the good of the commonwealth was a traitor. They had to be eliminated. Though persecution was sporadic, it was significant enough that the early church developed a theology of two baptisms: the first by water and the second by blood. Baptism, in the early church, was concretely connected to death because a convert knew that the sanctifying waters of baptism could also lead to the spilling of his or her own blood. This made sense to many of the early Christians, for if Jesus' blood was spilled, then so too should it be with his followers.

All of this changed in the early part of the fourth century. Only a decade or so after the beheading of Maximilian, Galerius decriminalized

11. Cf. Budde and Scott, *Witness of the Body*, 21–22.

Christianity in 311 CE. Roman citizens were required to be tolerant of all religious creeds. Shortly after, following a vision and a military victory that Constantine attributed to the God of the Christians, Constantine and Licinius issued the Edict of Milan in 313 CE. This edict not only furthered the tolerance of Christianity, but opened the door to a closer relationship between the church and the empire. Due to Constantine's eventual conversion, the church began to enjoy the political and social privileges concomitant with an emperor's favor. Christian existence in the world became more secure. Christians suddenly found themselves in positions of power, making decisions that shaped both the church and the empire.[12]

This period is often referred to as Constantinianism (which describes not so much a particular person as a specific era). Beginning a few years prior to the disputed "conversion" of Constantine, and not ending until a century or so after him, Constantinianism refers to the cataclysmic transition that occurred primarily during the fourth century. During this time, Christianity eventually became the state religion. As one can well imagine, things drastically changed. The first three centuries of Christianity enjoyed a period in which the Christian response to violence was modeled after the response given by Jesus. Christians turned the other cheek, did not resist evil, and, through suffering persecution, actually increased in number.[13] After Constantine, the persecution of Christians ceased, but at the expense of Christianity's nonviolent witness. Many adjustments were made, chief among them being that Christians were now in charge.

By the end of the fourth century, through the might of the emperor Theodosius, Christianity became the official state religion. It was under his reign that Christianity became the primary religious option.[14] Christianity no longer required conversion as much as it simply required being born. Baptism, which once required training, education, and a

12. Ibid.

13. Hence the occasion for Tertullian's famous adage, "The blood of the martyrs is the seed of the church."

14. Though one was "free" to not be a Christian, such people suffered many civil and political disadvantages that made choosing to be anything other than Christian absurd. Not that many people had a choice, hence the institutionalizing of infant baptism.

commitment to the possibility of an early death, now became an exclusive birthright.[15] As being a good Christian became synonymous with being a good Roman, other things had to change as well. Instead of the early Christian's peace witness forever altering the empire, the empire forever altered Christianity's peace witness. In just a few short years, a military that once killed Christians—and in which Christians were often forbidden to serve—was, by 416 CE, made up *only* of Christians.

Many Christians have historically viewed this transition in a positive light. Is this not a case of Christ triumphant? Isn't Christianity supposed to spread to all nations? What better way to spread the Gospel than by Rome becoming Christian (it makes missionary work a whole lot easier when you have imperial protection). Plus, it is certainly a good thing that religious persecution came to an end, right? Of course, we know better than to assume that religious persecution came to end. Unfortunately, as many opponents of Christianity often point out, Christians *became* the persecutors (oftentimes against one another!).[16] In the oddest of reversals, a once persecuted minority capable of loving their enemies as Christ did, who suffered horrid executions and unspeakable tortures, was now on the giving end. Could this really be Christ triumphant? Christian discipleship was hardly optional, and, yes, almost everyone became "Christian," but at what price?

After Christians found themselves in control, certain aspects of discipleship were no longer possible. One particular aspect among many was the refusal to carry the sword (such exceptions primarily included the clergy and monastics—many of whom assumed the necessity of the sword even if they did not wield it). What Jesus had demanded, and what the early church forbade, now became common practice. Christians were now in charge. To rule effectively, Christians could no

15. I am not attempting to make an argument for or against certain modes of baptism (be it infant or believer's—and by "believer's baptism" I mean the person being baptized, not the faith of his or her parent). I am simply noting what is surely a significant change in terms of how Christians were prepared and trained for the Christian life. To read more about the significance of infant versus believer's baptism in terms of discipleship, see James W. McClendon's *Systematic Theology*, 2:386–397.

16. Christians did not need to wait until the sixteenth century to start killing one another. They were already doing it, as in the case with the Donatists, by the end of the fourth century.

longer love their enemies as Jesus did; rather, they had to conquer, imprison, torture, and kill them. Empires that do not kill their enemies do not last long (of course, those that do kill their enemies don't always last that long either). For the good of the empire, and for the good of others, it became one's responsibility to brandish the sword. What was taken away from them, in arguably the most radical idea anyone ever offered as a response to violence, was once again a possibility. Indeed, it was more than a possibility; it became a necessity.

This did not mean that the fourth-century church easily took to the sword. Due to the centuries-long commitment to nonviolence, those in the church carried with them a predilection toward peaceableness that required a robust defense of violence. The theory of just war was created in order to defend the use of violence[17]—the assumption being that any use of violence, whether it was for war or capital punishment, had to be painstakingly justified. Peace was assumed to be the normative state of the Christian, but the practice of it could no longer be realistically expected when it came to issues of national defense, the protection of third-party innocents, or the common good. Christians now had the task of making sure the world came out right. Their newfound responsibility, unfortunately, demanded that the path of Jesus no longer be followed. The empire had not become Christian; Christianity had become the empire.

What is important to understand is how the life and teachings of Jesus were shaped and altered by this significant historic change.[18]

17. It should be noted that Augustine, one of the foremost proponents of the just war tradition, did not think it was possible for Christians to practice self-defense. Violence, for Augustine, could only be practiced for the sake of others. At the same time, Augustine participates in a reversal of the Christian response as represented in Maximilian. Augustine argues that soldiers can and must obey the commands of their leaders even if those commands are wrong (especially since government is viewed as an instrument of God). The leader suffers the guilt, not the soldiers. Apparently, Augustine, we can infer, would argue that you can't fault Nazi soldiers for doing exactly what they were supposed to do: kill Jews. After all, they were being obedient to those God had put in command. To refuse to kill Jews, when commanded to by one of God's ordained/appointed leaders, would be antithetical to what it means to be a Constantinian Christian. If this seems like a gross generalization, then ask a holocaust survivor for their opinion on Christianity's complicity with state power.

18. This is, of course, an incredibly (and embarrassingly so) brief summation of

The early church, along with the disciples, responded to their enemies with love, forgiveness and nonviolence. After the Constantinian shift, this could no longer be the primary response (if even a response at all). Christians, for the good of others, were required to respond differently than Jesus. They could no longer follow or imitate him in matters dealing with enemies, but rather had to "admire" what he said while making "tough moral decisions" that justified their ignoring of what he said. The primary Christian response to one's enemies was to undo what Jesus did to Peter: Christianity put the sword back into Peter's hands.

### Who Do You Say that I Am? (Jesus or Apollo or Ares or . . . ?)

One may feel that, in the name of honesty, Christians ought either quit fighting or quit calling themselves Christians.

—WENDELL BERRY

Earlier, I drew attention to the manner by which Christians live and how this must be connected to our proclamation that Christ is Lord. If it is the case that Christ is Lord, then how we embody this claim describes to the non-Christian the character of the one we declare Lord. I suggested that Christians engage in those activities imagined to be exemplary of the character of God. That is, to repeat, if you find yourself giving aid to the poor or visiting those in prison, it is because you think that God cares for the poor and the imprisoned. If you do not do such things, it is because you assume that such practices are not indicative of who God is—or at least not important to discipleship. Our actions speak truthfully in regards to whom we think we worship. For it is by no means clear that we worship whom we claim to worship. If our actions

---

the significant shift that occurred in the practices and habits of the church in the fourth century. For a far more nuanced and descriptive account of the positive and negative repercussions following this period, see Oliver O'Donovan's *The Desire of the Nations* and John Howard Yoder's *For the Nations*. Both books represent a good place to start in terms of attempting to adjudicate contrasting accounts of what it means, in terms of discipleship, for the empire to "convert" to Christianity. Also, Lee Camp's *Mere Discipleship* includes a detailed account of how Constantinianism continues to shape how we read Scripture.

are the true guarantor of our convictions, then what we do determines to whom we belong.

For example, which "god" do we really worship based on our response to our enemies? We may say it is Jesus, but if our response is the opposite of that which Jesus commands then we are lying (or at least wrong about which god we are serving). When Christians submit their bodies, as they do in the military, to learn how to wound, maim, and kill their enemies, they do so because they imagine that God not only endorses such behavior but would do so as well—even in the form of Jesus. Why else would I see cars with bumper stickers saying, "God Bless Our Snipers?"[19] On this point, the incredibly trendy question that revealed itself on jewelry and T-shirts a few years ago is quite applicable in this situation: what *would* Jesus do?[20] A Christian serving in the military has already answered this question by imagining that Jesus would bear guns, grenades, and knives in order to resist, beat into submission, and eliminate his enemies. The Christian soldier *must* think this about Jesus; otherwise he or she would not nor could not serve in the military. If Jesus would not shoot, maim, or kill his enemies, then the Christian, as one who follows and imitates Jesus, cannot engage in this behavior either.[21]

Then why are so many of us in the military? Why do we assume that the God of Jesus blesses or endorses our military (or that of any other nation)? Didn't Jesus say that those who live by the sword shall die by the sword? Was this not, especially given the context in which this statement is uttered, an indictment against carrying the sword?

19. The vehicle in question also exhibited a fish emblem so that no one would mistake the owner for being anything other than Christian. Of course, I'm not sure how many Christians would actually find anything wrong with being a Christian sniper. As Wendell Berry astutely points out, we have a habit of calling ourselves Christian and then assuming that whatever it is we do is, de facto, Christian. See his *Blessed Are the Peacemakers*, 49–68.

20. So-called witness wear, I contend, is part of the problem. Such blandly uncreative marketing that dupes us into purchasing "Jesus wear" is but one more means that relieves us from the burden of actually being a witness to Christ. Anyone who actually takes the Sermon on the Mount seriously will not need clothes telling others that he or she is a Christian.

21. On this point, I am leaning heavily on my "Who Mourns the Gods? Part II" in my *Third-Way Allegiance*, 100–106.

Why do so many of us think it is possible to follow Jesus while being willing to do violence to those Jesus demands we love? Do we really envision Jesus carrying a rifle, a nightstick, a can of mace, or owning a guard dog? Have we simply fallen prey to the same mentality that led so many people in the first century to reject Jesus because he did not rule like King David—by the sword? We need to be clear on this: does our version of Jesus rule by the sword or the cross? We cannot have them both. If it is the case that the prophets foretold the coming of the one who would put an end to war (Isa 2:4; Mic 4:3; Zech 9:10), then were the prophets wrong? Were those people in the first century who rejected Jesus because he did not initiate a military rebellion right to reject him? Based on this mentality, wouldn't the same people who presently assert their devotion to Jesus be the same ones who would have rejected him in the first century? After all, Jesus not only had some incredibly peculiar and counter-cultural ways of dealing with enemies—in fact, his ways were, and obviously still are, downright offensive. According to Jesus, Peter, John, as well as that once homicidal apostle who wrote a large chunk of the New Testament, Paul, here are some of their not so common "commonsense" teachings on the proper way to treat enemies:

> Blessed are the peacemakers, for they will be called children of God. (Matt 5:9)

> You have heard it that it was said, "An eye for an eye and a tooth for a tooth." But I say to you, Do not resist an evildoer. But if anyone strikes you on the right cheek, turn the other also . . . You have heard that it was said, "You shall love your neighbor and hate your enemy." But I say to you, Love your enemies and pray for those who persecute you, so that you may be children of your Father in heaven. (Matt 5:38–39, 43–45a)

> Then Jesus said to him, "Put your sword back into its place; for all who take the sword shall perish by the sword." (Matt 26:52)

But I tell you who hear me: Love your enemies, do good to those who hate you, bless those who curse you, pray for those who mistreat you. (Luke 6:27–28)

Bless those who persecute you; bless and do not curse. (Rom 12:14)

Do not repay anyone evil for evil. Be careful to do what is right in the eyes of everybody. If it is possible, as far as it depends on you, live at peace with everyone. Do not take revenge, my friends, but leave room for God's wrath, for it is written: "It is mine to avenge; I will repay, says the Lord." On the contrary: "If your enemy is hungry, feed him; if he is thirsty, give him something to drink. In doing this, you will heap burning coals on his head." Do not be overcome by evil, but overcome evil with good. (Rom 12:17–21)

We work hard with our own hands. When we are cursed, we bless; when we are persecuted, we endure it. (1 Cor 4:12)

Do not repay evil with evil or insult with insult, but with blessing, because to this you were called so that you may inherit a blessing. (1 Pet 3:9)

But they have conquered him by the blood of the Lamb and by the word of their testimony, for they did not cling to life even in the face of death. (Rev 12:11)

Despite the varied approaches we may adopt in order to interpret Scripture, one thing seems clear: the New Testament demands a radically different way of treating our enemies than killing them. It may be the case, on this very point, that the heart of what makes Christianity so unusual and thoroughly scandalous is its understanding of its enemies. Jesus has given us a new way to deal with our adversaries: to forgive them.[22]

22. Ibid., 103–4. In anticipation of a common objection, one cannot reconcile forgiving someone while killing him (as some people suggest in light of capital punishment). Such an intangible form of forgiveness makes a mockery of our relationship with Jesus and the relationship Jesus demands we have with others. God's forgiveness

Unfortunately, we are too much like James and John, who wanted to call forth fire from the heavens in order to kill those Samaritans who would not welcome Jesus. Instead of rebuking the Samaritans, Jesus immediately rebuked his own disciples (Luke 9:51–56). Jesus' kingdom will be built on suffering, servanthood, nonviolence, love of the enemy, and a rejection of the manner by which Gentiles rule (Matt 20:25). It will be unlike any other kingdom we can create or vote into existence.

It seems we have strayed a long way from the path of Jesus. We are told by politicians, moviemakers, and no shortage of priests and ministers that the only good, responsible, and moral way to deal with our enemies is through violence. That Christians ever found themselves in a position of having to have a discussion on the ethics of waterboarding, much less stockpiling nuclear arms, is proof that our understanding of God certainly has nothing in common with Jesus. Jesus freely gave his life for his enemies and then, no surprise, demanded that we do the same. For what else could he have meant when he commanded us to pick up our cross and follow him?

My real fear is that those who imagine a Jesus willing to bless their rifles and grenades may have more in common with the Greek god Ares than Jesus of Nazareth. Ares was the god of war and bloodlust. He never met a skirmish he didn't like. He pursued violence and engaged in one bloody conflict after another. Likewise, worshippers of Ares would often look to him (and many more looked to his half-sister, Athena) for blessings on their noble crusades.[23] Ares was the deity some Greeks called upon when they sought aid against their adversaries. Because Phobos and Deimos (Fear and Terror) were connected to Ares, he was a risky deity to invoke, but if you wanted to drive your enemies into the ground and forever erase their presence, he was often worth the risk.[24]

---

of us is completely predicated upon our forgiveness of others (Matt 6:14). Therefore, let's hope God's forgiveness is nothing like the person who suggests you can forgive someone while simultaneously executing or killing him. If so, we are all in serious trouble.

23. Ibid.

24. Athena, because she was seen as being more successful, was invoked more often than Ares. Ares, however, was certainly popular as he represented the incredibly violent aspects of warfare that attracted many warriors. Granted, I understand that such ruthless violence is not the mindset of those Christians indebted to the just

When the Greeks succeeded in killing their enemies, especially one of high priority (say, an Osama bin Laden kind of enemy), they praised their war deities and fervently celebrated the victory their gods gave them. As history shows, there is no shortage of such celebrations. There is also no shortage of gods to call upon for such celebratory killings. Take your pick: Ares, Mars, Bellona, Enyo, Virtus, Odin, Thor, Agurzil, Mixcoatl, Mextli, Badb, Andarta, Neit, Segomo, Tyr, Chi You, Horus, Laran, Mangala, Indra, Hanuman, Al Quam, *ad infinitum ad nauseum*. Apparently, Jesus is but one more name we can now add to the ever-expanding list of war gods to call upon as we plunge our swords deep into the bodies of others.

I do not intend to belittle the incredible sacrifices that soldiers of all stripes and nations have made throughout history. There is truly honor and nobility, especially according to Homeric wisdom, in such sacrifices. Yet, this is not the kind of sacrifice that Christians are called to make. We are not called to be heroes. We are not the Dirty Harrys, Rambos, and Achilles of the world. We are called to be those who would offer an alternative to the never-ending warring declared to be our lot in life. Though there may always be warring in this world, just like adultery and theft, we are not called to participate in it. We know that there are no acts of redemptive violence or sacrifice because Christ's resurrection trumps the need for us to continue killing to preserve ourselves or others. Instead, we have as an alternative the ability to forgive our enemies, to absorb the violence, and, if necessary, to practice martyrdom.

## No One Said It Would Be Easy

It is so hard to believe because it is so hard to obey.

—SØREN KIERKEGAARD

In the beginning of this chapter I suggested that there is a sense in which we are capable of making a statement, such as "Christ is Lord," either true or false. This does not mean that Christ's lordship is dependent

---

war tradition. But since just war theory is fairly irrelevant for the vast majority of Christians who take up arms, such wording as above is aimed toward the crusading mentality that desires the complete annihilation of one's foes.

upon my confession. What it means is that if I claim that Christ is Lord, yet I live a life that does not correlate to this claim, then I am speaking a false reality. If Jesus, Paul, and John are correct, that is, if we know the truthful ones by the lives they live, then the teachings of Jesus are non-negotiable. What he said about money, marriage, forgiveness, violence, the poor, and the alien, must be practiced if we can legitimately call ourselves his followers. For if we do not obey him, then not only do we lie to ourselves, but we convey a false reality to others. For if they cannot see the truth that we claim, then it does not exist in any meaningful way by which it can be named. We end up presenting a false image, a "god" that has more in common with Ares and Odin than Jesus. In doing so, we do more harm than not witnessing at all. There simply is a qualitative difference between the claims of a person who, for instance, turns the other cheek and one who does not. The former makes the claim "Christ is Lord" true in a way that the latter is incapable of doing.[25] For the one who does turn the other cheek, Christ truly is Lord. The person who does not turn the other cheek, thereby disobeying Christ, negates the authenticity of the claim of Christ's lordship over his or her life.

As stated earlier, our witness is our best argument for the existence of God. We must live in such a way that if Christ were not resurrected from the dead then our manner of life would be unintelligible. We can see then see how refusing to return violence for violence is, ultimately, evangelical. It is missional. It is, in the lives of those who do it, a reflection of Christ's lordship. It is a performative moment in truth. When Maximilian called Christ his Lord, he was speaking and living the truth. Those around him knew it. They were not, like the Muslims mentioned earlier, surprised to discover that Maximilian was peaceable. His commitment to the gospel of peace was the reason that he had to be killed. Such an alternative in the world exposes the principalities and powers

25. I am reflecting here on George Lindbeck's *Nature of Doctrine*. Lindbeck argues that truth is performative. It is not some objective reality that exists "out there," rather what we deem "truth" hinges upon the embodiment of those making such claims. For example, there is a difference between a crusader who shouts, "Christ is Lord!" while cleaving the skull of his enemy, and a martyr who shouts "Christ is Lord!" while burning at the stake for his or her confession. The latter speaks a truth that is indiscernible in the case of the former because the crusader's actions negate the claim while the martyr's actions substantiate it (64–65).

for what they truly are—in rebellion against their Creator. This is why he had to be killed. Truth is rarely welcomed. The prophets were hated, almost all of the disciples were killed, and those today who strive to take Jesus at his word continue to find harassment. To be a truth-teller like Maximilian is dangerous and, today, often surprising. Granted, there are a few Christians who continue to find ways to surprise us. Think of the Amish response to the killings of their children at West Nickel Mines School: forgiveness, no desire for revenge, and aid extended to the killer's own family. More importantly, think of the reaction that so many Christians had to the Amish response. They were shocked, baffled, and confused. What made bigger news—the killing of the children or that Christians would forgive a killer—is difficult to determine. This "Christian nation" was as visibly perplexed by the Amish response as were our two Muslim brothers by Murphy's presentation. I just wonder what this has to say, if anything, about our claims of following the Prince of Peace.

# Afterword

Shane Claiborne

WE HAVE THREE DIFFERENT bookshelves in our community in Philadelphia. There's the top "Do Not Remove" shelf of our favorites. There's the "Read and Return" shelf of books we like and we let folks borrow. And then there's the "Free" shelf, which are books that are, well . . . they are worth giving away.

The book you are holding is going on the "Do Not Remove" shelf.

I've always liked the old saying of pacifist Ammon Hennacy: "Love without courage and wisdom is sentimentality, as with the ordinary church member. Courage without love and wisdom is foolhardiness, as with the ordinary soldier. Wisdom without love and courage is cowardice, as with the ordinary intellectual. But the one who has love, courage, and wisdom moves the world."

This book is filled with love, courage, and wisdom. It is a long overdue apologetic for nonviolence (not apology, but apologetic).

It has been said that bad theology gets people killed. It is poisonous and deadly. No one kills as passionately as people who kill in the name of God.

It has also been said that the answer to bad theology is not no theology but good theology. This book is filled with good theology. It is a rebuttal to the best arguments against Christian pacifism (and there are some very good ones).

This book is like a theological cage match—of the most nonviolent sort, of course.

Every worldview has obstacles and objections and it is our duty, whoever we are, to take those objections seriously. It is our responsibility to wrestle with the verses that trouble us as much as we preach the verses that inspire us. That's what I love about this book. These authors take opposition so seriously that they have devoted an entire book to responding to critics and sparring partners. Our critics are not bad people . . . they are just wrong. And hopefully they think the same of us.

Sometimes nonviolence begins by realizing that our critics are our best teachers. As important as it is to be right, it is just as important to be nice. And there are plenty of liberals and conservatives who can teach us that you can have lots of good ideas and still be mean. It is my hope that this book is a landmark on the journey towards thoughtful, civil dialogue around issues of violence. For those of us who are Christian, one of the best things we can do is learn to disagree well. We have to remember that both a tax collector and a Zealot were welcome at the table of Christ. As our brother Desmond Tutu says, "God's revolution is big enough to set both the oppressed and oppressors free."

Let us resolve to end this book by beginning a conversation, perhaps with someone we might not see eye to eye with . . . and resolving to disagree well.

Many of the contributors to this book are close personal friends, mentors, and coaches—and they are midwives of an entire movement in the Church of Christians who have grown tired of militarism and violence.

This conversation about violence is one of the most urgent conversations of our day. We have tried the "eye for an eye" thing over and over. We have learned the "pick up the sword, die by the sword" lesson all too well. We see the collateral damage of the myth of redemptive violence nearly every day—in Iraq, Afghanistan, Israel-Palestine, and among the soldiers themselves whose suicide deaths outnumber combat deaths. But, as Jesus promises us: "there is a better way."

In 2003, I was in Iraq with the Christian Peacemaker Teams where we lived in Baghdad during the shock and awe bombing. I saw some of the most violent and terrible things I could ever imagine, and so much of it was baptized with language of God and blessing and prayer. I remember seeing one woman throw her hands into the air and say, "I am done with God." As we talked a little more, she explained that she had been raised Muslim and then was drawn to the Christian message of grace—but as she watched the war, she had given up on God because, in her words, "What kind of God blesses bloodshed?" She went on to say, "My government and your government are both doing the same thing: creating terrible violence and asking God to bless it. I want nothing to do with that kind of God."

I learned in Iraq that what is at stake today with all of our bad theology is not just the reputation of America, but the reputation of our faith and the integrity of the Christian message.

We have seen violent religious extremists of all stripes—Muslim, Jewish, Christian. They distort the best that our faiths have to offer and hijack the news with stories of hatred. When we hear someone singing really badly, we don't stop singing. We just sing a better song. The chapters of this book show us the promise that God is doing a new thing. There is a wave of Christians who are thoughtfully nonviolent and whose message is more compelling and more attractive than the type of Christianity that blows up abortion clinics, blesses bombs, burns the Koran, or holds signs that read, "God hates fags."

I am excited to be alive today. Books like this one point us towards a new kind of Christianity—one that is actually very old. They remind us that the first few hundred years of our faith were marked by pacifism and enemy-love.

It must also be said that our great challenge today is not just right thinking but right living. Our ideologies come with responsibility. We are not just against war, we are for peace—and that could cost us our lives. In his 1984 message that helped catalyze the Christian Peacemaker Teams, evangelical pacifist Ron Sider said:

> Unless we are prepared to risk injury and death in non-violent opposition to the injustice our societies foster, we don't dare even whisper another word about pacifism to our sisters and brothers in those desperate lands. Unless we are ready to die . . . we should confess that we never really meant the cross was an alternative to the sword . . . Making peace is as costly as waging war. Unless we are

> prepared to pay the cost of peacemaking, we have no right
> to claim the label or preach the message.[1]

So our challenge today is one both of right thinking and of right living.

Let us not forget that the seeds of nonviolence begin very small. We must work hard at trying to change what we can change—ourselves. We must look for the worst in ourselves and the best in others. We must create holy habits and be filled with the Spirit so that those things that are God—like love, joy, peace, patience, gentleness, goodness, kindness, faithfulness, and self-control—become more a part of who we are.

There is no doubt in my mind that *A Faith Not Worth Fighting For* will become a classic, a handbook for Christian peacemakers around the world. It is bound to get the attention of scholars and activists, skeptics and cynics, old school liberals and new school conservatives.

It will energize the traditional peace churches and put fresh wind in the sails of a postmodern generation that is quickly moving away from the triumphalistic, militant, God-and-country Christianity of American theocracy and toward the peaceable, humble, uncompromisingly nonviolent Christianity of Christ again.

At the end of the day, that's what we need—a Christianity that looks like Jesus again, and that takes the cross seriously. After all, we can look at the Bible and find verses that justify violence and nonviolence. We can look at history and find strong arguments to make a case for war and to make a case for pacifism. But in the end we must ask, what looks the most like Jesus?

If we want to see what love looks like as it stares evil in the face, we need only look at the cross. It is the cross that shows us the nonviolent love of God, a God who loves enemies so much he dies for them . . . for us. It is that cross that makes no sense to the wisdom of this world and that confounds the logic of smart bombs. That triumph of Christ's execution and resurrection was a victory over violence, hatred, sin, and everything ugly in the world. And it is the triumph of the glorious res-

---

1. Sider gave this message at the General Assembly of Mennonite World Conference in Strasbourg, France. For a history of Christian Peacemaker Teams, see Kern, *In Harm's Way*.

urrection that fills us with the hope that death is dead—if only we will let it die.

As the early Christians said, "For Christ we can die but we cannot kill." That is a truth at the heart of the Gospel: there is something worth dying for, but nothing in the world worth killing for.

Jesus, give us the courage to follow you.

# Contributors

**Andy Alexis-Baker** is a PhD candidate at Marquette University in Systematic Theology and Ethics. He is the coeditor of *Christian Attitudes to War, Peace, and Revolution*, and the cofounder of Jesus Radicals.

**Justin Bronson Barringer** is a graduate student at Asbury Theological Seminary where he also works for the Office of Global Community Formation. He has been a missionary in China and Greece, worked extensively among homeless people in Nashville, and served at mercy and justice organizations like The Dream Center and Sojourners.

**Gregory A. Boyd**, PhD, is the Senior Pastor of Woodland Hills Church in St. Paul, Minnesota. He is the author of *Letters from a Skeptic, The Myth of a Christian Nation*, and *The Myth of a Christian Religion*. He has been featured on the front page of *The New York Times* and on *The Charlie Rose Show*, CNN, NPR, and BBC.

**Robert Brimlow**, PhD, is Associate Professor of Philosophy, St. John Fisher College. He has authored and edited numerous books including *What about Hitler?*, *Christianity Incorporated*, and *The Church as Counterculture*.

**Lee C. Camp**, PhD, is Professor of Theology and Ethics, Lipscomb University. He is the author of *Mere Discipleship* and *Who Is My Enemy?* He is a minister in the Church of Christ.

**Shane Claiborne** is the author of several books including *Jesus for President, The Irresistible Revolution, Follow Me to Freedom,* and *Becoming the Answer to Our Prayers.* He is also one of the founding members of the new monastic community/alternative seminary known as "The Simple Way."

**John Dear**, SJ, is a Jesuit priest and a peace activist who has been arrested more than seventy-five times for acts of civil disobedience. He is the author of more than twenty books including his recent autobiography, *A Persistent Peace: One Man's Struggle for a Nonviolent World.* In 2008, Archbishop Desmond Tutu nominated John Dear for the Nobel Peace Prize. He is featured in the DVD film *The Narrow Path.*

**Amy Laura Hall**, PhD, is Associate Professor of Christian Ethics, Duke University. Author of *Conceiving Parenthood* and *The Treachery of Love,* she is an ordained minister in the United Methodist Church.

**Stanley Hauerwas**, PhD, is the Gilbert T. Rowe Professor of Theological Ethics at Duke Divinity School, Duke Unviersity. Hauerwas is the author of dozens of books, and was named by *Time* magazine as America's Best Theologian.

**J. Nelson Kraybill**, PhD, is president emeritus of Associated Mennonite Biblical Seminary (Elkhart, Indiana), lead pastor at Prairie Street Mennonite Church (Elkhart, Indiana), and author of *Apocalypse and Allegiance: Worship, Politics, and Devotion in the Book of Revelation.*

**Ingrid E. Lilly**, PhD, is Assistant Professor of Religious Studies at Western Kentucky University, where she teaches courses in Hebrew Bible, Judaism, and Cultural Approaches to Religion.

**D. Stephen Long**, PhD, is Professor of Systematic Theology, Marquette University. He is the author of numerous books including *The Goodness of God, The Truth about God,* and *Divine Economy.* Long is also an ordained minister in the United Methodist Church.

**Gerald W. Schlabach**, PhD, is Associate Professor of Theology at the University of St. Thomas. He is the author and editor of numerous books including *Just Policing, At Peace and Unafraid,* and *For the Joy Set Before Us.* He worked in Central America with the Mennonite Central Committee—an organization dedicated to issues pertaining to peace and justice.

**Kara Slade**, PhD, is a student at Duke Divinity School. A former specialist in the physics of aircraft and satellites, she served on the faculty of the Pratt School of Engineering at Duke University and worked in research and development for the federal government. She is preparing for ordination to the priesthood in the Episcopal Church.

**C. Rosalee Velloso Ewell**, PhD, is a theologian from São Paulo, Brazil. She serves as executive director of the Theological Commission for the World Evangelical Alliance, and is the New Testament editor for the Latin American Bible Commentary project. Rosalee and her family currently live in Birmingham, United Kingdom.

**Samuel Wells**, PhD, is the Dean of Duke University Chapel. He is the author and editor of more than half a dozen books including *The Blackwell Companion to Christian Ethics* and *Transforming Fate into Destiny.*

**Tripp York**, PhD, teaches in the Religious Studies Department at Virginia Wesleyan College in Norfolk, VA. He is the author and editor of numerous books including *Third Way Allegiance, Living on Hope While Living in Babylon,* and *The Devil Wears Nada.*

# Bibliography

Ackerman, Peter, and Jack DuVall. *A Force More Powerful: A Century of Nonviolent Conflict*. New York: St. Martin's, 2000.

Alexis-Baker, Andy. "Community, Policing and Violence." *Conrad Grebel Review* 26:2 (2008) 102–16.

———."The Gospel or a Glock? Mennonites and the Police." *Conrad Grebel Review* 25:2 (2007) 28–29.

———. "Just Policing: A New Face to an Old Challenge." In *Peace Be with You: The Church's Benediction amid Empire*, edited by Michael Hardin, 80–99. Telford, PA: Cascadia, 2010.

———. "Policing and Christian Forgiveness." In *Christian Peace and Nonviolence: A Documentary History*, edited by Michael Long, 327–30. Maryknoll, NY: Orbis, 2011.

———. "Unbinding Yoder from Just Policing." In *Power and Practices: Engaging the Work of John Howard Yoder*, edited by Jeremy M. Bergen and Anthony G. Siegrist, 147–66. Waterloo, Ontario: Herald, 2009.

Allen, Leonard C. *The Cruciform Church: Becoming a Cross-Shaped People in a Secular World*. Abilene, TX: Abilene Christian University Press, 1990.

Augsburger, David. *Dissident Discipleship: A Spirituality of Self-Surrender, Love of God, and Love of Neighbor*. Grand Rapids: Brazos, 2006.

Bainton, Roland. *Christian Attitudes Toward War and Peace*. Nashville: Abingdon, 1979.

Barth, Karl. *A Shorter Commentary on Romans*. Translated by D. H. van Daalen. London: SCM, 1959.

Barton, Stephen C. *Discipleship and Family Ties in Mark and Matthew*. Cambridge: Cambridge University Press, 1994.

Bell, Daniel M. *Just War as Christian Discipleship: Recentering the Tradition in the Church Rather than the State*. Grand Rapids: Brazos, 2009.

Berry, Wendell. *Blessed Are the Peacemakers*. Emeryville, CA: Shoemaker & Hoard, 2005.

Black, David. *Christian Archy*. Gonzalez, FL: Energion, 2009.

Bond, Helen K. *Pontius Pilate in History and Interpretation*. Cambridge: Cambridge University Press, 2004.

Bonhoeffer, Dietrich. *Ethics*. Minneapolis: Fortress, 2005.

Boyd, Gregory A. *God at War: The Bible and Spiritual Conflict*. Downers Grove, IL: InterVarsity, 1997.

———. "The Kingdom as a Political-Spiritual Revolution." *Criswell Theological Review* 6 (2008) 23–41.

———. *The Myth of a Christian Nation: How the Quest for Political Power Is Destroying the Church.* Grand Rapids: Zondervan, 2005.

Braght, Thieleman, J. van. *The Bloody Theater, or, Martyrs Mirror of the Defenseless Christians.* 2nd English ed. Scottdale, PA: Herald, 2001.

Brandon, S. G. F. *Jesus and the Zealots.* Manchester: Manchester University Press, 1967.

Brimlow, Robert. *What about Hitler? Wrestling with Jesus' Call to Nonviolence in an Evil World.* Grand Rapids: Brazos, 2006.

Brnjas, "What About Peter? A Response to 'The Gospel or a Glock.'" *Conrad Grebel Review* 26:2 (2008) 9–18.

Brock, P. *Varieties of Pacifism: A Survey from Antiquity to the Outset of the Twentieth Century.* Syracuse: Syracuse University Press, 1998.

Bruner, Frederick Dale. *The Christbook: A Historical/Theologial Commentary: Matthew 1–12.* Grand Rapids: Eerdmans, 2004.

Budde, Michael L., and Karen Scott, editors. *Witness of the Body: The Past, Present, and Future of Christian Martyrdom.* Grand Rapids: Eerdmans, 2011.

Camp, Lee C. *Mere Discipleship: Radical Christianity in a Rebellious World.* 2nd ed. Grand Rapids: Brazos, 2003.

———. *Who Is My Enemy? Questions American Christians Must Face about Islam—and Themselves.* Grand Rapids: Brazos, 2011.

Carroll, James. *Jerusalem, Jerusalem: How the Ancient City Ignited Our Modern World.* Boston: Houghton Mifflin Harcourt, 2011.

Carter, Warren. *Matthew and the Margins: A Sociopolitical and Religious Reading.* Sheffield: Sheffield Academic, 2000.

Cavanaugh, William T. "Killing for the Telephone Company: Why the Nation-State Is Not the Keeper of the Common Good." *Modern Theology* 20:2 (2004) 243–74.

Chase, Kenneth R., and Alan Jacobs, editors. *Must Christianity Be Violent? Reflections on History, Practice, and Theology.* Grand Rapids: Brazos, 2003.

Christoyannopoulos, Alexandre. *Christian Anarchism: A Political Commentary on the Gospel.* Abridged ed. Exeter: Imprint Academic, 2011.

Claiborne, Shane, and Chris Haw. *Jesus for President.* Grand Rapids: Zondervan, 2008.

Cochrane, Arthur C. *The Church's Confession under Hitler.* Philadelphia: Westminster, 1962.

Colson, Charles. *God and Government.* Rev. ed. Grand Rapids: Zondervan, 2007.

Conway, John S. *The Nazi Persecution of the Churches, 1933–45.* London: Weidenfield & Nicolson, 1968.

Crim, Keith, editor. *The Interpreter's Dictionary of the Bible, Supplementary Volume.* Nashville: Abingdon, 1976.

Crofford, Gregory. *Streams of Mercy: Prevenient Grace in the Theology of John and Charles Wesley.* Lexington: Emeth, 2010.

Cross, Frank Moore. *Canaanite Myth and Hebrew Epic: Essays in the History of the Religion of Israel.* Cambridge: Harvard University Press, 1973.

Cullman, Oscar. *The State in the New Testament.* New York: Scribner's, 1956.

Davies, W. D., and Dale C. Allison. *A Critical and Exegetical Commentary on the Gospel according to Saint Matthew.* Vol. 2., *Commentary on Matthew 8–18.* International Critical Commentary. Edinburgh: T. & T Clark, 1991.

Day, John. *Yahweh and the Gods and Goddesses of Canaan*. Sheffield: Sheffield Academic Press, 2000.

D'Este, Carlo. *Patton: A Genius for War*. New York: Harper Collins, 1995.

DeYoung, C. G., J. B. Hirsh, M. S. Shane, X. Papademetris, N. Rajeevan, and J. R. Gray. "Testing Predictions from Personality Neuroscience: Brain Structure and the Big Five." *Psychological Science* 21 (2010) 820–28.

Drake, H. A. "Lions into Lambs: Explaining Early Christian Intolerance." *Past and Present* 153 (1996) 3–36.

Driver, John. *How Christians Made Peace with War: Early Christian Understandings of War*. Scottdale, PA: Herald, 1988.

Eisenhower, Dwight D. "Address at the Freedoms Foundation." December 22, 1952. Online: http://www.eisenhower.archives.gov/all_about_ike/quotes.html.

———. "Statement by the President upon Signing Bill to Include the Words 'Under God' in the Pledge to the Flag." June 14, 1954. Online: http://www.presidency.ucsb.edu/ws/index.php?pid=9920#axzz1eNv7jQU8.

Eliot, T. S. *Murder in the Cathedral*. New York: Harcourt, Brace, 1963.

Eller, Vernard. *Christian Anarchy: Jesus' Primacy Over the Powers*. Eugene, OR: Wipf & Stock, 1999.

———. *The Most Revealing Book of the Bible: Making Sense Out of Revelation*. Grand Rapids: Eerdmans, 1974.

Ellul, Jacques. *Anarchy and Christianity*. Translated by G. W. Bromiley. Grand Rapids: Eerdmans, 1991.

———. *The Ethics of Freedom*. Translated and edited by G. W. Bromiley. Grand Rapids: Erdmans, 1976.

———. *The Political Illusion*. Translated by K. Kellen. New York: Vintage , 1972.

———. *The Subversion of Christianity*. Translated by G. W. Bromiley. Grand Rapids: Eerdmans, 1986.

———. *Violence: Reflections from a Christian Perspective*. Translated by Cecilia Gaul Kings. New York: Seabury, 1969.

Finkelstein, Israel, and Neil Silberman. *The Bible Unearthed: Archaeology's New Vision of Ancient Israel and the Origin of Sacred Texts*. New York: Simon & Schuster, 2001.

France, R. T. *The Gospel of Matthew*. New International Commentary on the New Testament. Grand Rapids: Eerdmans, 2007.

Frend, William H. C. *Martyrdom and Persecution in the Early Church*. Garden City, NY: Anchor, 1967.

Fretheim, Terrence. *Creation Untamed: The Bible, God, and Natural Disasters*. Grand Rapids: Baker Academic, 2010.

———. "God and Violence in the Old Testament." *Word & World* 24 (2004) 18–28.

———. "'I Was Only a Little Angry': Divine Violence in the Prophets." *Interpretation* 58 (2004) 365–75.

Friesen, Duane K. "Peacemaking as an Ethical Category: The Convergence of Pacifism and Just War." In *Ethics in the Nuclear Age: Strategy, Religious Studies, and the Churches*, edited by Todd Whitmore, 161–80. Dallas: Southern Methodist University Press, 1989.

Friesen, Duane K., and Gerald W. Schlabach, editors. *At Peace and Unafraid: Public Order, Security, and the Wisdom of the Cross*. Scottdale, PA: Herald, 2005.

Funk, John F. *Warfare: Its Evils, Our Duty*. Chicago: Charles Hess, 1863.

Gnilka, Joachim. *Das Matthäusevangelium*. Freiburg: Herder, 1986.

Gorman, Michael J. *Cruciformity: Paul's Narrative Spirituality of the Cross.* Grand Rapids: Eerdmans, 2001.

Gray, J. R., and P. M. Thompson. "Neurobiology of Intelligence: Health Implications?" *Discovery Medicine* 22 (2004) 157–62.

Green, Joel B. *1 Peter.* Two Horizons New Testament Commentary. Grand Rapids: Eerdmans, 2007.

———. *The Gospel of Luke.* New International Commentary on the New Testament. Grand Rapids: Eerdmans, 1997.

Griswold, Charles. "Forgiveness and Apology: What, When, Why?" *Tikkun*, March/April 2008, 21–26.

Groff, Anna. "Protester Sparks Look at Safety Practices." *The Mennonite,* 17 November 2009, 24.

Gunning, Sandra. *Race, Rape, and Lynching: The Red Record of American Literature, 1890–1912.* Oxford: Oxford University Press, 1996.

Hall, Amy Laura. "Unwanted Interruptions." *Christianity Today,* July 2004. Online: http://www.christianitytoday.com/ct/2004/july/9.30.html.

Hallie, Philip. *Lest Innocent Blood Be Shed: The Story of the Village of Le Chambon and How Goodness Happened There.* New York: HarperPerennial, 1994.

Harmon, William, editor. *The Classic Hundred Poems: All-Time Favorites.* New York: Columbia University Press, 1998.

Hatfield, Mark. *Between a Rock and a Hard Place.* New York: Pocket, 1977.

Hauerwas, Stanley. *After Christendom? How the Church Is to Behave if Freedom, Justice, and a Chrsitian Nation Are Bad Ideas.* Nashville: Abingdon, 1991.

———. *Against the Nations: War and Survival in a Liberal Society.* Notre Dame: University of Notre Dame Press, 1992.

———. *The Hauerwas Reader.* Edited by J. Berkman and M. Cartwright. Durham: Duke University Press, 2001.

———. *The Peaceable Kingdom.* Notre Dame: University of Notre Dame Press, 1983.

———. *Performing the Faith: Bonhoeffer and the Practice of Nonviolence.* Grand Rapids: Brazos, 2004.

———. *With the Grain of the Universe: The Church's Witness and Natural Theology.* Grand Rapids: Brazos, 2001.

Hauerwas, Stanley, et al., editors. *The Wisdom of the Cross: Essays in Honor of John Howard Yoder.* Grand Rapids: Eerdmans, 1999.

Hauerwas, Stanley, and William Willimon. *Resident Aliens: Life in the Christian Colony.* Nashville: Abingdon, 1989.

Hays, Richard. *The Moral Vision of the New Testament.* San Francisco: HarperSanFrancisco, 1996.

Helgeland, John, Robert J. Daly, and J. Patout Burns. *Christians and the Military: The Early Experience.* Philadelphia: Fortress, 1985.

Hengel, Martin. *Crucifixion in the Ancient World and the Folly of the Message of the Cross.* Translated by John Bowden. Philadelphia: Fortress, 1977.

Hippolytus. *On the Apostolic Tradition.* Introduction and commentary by Alistair Stewart-Sykes. Crestwood, NY: St. Vladimir's Seminary Press, 2001.

Hobbes, Thomas. *Leviathan: With Selected Variants from the Latin Edition of 1668.* Edited by Edwin Curley. Indianapolis: Hackett, 1994.

Holloway, Steven W. *As[set breve over s]s[set breve over s]ur is King! As[set breve over s]s[set breve over s]ur is King! Religion in the Exercise of Power in the Neo-Assyrian Empire.* Boston: Brill, 2002.

Hornus, Jean-Michel. *It Is Not Lawful for Me to Fight: Early Christian Attitudes toward War, Violence and the State.* Scottdale, PA: Herald, 1980.

Howard-Brook, Wes. *Becoming Children of God: John's Gospel and Radical Discipleship.* Maryknoll, NY: Orbis, 1993.

Huebner, Chris K. *A Precarious Peace: Yoderian Explorations on Theology, Knowledge, and Identity.* Scottdale, PA: Herald, 2006.

Hunter, D. G. "A Decade of Research on Early Christians and Military Service." *Religious Studies Review* 18:2 (1992) 87–94.

Jackson, Dave. *Dial 911: Peaceful Christians and Urban Violence.* Scottdale, PA: Herald, 1981.

Jobling, David, and Tina Pippin et al., editors. *The Postmodern Bible Reader.* Malden, MA: Blackwell, 2001.

Johns, Loren L. *The Lamb Christology of the Apocalypse of John.* Tübingen: Mohr Siebeck, 2003.

Jüngel, Eberhard. *God as the Mystery of the World: On the Foundation of the Theology of the Crucified One in the Dispute between Theism and Atheism.* Grand Rapids: Eerdmans, 1983.

Keener, Craig. *The IVP Background Commentary: New Testament.* Downers Grove: InterVarsity, 1993.

Kemp, K. "Personal Pacifism." *Theological Studies* 56 (1995) 21–38.

Kern, Kathleen. *In Harm's Way: A History of Christian Peacemaker Teams.* Eugene, OR: Cascade, 2009.

Kierkegaard, Søren. *Works of Love.* Translated by Howard V. Hong and Edna H. Hong. Princeton: Princeton University Press, 1995.

Kistemaker, Simon J. *New Testament Commentary: Exposition of the Epistles of Peter and of the Epistle of Jude.* Grand Rapids: Baker, 1987.

Krahn, Cornelius. "Government of Mennonites in Russia." In *The Mennonite Encyclopedia,* vol. 2, 556–57. Hillsboro, KS: Mennonite Brethren Publishing House, 1955–1990.

Kraybill, Donald B., Steven M. Nolt, and David L. Weaver-Zercher. *Amish Grace: How Forgiveness Transcended Tragedy.* San Francisco, CA: Jossey-Bass, 2007.

Kraybill, Nelson J. *Apocalypse and Allegiance: Worship, Politics, and Devotion in the Book of Revelation.* Grand Rapids: Brazos, 2010.

Kreider, Alan. *The Change of Conversion and the Origin of Christendom.* Eugene, OR: Wipf & Stock, 2007.

Kistemaker, Simon J. *New Testament Commentary: Exposition of the Epistles of Peter and of the Epistle of Jude.* Grand Rapids: Baker, 1987.

Kurlansky, Mark. *Non-Violence: The History of a Dangerous Idea.* New York: Random House, 2006.

Lakey, George. "Nonviolent Action as the Sword that Heals." Online: http://www.trainingforchange.org/nonviolent_action_sword_that_heals.

———. *Powerful Peacemaking: A Strategy for a Living Revolution.* Philadelphia: New Society Publishers, 1987.

Lasserre, Jean. *War and the Gospel.* Eugene, OR: Wipf & Stock, 1998.

Lawrence, D. H. *Apocalypse and the Writings on Revelation*. Edited by Mara Kalnins. Cambridge: Cambridge University Press, 1980.

Leithart, Peter J. *Defending Constantine: The Twilight of an Empire and the Dawn of Christendom*. Downers Grove, IL: InterVarsity, 2010.

Lepard, Bryan D. *Rethinking Humanitarian Intervention: A Fresh Legal Approach Based on Fundamental Ethical Principles in International Law and World Religions*. University Park: Pennsylvania State University Press, 2002.

Lind, Millard C. *Yahweh Is a Warrior: The Theology of Warfare in Ancient Israel*. Scottdale, PA: Herald, 1980.

Lindbeck, George. *The Nature of Doctrine: Religion and Theology in a Postliberal Age*. Philadelphia: Westminster, 1984.

Lipscomb, David. *Civil Government: Its Origin, Mission, and Destiny, and the Christian's Relation to It*. Nashville: McQuiddy Printing, 1913.

Lohfink, Gerhard. *Jesus and Community*. Translated by John P. Galvin. Philadelphia: Fortress, 1984.

Long, D. Stephen. *John Wesley's Moral Theology: The Quest for God and Goodness*. Nashville: Kingswood, 2005.

Long, Michael G. *Christian Peace and Nonviolence: A Documentary History*. Maryknoll, NY: Orbis, 2011.

Lüdemann, Gerd. *The Unholy in Holy Scripture: The Dark Side of the Bible*. Translated by John Bowden. Louisville: Westminster John Knox, 1997.

Luther, Martin. *Commentary on the Epistle to the Romans*. Translated by J. Theodore Mueller. Grand Rapids: Zondervan, 1954.

———. *Faith and Freedom: An Invitation to the Writings of Martin Luther*. Edited by John F. Thornton and Susan B. Varenne. New York: Vintage, 2002.

Luz, Ulrich. *Matthew 8–20*. Translated by James E. Crouch. Hermeneia. Minneapolis: Augsburg, 1989.

MacMullen, Ramsay. *Christianizing the Roman Empire (A.D. 100–400)*. New Haven: Yale University Press, 1984.

McClendon, James W. *Systematic Theology*. Vol. 2, *Doctrine*. Nashville: Abingdon, 1994.

McMaster, Neil. "Torture from Algiers to Abu Ghraib." *Race and Class* 46:2 (2004) 1–21.

Miller, Keith D. *Voice of Deliverance: The Language of Martin Luther King, Jr., and Its Sources*. Athens: University of Georgia Press, 1998.

Miller, Patrick. *Divine Warrior in Early Israel*. Cambridge: Harvard University Press, 1973.

Murphy, Jeffrie G., and Jean Hampton. *Forgiveness and Mercy*. Cambridge: Cambridge University Press, 1988.

Myers, Ched. *Binding the Strong Man: A Political Reading of Mark's Story of Jesus*. Maryknoll, NY: Orbis, 1987.

Niebuhr, Reinhold. *Christianity and Power Politics*. New York: Scribner's, 1940.

———. *Moral Man and Immoral Society: A Study of Ethics and Politics*. Louisville: Westminster John Knox, 2002.

Nippel, Wilfried. *Public Order in Ancient Rome*. Cambridge: Cambridge University Press, 1995.

O'Donovan, Oliver. *The Desire of the Nations*. Cambridge: Cambridge University Press, 1999.

O'Gorman, Angie. *The Universe Bends towards Justice*. Philadelphia: New Society Publishers, 1990.

Penton-Voak, I. S., and D. I. Perrett. "Female Preference for Male Faces Changes Cyclically; Further Evidence." *Evolution and Human Behavior* 21 (2000) 39–48.

Pinnock, Clark H. *Flame of Love: A Theology of the Holy Spirit*. Downers Grove, IL: InterVarsity, 1996.

Pliny the Younger. *Letters and Panegyricus*. Vol. 2. Translated by Betty Radice. Loeb Classical Library 59. Cambridge: Harvard University Press, 1969.

Rad, Gerhard von. *Holy War in Ancient Israel*. Translated and edited by Marva J. Dawn. Grand Rapids: Eerdmans, 1991.

Roberts, Dorothy. "Torture and the Biopolitics of Race." *University of Miami Law Review* 62 (2008) 229–47.

Robinson, James Harvey, editor. *Readings in European History*. Vol. 1, *From the Breaking Up of the Roman Empire to the Protestant Revolt*. Boston: Ginn, 1904.

Römer, Thomas. *Dieu obscur: Le sexe, le cruauté et la violence dans l'Ancien Testament*. Geneva: Labor et Fides, 1996.

Roth, Jonathan. "Jewish Military Forces in the Roman Service." Paper delivered at the annual meeting of the Society for Biblical Literature, San Antonio, TX, November 23, 2004. Online: http://pace.mcmaster.ca/media/pdf/sbl/Roth%20Jewish%20 Forces.pdf.

Rowlett, Lori L. *Joshua and the Rhetoric of Violence: A New Historicist Analysis*. Sheffield: Sheffield Academic Press, 1996.

Russell, Bertrand. "The Future of Pacifism." *The American Scholar* 13 (1943) 7–13.

Russell, F. H. "Love and Hate in Medieval Warfare: The Contribution of Saint Augustine." *Nottingham Medieval Studies* 31 (1987) 108–24.

Russell, Stephen M. *Overcoming Evil God's Way: The Biblical and Historical Case for Nonresistance*. Guys Mills, PA: Faithbuilders Resource Group, 2008.

Schlabach, Gerald W. "Beyond Two- Versus One-Kingdom Theology: Abrahamic Community as a Mennonite Paradigm for Engagement in Society." *Conrad Grebel Review* 11:3 (1993) 187–210.

Schlabach, Gerald W., editor. *Just Policing, Not War: An Alternative Response to World Violence*. Collegeville, MN: Liturgical, 2007.

Schoenfeld, Andrew J. "Sons of Israel in Caesar's Service: Jewish Soldiers in the Roman Military." *Shofar: An Interdisciplinary Journal of Jewish Studies* 24:3 (2006) 115–26.

Smend, Rudolf. *Yahweh War and Tribal Confederation: Reflections on Israel's Earliest History*. Translated by M. G. Rogers. Nashville: Abingdon, 1970.

Smith, Nathan Rex. "The First Question about Pacifism Which I Will Never Answer Again." Online: http://www.associatedcontent.com/article/283441/the_first_ question_about_pacifism_which.html?cat=60.

Soderlund, Sven K., and N. T. Wright, editors. *Romans and the People of God*. Grand Rapids: Eerdmans, 1999.

Stark, Rodney. *The Rise of Christianity*. Princeton: Princeton University Press, 1996.

Stephey, M. J. "Top 10 Memorable Debate Moments." *Time*. Online: http://www.time. com/time/specials/packages/article/0,28804,1844704_1844706_1844712,00. html.

Stevenson, William R. *Christian Love and Just War: Moral Paradox and Political Life in St. Augustine and His Modern Interpreters*. Macon: Mercer University Press, 1987.

Stone, L. G. "Ethical and Apologetic Tendencies in the Redaction of the Book of *Joshua*." *Catholic Biblical Quarterly* 53 (1991) 25–35.

Stout, Jeffrey. *Blessed Are the Organized: Grassroots Democracy in America.* Princeton: Princeton University Press, 2010.

Stringfellow, William. *An Ethic for Christians and Other Aliens in a Strange Land.* Eugene, OR: Wipf & Stock, 2004.

Swift, Louis J. *The Early Fathers on War and Military Service.* Wilmington: Glazier, 1983.

Tannehill, R. C. *The Sword of His Mouth: Forceful and Imaginative Language in Synoptic Sayings.* Semeia Supplements 1. Philadelphia: Fortress, 1975.

Travis, Stephen. *Christ and the Judgment of God: The Limits of Divine Retribution in New Testament Thought.* Peabody, MA: Hendrickson, 2009.

Trible, Phyllis. *Texts of Terror: Literary-Feminist Readings of Biblical Narratives.* Minneapolis: Fortress, 1984.

Trocmé, Andre. *Jesus and the Nonviolent Revolution.* Maryknoll, NY: Orbis, 2004.

Trzyna, Thomas. *Blessed Are the Pacifists.* Scottdale, PA: Herald, 2006.

Turner, E. G. "Tiberius Julius Alexander." *Journal of Roman Studies* 44 (1954) 54–64.

Vaux, Roland de. *Ancient Israel.* Vol. 1, *Social Institutions.* Translated by John McHugh. New York: McGraw-Hill, 1965.

Water, Mark. *The Encyclopedia of Christian Martyrs.* Grand Rapids: Baker, 2001.

Weaver, A. E. "Unjust Lies, Just Wars? A Christian Pacifist Conversation with Augustine." *Journal of Religious Ethics* 29 (2001) 51–78.

Weaver, Dorothy Jean. "Power and Powerlessness: Matthew's Use of Irony in the Portrayal of Political Leaders." In *Society of Biblical Literature 1992 Seminar Papers*, edited by E. H. Lovering, 454–66. Atlanta: SBL, 1992.

Weinfeld, Moshe. *The Promise of the Land: The Inheritance of the Land of Canaan by the Israelites.* Berkeley: University of California Press, 1993.

"What an Ovulating Girl Wants: Manly Men." *LiveScience, msnbc.com.* Online: http://www.msnbc.msn.com/id/18077810/ns/health-livescience/t/what-ovulating-girl-wants-manly-men/.

Whitmore, Todd. *Ethics in the Nuclear Age: Strategy, Religious Studies, and the Churches.* Dallas: Southern Methodist University Press, 1989.

Wink, Walter. *Engaging the Powers: Discernment and Resistance in a World of Domination.* Minneapolis: Augsburg Fortress, 1992.

Winright, Tobias. "The Challenge of Policing: An Analysis in Christian Social Ethics." PhD diss., University of Notre Dame, 2002.

Wright, N. T., and Sven K. Soderlund, editors. *Romans and the People of God.* Grand Rapids: Eerdmans, 1999.

Yoder, John Howard. *Christian Attitudes to War, Peace, and Revolution.* Edited by Theodore J. Koontz and Andy Alexis-Baker. Grand Rapids: Brazos, 2009.

———. *The Christian Witness to the State.* Newton, KS: Faith and Life, 1964.

———. *The Christian Witness to the State.* Scottdale, PA: Herald, 2002.

———. *For the Nations.* Eugene, OR: Wipf & Stock, 2002.

———. *For the Nations: Essays Evangelical and Public.* Grand Rapids: Eerdmans, 1997.

———. *The Original Revolution: Essays on Christian Pacifism.* Scottdale, PA: Herald, 1971.

———. "'Patience' as Method in Moral Reasoning: Is an Ethic of Discipleship 'Absolute'?" Unpublished, drafted September 1992. Online: http://theology.nd.edu/people/research/yoder-john/documents/PATIENCE.pdf.

———. *The Politics of Jesus.* 2nd ed. Grand Rapids: Eerdmans, 1994.

———. *The Royal Priesthood: Essays Ecclesiological and Ecumenical.* Edited by Michael G. Cartwright. Grand Rapids: Eerdmans, 1994.

———. *The Schleitheim Confession.* Scottdale, PA: Herald, 1973.

———. *What Would You Do? A Serious Answer to a Standard Question.* Scottdale, PA: Herald, 1992.

York, Tripp. *The Purple Crown: The Politics of Martyrdom.* Scottdale, PA: Herald, 2007.

———. *Third Way Allegiance: Christian Witness in the Shadow of Religious Empire.* Telford, PA: Cascadia, 2011.

Zunes, Stephen, et al., editors. *Nonviolent Social Movements: A Geographical Perspective.* Malden, MA: Blackwell, 1999.